Millennials

IN THE **WORKPLACE**

HUMAN RESOURCE STRATEGIES FOR A NEW GENERATION

IMPLICATIONS FOR EDUCATORS,
EMPLOYERS, AND POLICY MAKERS

Howe, Neil with Reena Nadler
Millennials in the Workplace
ISBN: 978-0-9712606-4-1

Table of Contents

Nearly twenty-five years have passed since Bill Strauss and I first began studying the Millennials, back when the oldest of them were still in preschool. Nearly twenty years have passed since we wrote *Generations* (1991), in which we first gave this generation its "Millennial" label. Around the same time, the Millennials became of interest to us for personal as well as professional reasons. We each became the parent of two, in both cases a boy and a girl.

Back when we wrote *Generations*, we described how the children then entering elementary school rode "a powerful crest of protective concern," how they were seen as "precious" by Boomer parents who wielded a "perfectionist approach to child nurture" in an adult world that was "rediscovering an affection and sense of responsibility for other people's children." In the early 1990s, when most youth assessments were downbeat, even grim, we forecast that, as these new children passed through adolescence, "substance abuse, crime, suicide, unwed pregnancy will all decline."

When these trends all came to pass, we were not surprised. There are good reasons, rooted in how the Millennials were raised and in the rhythms of history, for why this occurred.

Again and again over the centuries, in America and elsewhere, new generations arise that both correct the trends set in motion by their parents and fill the role being vacated by their grandparents. It is happening again. That's what these leading-edge Millennials are doing with a midlife "Boomer Generation" now approaching retirement and a "G.I. Generation" deep in elderhood.

When we published *Millennials Rising* (2000), we chose the subtitle "The Next Great Generation" in part because, as a group, Millennials exhibit qualities—confidence, optimism, teamwork, and trust in big institutions—not generally seen in American youth since today's "senior citizens" were themselves young workers. And just as today's elder Americans did in their own youth, Millennials are growing up seeing their needs and dreams climb to the top of the national agenda.

Millennials Rising proved to be something of a watershed. After it appeared, and as this Millennial Generation grew older, Bill and I were often asked to speak to or consult with a variety of institutions that found themselves in charge of these "special" young people. Each set of encounters resulted in a new book about Millennials. We were commissioned to write and publish *Recruiting Millennials* (2000) for recruiting officers and other personnel in the armed forces. We published *Millennials Go To College* (2003, second edition 2007) for the faculty, administrators, and recruiting and campus-life personnel at colleges and universities. We released *Millennials and the Pop Culture* (2006) for media, marketers, and the entertainment industry; and *Millennials and K–12 Schools* (2008) for primary and secondary school teachers and administrators.

The current volume, *Millennials in the Workplace*, thus marks our sixth book on this generation. How generations get along—or don't get along—in the workplace has always been a subject of great interest to us. Back in the 1990s, the main generational clash was between Boomers, who were moving into midlife managerial positions, and Gen Xers, who were still just coming on board. In the years since 2000, while the Boomer-Xer divide has not gone away, its significance has gradually receded with the arrival of Millennials, fresh out of school and college. What both older generations now want to know is: Who are these new kids? What do they want? Who do they trust? What motivates them? Once they are hired, why do they stay or leave—and what can we do about it? Many clients asked us to turn some serious attention to such questions. So we did.

We started *Millennials in the Workplace* in 2006 and have been working on it ever since. Along the way, we have done exhaustive literature, survey, and media reviews and have conducted dozens of interviews with HR professionals and managers. Where appropriate, we have also drawn from our other

Millennial research (especially on high school and college students). Indeed, our books on K–12 schools, colleges, and the workplace can be regarded as three "companion volumes"—all dealing with different aspects of the school-to-work transition in the Millennial youth era.

Brief excerpts from this book have been published elsewhere: in our 2007 *Harvard Business Review* article, "The Next Twenty Years: How Customer and Workforce Attitudes Will Evolve," and in *Helicopter Parents in the Workplace*, a 2007 report for the think tank New Paradigm.

In one respect, this book represents a continuation of a series—not just as our sixth book on Millennials, but as our ninth book on generational topics. Yet in another respect, it represents a painful break in that series. This is the first book I have written on generations that is not coauthored with Bill Strauss, who passed away after a long illness in December of 2007. Bill was not only a brilliant thinker and writer, but also a close friend. He and I collaborated closely on generations for over twenty years—so closely and for so long indeed that learning to work without him was not, for me, as easy task.

Fortunately, among the professionals working for and with LifeCourse Associates, LLC (my consulting firm), I have found others to assist me in producing this book. It is in this spirit that I will continue to refer to it as "our" publication.

Foremost, I need to mention Reena Nadler, who has been with LifeCourse Associates for four years and who has been centrally engaged in every aspect of the project, from research and outlining to writing and editing. A Millennial herself, Reena represents the very best of her generation at work—perceptive, articulate, systematic, and industrious. This book literally could not have happened without her, and I employ the phrase "with Reena Nadler" in the title in grateful recognition of her critical role.

Let me acknowledge other LifeCourse personnel who have made important contributions: Rick Delano, for his deep familiarity (and contacts) with the world of career counseling, career academies, and career technical education; Jack Congdon, for assisting in our research and conducting extensive management interviews; and Victoria Hays, without whose fact-checking help our text would have contained many errors.

Several friends of LifeCourse have also lent a hand. These include Bob Filipczak, himself a coauthor of a book on generations in the workplace, who informs us of new trends; Paula Santonocito, a business journalist on workplace issues, who sends us breaking news; John Williams, former Michigan state director of career technical education, who briefed us on the "career cluster" movement; John Geraci, president of Crux, Inc., a youth survey firm with whom we often collaborate; and Mike Dover, vice president at New Paradigm in Toronto, Canada, an established thought leader on the role of IT in the workplace.

A final note for readers who want to know more about what we have written on Millennials or on generations and history: Please go to *www.lifecourse. com* and look over the books, articles, and DVDs listed there. We have written many recent books about various aspect of the Millennial Generation. Our one comprehensive book about this generation remains *Millennials Rising* (2000). For generations and history, see *Generations* (1991), *The Fourth Turning* (1997), and other more recent publications and DVDs.

We invite readers with comments or questions to contact us at authors@ lifecourse.com.

Neil Howe
April, 2010

Introduction:
A New Generation
Enters the
Workplace

"Millennials are fast becoming an influential factor
in the workplace—and an increasingly important
part of its future…. Organizations of all shapes
and sizes have much to learn if we are to attract
and keep the talent we need to succeed."

— **W. STANTON SMITH**, NATIONAL DIRECTOR OF NEXT
   GENERATION INITIATIVE, DELOITTE & TOUCHE USA LLP (2008)

"Meet the Millennials, and rejoice."

— **ANNA QUINDLEN**, *NEWSWEEK* (2000)

Introduction:
A New Generation Enters the Workplace

As the Millennial Generation (born since 1982) graduates from schools and colleges and fills the ranks of the entry-level workforce, older Americans are beginning to take notice. What are they saying about these Millennials? Actually, a great variety of things.

Many express sympathy about record-high youth unemployment. Some know young relatives who are looking for a good job but cannot find one or have moved in with mom and dad to save money. They've heard of job fairs where hundreds show up but only a handful are hired.

Many say, wow, a lot of these kids are smart, especially with digital gadgets—just look at how they're wired 24/7 to all their friends. Some have sons or daughters in college who compete for prizes in fields they've never even heard of, like nanotoxicology or evolutionary robotics.

Many are mystified, and maybe amused, by how much the world of teens and twenty-somethings has changed over the years. The teen lifestyle used to be about musclecars and malls. Now, it's about scooters and social networks. Starting a career used to be about tryouts, freelancing, cash bonuses—and getting away from your parents. Now it's about résumé-building, interning, certificates—and getting your parents' daily feedback.

Yet if you ask older Americans specifically how they think Millennials perform on the job, their comments become more critical and concerned. Many talk about young employees who think they're so special they expect to be promoted tomorrow, without "paying their dues." Or who, when given a task, always ask "why" rather than just get it done. Or who can't dress properly, write a proper memo, or show "respect" for their supervisors. Or who require exhaustive amounts of direction and encouragement just to make it through the day.

A decisive majority of American workers agree, in surveys repeatedly conducted by *Wired, Fortune,* JWT, and others, that there is indeed a "real generational divide" that causes "problems in your workplace" (or words to that effect). The JWT survey even asks workers whether "generational differences aren't so big as they've been hyped by the media." Only a third say the differences are over-hyped. Respondents usually identify the source of the problem as the youngest generation. Americans of all ages overwhelmingly believe (74 percent of them, according to a 2009 Pew Research Center survey) that the "work ethic" is stronger in older workers than in younger workers.

The educators and managers who train, counsel, and supervise on-the-job Millennials are even more pointedly negative about them. Experts in human resources have even coined special phrases to sum up their disappointment about today's young workers. They describe a pervasive "soft-skills deficiency" to explain why Millennials don't dress, talk, meet, eat, write, email, text, handle the phone, or show respect as they should. They identify a deepening "entitlement ethic" among Millennials to account for their alleged crass ambition to get to the top—or alternatively, their nonstop craving for positive feedback. They often cite "declining work centrality" as the reason so many Millennials are failing to emulate the obsessive work-focus of their Boomer managers.

Why Most Experts Sound So Negative

It's no mystery why older workers tend to be critical about anything they perceive as unexpected in the rising generation. We all like our comfort zone. Without compelling reasons to the contrary, we expect newcomers to adjust to us, not the other way around.

It's harder to explain why the educators, managers, and HR experts—those who are supposed to be the most focused on who these young people are and what motivates them—are often the most downbeat of all. Perhaps it's the echo-chamber effect, where each caustic observation feeds another, growing steadily in the retelling. Repeated stories about flip-flops, calls to mom, silly questions, Facebook breaks, quitting without notice, overuse of the word "like," and tearful responses to the words "do over" have a way of turning this generation into a difficult and perhaps insurmountable challenge.

Over the last few years, a small library of books and articles has arisen trying to instruct human resource professionals about how to "deal with" or "handle" Millennial trainees and employees. For the most part, these how-to authors simply amp up the echo-chamber negativity to a louder volume. Readers learn about Millennials in descriptions that are riddled with caustic or, at best, condescending adjectives—such as *me-oriented, coddled, distractible, fragile, pushy, needy, rude, impatient, thin-skinned, ruthless, irresponsible, reckless, overprogrammed,* and *timid.* (Never mind that some of these seem contradictory.)

One of these authors memorably divides all Millennial job seekers into four groups: the *clueless,* the *aimless,* the *directionless,* and (only "25 percent of them") the *directed.* Most support their findings by quoting, sometimes at length, from the well-known psychologist Jean Twenge (whom we will encounter again briefly in Chapter 1). Twenge is most famous for her remark that "young people born after 1982 are the most narcissistic generation in recent history"—and in case anyone misses the point, she elsewhere explains that "narcissism is one the few personality traits that psychologists agree is almost completely negative."

Nearly all of these how-to authors base their understanding of Millennials primarily on interviews with irritated educators in the classroom and frustrated managers in the office. From time to time, they may cite surveys of workers of different ages. They rarely look at what is going on the lives of Millennials outside work or at any of the forces that have shaped their lives before they arrived in the workplace. Finally, they don't often have much practical advice to impart—since after all, not a lot can be done with the "impatient" and "me-first" young workers they describe. And even if there were, what teachers or supervisors are going to be inspired to invest much time in them? Many of the recommendations have the feel of damage control and diversion: Keep the lessons short, reward them often, distract them with games, resign yourself to high turnover rates, and so on.

A few dissident experts argue that the basic generational premise of these authors is mistaken. It's not that each older generation finds new failings in each younger generation, they say, it's just that the old are always complaining about the young—who eventually mature and become just like the old were. It's not about generations, just about phase of life.

This phase-of-life approach offers a welcome alternative to the negativity of the dominant generational school. Unfortunately, it just doesn't hold up under inspection. It assumes that the failings of every youth generation are the same, which seems implausible given historical data showing vast changes in youth attitudes and behavior from one era to the next. Hardly anybody would claim that the way older people saw the young "New-Deal" G.I. Generation in the 1930s was similar to the way older people saw young "flower-power" Boomers in the 1970s or young "free-agent" Gen-Xers in the 1990s. Nor would anybody claim that these generations, as they aged, matured into the same kinds of parents and leaders.

Surveys confirm that most Americans explicitly reject the phase-of-life explanation. When asked if the problems they observe in their workplace are really generational or just due to age differences, "generational" wins, hand down. That's probably why these problems stir such strong emotions. What most worries Boomer or Gen-X supervisors is not the Millennial behavior they recognize (because, sure, I was like that at that age), but rather the behavior they don't—because, wait, *I was never like that* at that age. Millennials, looking up the age ladder, feel the same apprehension: I'm pretty sure *I never will be like that* at that age.

Across a generational divide, people often find it hard to recognize or understand each other, and those in charge can no longer presume that the young will grow older the same way they did. To quote the high school principal in *The Breakfast Club* (1985) on the subject of Gen-X teens: "Now this is the thought that wakes me up in the middle of the night. That when I get older, these kids are going... to be running the country and take care of me." The movie resonated with audiences of all ages because the basic message struck home: The principal knew he was never like those kids, and the kids were pretty sure they would never be like the principal.

The stark pessimism of the principal's prediction, of course, takes us right back to the negativity of the generational approach. Yet does it have to be this way? In retrospect, Gen Xers have matured into midlife leaders and parents who are obviously different from the midlifers they knew as kids, but probably no worse overall (and in some ways better). Isn't it possible that today's Millennial youth will likewise mature into leaders and parents who are different—but also no worse overall (and in some ways better)—than the Gen Xers and Boomers they look up to today?

We believe such a future is not only possible, but nearly certain.

How Our Approach is Different

This book intends to bridge the generational divide between Millennials and older generations in the workplace. Unlike the phase-of-life dissidents, we don't dismiss this generational divide. We insist on it. Millennials are a new generation. And, like every new generation, they bring with them unfamiliar attitudes, beliefs, life aspirations, and motivational triggers. Millennials often surprise older people, just as every earlier generation—most recently, the Silent, Boomers, and Gen Xers—surprised plenty of older people when they first arrived.

Yet unlike most of the mainstream how-to literature, we try to look across the generational divide without pessimism or condescension. We find—and we think readers will also find—that the more one understands Millennials as a generation, the more reasons one finds to be positive about them as workers and optimistic about their future. Likewise, we don't use the complaints and frustrations of educators and managers as our starting point. Our purpose is not to commiserate with our readers, but to assist them. And to do that, we start out by taking them out of their own world and into the Millennials'.

To help educators and employers manage, guide, and work with Millennials more effectively, we offer three basic learning steps.

First, the fundamentals: Learn who the Millennials are.

Understanding Millennials means getting acquainted with everything that goes on in their day-to-day lives, from their racial and ethnic diversity to how they view the gender divide, from where they live to how they pay for their schooling, from how they see their parents to what they do with their friends. It also means understanding how they got where they are today. What was going on in families, in schools, in politics, and in popular culture while the

Millennials were children? How did all of this shape them into the young-adult generation that is now emerging?

As readers learn more about this generation's collective biography, they will be struck by many positive trends that most Americans seldom hear about. Millennials, for example, have spurred a dramatic decline in juvenile crime, teen pregnancy, and youth risk-taking of nearly every variety. They have propelled an equally dramatic climb, among young people, in community service, voting rates, and institutional trust. Compared to Boomers or Gen Xers at the same age, Millennials are closer to their parents and more motivated to meet conventional benchmarks of success. And they are graduating from high school, attending college, and earning college degrees at the highest per-capita rates in American history.

Some readers may even be tempted to reverse the usual question and ask themselves: How did my generation at that age match up to the Millennial standard?

Second, the problem: Learn why Millennials and older generations misperceive each other.

Understanding Millennials can help educators and employers correctly interpret what this generation is saying and doing. Misperception typically occurs when older people evaluate the lives of younger people using their own (recollected) youth as the standard of comparison. Today, Boomers and Xers often assume that whatever Millennials are thinking or doing must be a continuation of youth trends that prevailed when they were that age.

The truth dies hard. In 2007, the Collegiate Employment Research Institute (CERI) at Michigan State University asked college students which characteristics they valued most in a job. Then they asked corporate recruiters what they *expected* these students would value most. Revealingly, the recruiters gave high rankings to factors Gen Xers had valued as young workers and entirely missed the Millennials' new top priorities. For example, recruiters thought students would rank "high income" (a key Xer priority) fourth out of fifteen characteristics—when Millennials actually ranked it way down in eighth place. Recruiters also thought students would rank "good benefits" and "job security" down in fifth and seventh place—while Millennials actually ranked these factors second and third.

As CERI discovered, recruiters can fundamentally misunderstand what the young are looking for in the workplace. Such disconnects create enormous problems. Nor are these problems restricted to recruiters. Misperceptions of Millennials abound both in the classroom and in the workplace itself. Consider the following examples:

* *Perception:* Millennial employees dress inappropriately, show up late, chatter on cell phones, and flub formal business letters because they disrespect their bosses and the rules of the office. *Reality:* Many Millennials have never been taught "soft" workplace skills like appropriate dress and communication, or don't know when or where to apply them. When asked, young workers are astonished to find that their t-shirts or casual emails are interpreted as disrespect.

* *Perception:* It's not worth investing much in Millennial employees because they are easily distractible, have short time horizons, and can't wait to "job hop" at the first opportunity. *Reality:* Surveys show that most Millennials want to bond with an employer who will partner with them to achieve their lifelong career goals. They typically job hop only when they're convinced that their employer is not offering any serious and challenging long-term opportunity.

* *Perception:* Millennials demand lots of unrealistic praise and encouragement from managers because they are entitled, egotistical, and self-oriented. *Reality:* Millennials want tight cycles of feedback to ensure that they're doing exactly what their managers want. Many also believe that a culture of positive recognition would benefit today's workplaces, in which (they feel) management is too apt to be cynical both about their own jobs and the organization's overall purpose.

As these frequent misperceptions show, most managers just don't know what to make of the Millennials—and in their confusion, they end up seeing them as a burden, a challenge, or a sheer liability. Once you begin to interpret Millennials' behavior and motivations correctly, you can move beyond this "damage control" mentality. You can, instead, view this generation as potential to be unleashed or as energy to be harnessed.

Third, the solution: Learn how to teach and manage Millennials more effectively.

Once educators and managers correctly perceive what motivates Millennials, they can design effective solutions to any problems that arise. In this book, we outline many of these solutions and describe the best practices of forward-thinking schools, colleges, and employers. For example:

* We show how many employers have remedied soft-skills deficiencies by developing explicit policies about required dress and behavior, and by formally training young workers who are grateful to acquire new skills.

* We show how many employers have stopped high turnover by demonstrating to young workers that they are committed to their long-term career paths and can offer them variety in a secure, structured environment.

* We show how many employers have solved the "praise me" problem by getting supervisors to provide frequent feedback and positive reinforcement—in a way that doesn't inflate egos, but does make young workers feel positive about their contribution and proud of their organization.

Our book offers educators and managers a multitude of solutions and best-practice descriptions. Yet our goal is to give them something even more fundamental. We hope to impart to our readers a robust method of generational understanding and generational listening that will enable them to improvise or design *their own solutions* to any problem they encounter with this rising generation. By explaining the big picture of who Millennials really are, where they came from, and how they see themselves and the world of work, we want to make our readers not just better informed—but also more inspiring and effective as teachers or managers.

How This Book Is Organized

This book is organized into two parts. In Part I, "Meet the Millennials," we explain who the Millennials are and why older generations often misunderstand them. Although our focus is on young people in the United States, we discuss briefly how many of the same youth trends are drawing attention in societies and cultures from Europe to China. Global managers will find that they can apply many of the strategies that work for U.S. Millennials to their global Millennial workforce.

In Part II, "Millennials in the Workplace," we delve more concretely into the generational conflicts that emerge in the workplace environment. In keeping with our big-picture focus, we organize this discussion around the seven core traits of the Millennial generation, dedicating one chapter to each trait. Within each chapter, we discuss effective solutions and best practices for the three constituencies that make up our intended readership: (1) *Educators* at the secondary and postsecondary levels; (2) *Employers*, including managers, recruiters, and HR personnel of organizations that hire Millennials; and (3) the *Public Sector*, with a special focus on managers who deal with issues unique to the government workplace and on policymakers who design the laws and regulations that impact Millennial workers nationwide.

A deep understanding of a generation's past enables one to know more about who it is today. Likewise, knowing who it is today enables one to say something important about its future. In our Afterword, "America's Millennial Future," we offer our own predictions about how America is likely to change—and not just in its workplaces—as Millennials mature over the next thirty years into the nation's dominant generation of managers and educators, parents and consumers, voters and political leaders.

Flash back for a moment to the pessimistic reflections of that high school principal in *The Breakfast Club* about how "those kids" would turn out. Imagine that, back then, you could have found a balanced and forward-looking book about who those young Gen Xers were and how they were likely to reshape America's workplaces during the 1990s and 2000s. It would have been a book detailing everything about the Xers' resilient individualism, their attraction to markets and risk, their distrust of big institutions and grand causes, their instinctive survivalism, and their pragmatic focus on the bottom line. Imagine how useful that book would have been for the managers of that era who wanted to prepare for the future.

Now imagine that, today, you could find such a book about Millennials, a generation poised to transform America's workplaces in a very different direction during the 2010s and 2020s.

We hope you are holding that book.

PART ONE

MEET **THE MILLENNIALS**

01

The Millennial Surprise

"There has been a faulty portrayal of Millennials by the media—television, films, news, blogs, everything. These people are not the self-entitled, coddled slackers they're made out to be. Misnomers and myths about them are all over the place."

— **ANN MACK**, DIRECTOR OF TREND SPOTTING, JWT (2008)

"They are not individualistic risk takers like Boomers or cynical and disengaged like Generation X… Millennials are civic minded, trust in leaders, and are team oriented."

— **PETER LEYDEN**, DIRECTOR OF THE NEW POLITICS INSTITUTE (2007)

The Millennial Surprise

Meet today's young workers. "They are much more willing to ask for guidance," says Martha Burger, senior vice president for human resources at Chesapeake Energy Corporation. "The last thing older generations would do was ask their boss for help. This generation just seems more comfortable with authority figures."

Employers are noticing many new qualities in this rising crop of employees. "They are more concerned than previous generations about the future and where their careers are going" says Steve Canale, recruiting and staffing manager at GE. "They want to be more predictable. And they are the best 'teaming' workers we've ever had."

Up until recently, managers grew accustomed to young employees who viewed hands-on guidance as "micromanagement," preferred solo gigs to teamwork, and focused more on the next paycheck than the long-term payoff.

Now a new generation of young workers is turning this image on its head. They are planning careers before they get their braces off. They are newly attracted to teamwork and "helping" careers. They are keeping their parents highly involved every step of the way. And once they arrive at the office, they expect constant feedback and positive recognition from managers. "That's right," says Penelope Trunk, who covers the workplace beat for *BusinessWeek*, "Gen Y wants to be micromanaged... So stop judging and start micromanaging. Check in three times a day. Give goals that are daily and weekly and monthly."

The Changing Face of Youth

Teachers, career counselors, military officers, and corporate recruiters who work with youth often pride themselves on being the first to notice generational change when it occurs. These days many of them are giving workshops, writing editorials, or talking to the media. Your ears may be ringing with references to "Millennials," "Gen Y," or "Net Gen"—perhaps in comparison to older "Gen Xers," "Boomers," or "Traditionalists."

Yet even those in closest contact with the youth culture are often confounded by both the direction and timing of such change. Perhaps the most common mistake is to assume that generational change is gradual and linear, and that next year's new hires or college grads will be like last year's, only a bit more so. Most of the time that's true. But every two decades or so such linear projections prove to be drastically mistaken. That is the surprise that happens when the change is abrupt and nonlinear—in other words, when a new youth generation actually appears.

Consider the following expectations for youth at various times during the postwar era:

The Silent Generation came as a surprise.

In 1946, about the time General George Marshall declared the nation's victorious troops to be "the best damn kids in the world," Americans braced for fresh ranks of organized young workers who would take the mass mobilizations of the New Deal and World War II to a higher level of activism. These new youths were expected to be just like the world-conquering generation just before them—only this time they would energize unions, veterans, students, and party leaders to strive for even grander political goals.

This didn't happen. After the returning G.I.s flowed quickly into and out of the nation's campuses, everyone was surprised to learn that the next generation of young people seemed more interested in protecting their "permanent records" than in marching on Washington. Looking back, historian William Manchester wrote, "Never had American youth been so withdrawn, cautious, unimaginative, indifferent, unadventurous—and silent....They waited so patiently for everything that visitors to college campuses began commenting on their docility."

As young workers, this Silent Generation (born 1925–1942) didn't want to change the system (so went the quip), they wanted to "work within the system." A rising crop of "organization men" planned long careers with big organizations, donning gray flannel suits and climbing corporate ladders. They married early, bought homes in the suburbs, and kept their heads down.

Boomers came as a surprise.

By the early 1960s, Americans had grown used to talking about a "Silent Generation" of youth. As experts looked ahead to the onrushing bulge of children known as the "baby boom" who were about to arrive in the workplace, they foresaw a new corps of technocratic corporatists, a Silent Generation to the next degree, even more pliable and conformist than the "lonely crowd" right before them. They would plug into the system and build domed cities with monorails. "Employers are going to love this generation," University of California Berkeley's Clark Kerr declared in 1959. "They are going to be easy to handle. There aren't going to be any riots."

Events, to say the least, turned out otherwise. A new Boom Generation (born 1943–1960) came of age as flower-power protesters, campus rioters, and inner-city mobs. Entering the workplace, Boomers rejected big institutions, materialism, and "the system," striking out on their own to find meaningful "callings." They wouldn't take just any establishment career. They would consult their own conscience and "follow their bliss." Remarkably, none of the big-name social scientists—not even Erik Erikson or Margaret Mead—saw any hint of the youth explosion that was about to shake America.

Generation X came as a surprise.

Let's move forward another twenty years. By around 1980, youth experts agreed that young Boomers defined the new norm in adolescent attitudes and behavior. So the question was soon raised: What would the next crop be like? These were the "baby busters," kids who had no memories of the assassination of John F. Kennedy and no clear impression of Woodstock, Vietnam, or even Watergate. Once again, the expectation was linear, that these youths would be like Boomers, only more so. Demographic forecasters suggested that the teens in the 1980s and 1990s would be even more ideological, "holistic," and morals-driven—extending what *American Demographics* termed "an ongoing trend away from material aspirations toward non-materialistic goals."

Those predictions were rudely overturned when the scrappy, pragmatic persona of Generation X (born 1961–1981) emerged a few years later. Disco gave way to MTV, soul to hip hop, Sylvester Stallone to Tom Cruise, Robin Williams to Eddie Murphy. Long-haired ideologues were replaced by mohawked punks, suicidal grunge stars, goateed gamers, professional soldiers, gangsta rappers, and business school "power tools." The journey was no longer the reward; instead winning was "the only thing." Free-agent entrepreneurs struck out into the marketplace, taking risks, making deals, and looking out for the bottom line.

And the Millennials?

Millennials (born 1982–2004) are also coming as a surprise.

Today another twenty years have passed, and another generational change is on the doorstep. As a group, Millennials are unlike any young adults in living memory. More numerous, more affluent, better educated, and more ethnically diverse than those who came before, they are beginning to manifest a wide array of positive social habits that older Americans no longer associate with youth.

Yet most people's perception of youth still lags behind reality. As was true twenty, forty, and sixty years ago, a common adult view is that these young adults are like the prior batch (Gen X) taken to the next degree (alias Gen "Y"). One well-known consultant who specializes in managing younger workers literally refers this rising group as "Gen X on steroids."

Extrapolating from Gen-X trends, older adults generally take a dim view of the Millennials. This is not because there is anything wrong with Generation X, but rather because any set of personality traits, extended far enough, are ultimately perceived as negative. So the Gen Xers' trademark individualism becomes selfishness. Their skepticism becomes cynicism. Their bluntness becomes rudeness. Their pragmatism becomes apathy—or even dumbness.

A 2009 Pew study found that a majority of older Americans believe today's young adults are inferior to them in moral values, work ethic, and respect for others. One recent book (by Mark Bauerlein) calls them *The Dumbest Generation*. Another (by Jean Twenge) calls them *Generation Me*. Each month, new newspaper articles criticize young people for everything from poor grammar and short attention spans to spaghetti straps and freak dancing. According to the editors of the *Wall Street Journal*, they are "Generation E, for Entitled." According to Hillary Clinton, "they think work is a four-letter word."

In the business world, plenty of older managers report an equally downbeat impression of today's young workers. They have unleashed a storm of criticism about how this generation is entitled, needy, whiney, and even lazy. Drawing on memories of their own youth, Boomer and Gen-X supervisors assume that Millennials are even more rude than they were (that's why they wear flip-flops), even more disloyal than they were (just waiting for their chance to "job hop"), and even more dismissive of authority than they were (why else would they tell their boss there might be better way to get the job done?).

To believe all these accounts, you'd suppose America is being overrun by young people who can't read anything longer than a text message, spend their loose change on tongue rings, think about nothing but themselves, and couldn't care less who runs the country.

How depressing. And how wrong.

The Millennial Surprise

The truth is that the Millennial Generation is not following a trend. Like earlier generations coming of age, it is starting its own new trend. And that new trend happens to be fairly positive. Look closely at youth indicators, and you'll see that the Millennials' attitudes and behaviors represent a turnaround from many of the negative youth directions launched by Boomers in the 1960s and '70s and by Gen Xers in the '80s and '90s. The data are clear—and reflect a profound disconnect between the good news about today's youth and older adults' misperception of them.

Are the Millennials self-absorbed individualists? No. They are gravitating toward group activity and community life. In K–12 schools, they have come to expect team teaching, team grading, and group projects. In college, they are enrolling in "living-learning" communities. They leverage social networking technology to stay connected to their peers 24/7. The U.S. Army discarded its "Army of One" slogan to attract them. More than three-quarters of Millennial employees say the social aspects of work are very important to their workplace satisfaction, and one in four say they left a job because they felt disconnected from the organization—far more than any other generation.

Are they rule breakers? No, they're rule followers. Over the past fifteen years, rates of violent crime among teens have dropped by over 65 percent, rates of teen pregnancy and abortion by 40 percent, rates of high school sexual activity by 15 percent, and rates of alcohol and tobacco use in grades eight, ten, and twelve are hitting all-time lows. According to "Youth Risk Behavior" surveys run by the Centers for Disease Control and Prevention (CDC), risk-taking is down across the board for high school students—in everything from binge drinking to not buckling your seatbelt. In the workplace, surveys show that Millennials are more likely than prior generations to opt for secure, structured jobs and to value safety protocols, health insurance, and wellness guidance.

Are they pessimists? No. They're optimists. In a 2008 survey, fully 77 percent of high school students said they are "very confident" about reaching their career goals. Another 31 percent said "fairly confident." A large majority of students (especially large among minority students) think they will do better economically than their parents. Teen suicide rates are trending downward for the first time since World War II. Surveys show that today's young workers are more optimistic than older generations about the career opportunities their employers offer. Managers are noting that they expect to receive interesting tasks, opportunities to contribute, and plenty of positive feedback—but that they also have very high expectations for their own performance.

Figure 1 ▶

Violent Crime, 1973 to 2009, Rates for Youth Offenders and Youth Victims*

* 2009 estimated; violent crimes are murders, rapes, robberies, and assaults.

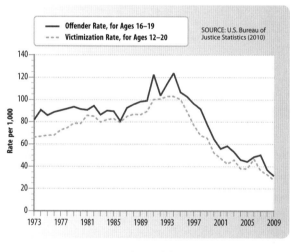

Are they alienated? No. They are invested in the community. A record-high 70 percent of college freshmen now say that it is "extremely important" to help others in need. The share of 16- to 24-year olds who volunteer in their community has doubled since 1989. Surveys show that today's youth are strongly attracted to "helping" professions like government careers, teaching, and non-profits—a remarkable shift away from the Gen-X preference for the private sector. Eight out of ten 13- to 25-year olds say they want to work for a company that cares about how it affects or contributes to society. It is a mistake to call them

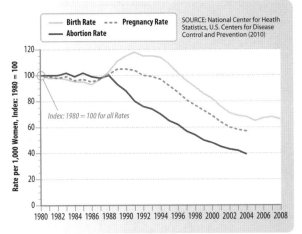

◄ **Figure 2**

Rates of Pregnancy, Abortion, and Birth for Girls Age 15 to 17, 1980 to 2008*

* Data unavailable past 2004 for pregnancies and abortions.

the "Me Generation" (a label invented for young Boomers in the 1960s). Better to call them the "We Generation."

Are they distrustful? No. They trust authority figures. A recent survey found 82 percent of teens reporting "no problems" with any family member—versus just 48 percent who said that back in 1974, when parents and teens were far more likely to argue and oppose one another's basic values. Even as Millennials enter young adulthood, they continue to report that parents are far and away their most trusted source of information about life choices and careers. Half say they trust government to do what's right all or most of the time—twice the share of older people answering the same question in the same poll. In school, they often want more life-guidance than guidance counselors are prepared to offer. On the job, Millennials thrive with older adult mentors and rank working with a boss they can respect and learn from as the number one attribute of the job they seek.

Are they aimless? No, they are highly directed and feel pressure to meet long-term goals in order to keep up with achievement-oriented peers. The majority of today's high school students say they have detailed five- and ten-year plans for their future. College students and their parents both agree, by a six-to-one margin, that the students spend more time planning for the future than their parents did at the same age. A rising number of high school seniors say they plan to hold only one or two jobs within their first ten years of employment—and those who do "job hop" tend to leave because they aren't finding the hands-on guidance and long-term growth opportunities they seek. Employers are noting that young workers prefer weekly or even daily feedback to ensure their work is on track.

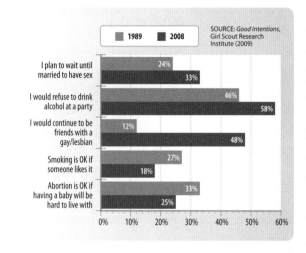

Figure 3 ▶

Questions Asked
of Students in
Grades 7 to 12:
Percent who Agree,
1989 and 2008

Are they slackers? No. They are the most achievement-oriented generation in memory. Since the late 1980s, grade school aptitude test scores have been rising or (at least) flat across all subjects and all racial and ethnic groups. The number of high school students who take and pass an Advanced Placement (AP) test has more than doubled in the past ten years. Fully 70 percent of high school students today say they want a four-year college degree. A growing share are taking the SAT or ACT. Even so, the average score on these national tests is the highest in thirty years. Eight in ten teenagers say that it is "cool to be smart." Three in ten say "knowledge" is what makes someone successful (twice the share who say that about "fame"). In the workplace, they continue to seek opportunities to learn and advance according to well-defined expectations—81 percent rate "opportunities for promotion" as a crucial characteristic when choosing a job, and 77 percent say the same for "learning new skills."

So why don't employers and HR professionals see who the Millennials really are? Very simple. They're looking at young workers as an age bracket—which, over the last forty years, has been dominated by Boomers and Gen Xers. They believe they understand the trends. They're not looking down the age ladder at the Millennial Generation, which will soon take over the young-worker age bracket and, as it does, redirect those trends. If they had been looking at Millennials, perhaps they would have noticed how public schools, colleges, and the military are beginning to interact with youth in entirely new ways— by involving parents, raising standards, stressing teamwork, offering instant feedback, and celebrating achievement. But not many are paying attention.

Since many managers and HR experts are themselves parents of Millennials, with an up-close view of this rising generation, you might think that they have noticed many of these new trends firsthand. Yet so jaded is the media stereotype that even these parents draw a sharp contrast between the young people they know personally (their own kids and their kids' friends: positive) and those they don't (youth in general: negative). This double vision shows up consistently in opinion research. In a recent California survey asking about parenting skills, for example, parents gave themselves a grade of A or B—but gave parents in general a D or F.

Observant employers might notice that even the entertainment industry is beginning to turn the negative Boomer and Xer stereotypes of young workers on their head. In the film *The Devil Wears Prada*, it's the Boomer fashion boss who is aggressively egotistical, while the pleasant young assistant struggles to please and fit in. In *Up in the Air*, it's the Boomer executive who leads a rootless life of workaholism and isolation, while his young associate aspires to a perfectly

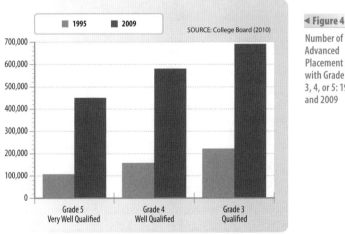

◄ **Figure 4**

Number of Advanced Placement Exams with Grade of 3, 4, or 5: 1995 and 2009

conventional minivan-and-suburban home lifestyle. In NBC's "The Office," it's the oddball Gen-X supervisor who fights with "corporate," while the youngest employees yearn for a normal work environment.

Educational Attainment, Then and Now

	All Young Adults Age 18 to 24...[1]	
	in 1985	in 2008
high school dropouts	14%	9%
enrolled in two-year college	7%	12%
enrolled in four-year college	20%	28%
taken at least one AP exam*	4%	30%
taken the SAT*	25%	41%
average SAT score*	999	1,022

	All Graduating High School Students...[2]	
	in 1982	in 2004
completed algebra II	40%	68%
completed biology and chemistry	29%	61%
completed 3 years+ in foreign language	9%	19%
completed calculus	5%	13%
completed engineering	1%	9%

* Average annual participation and score for all years in which the seven cohorts reached age 18
[1] Age 18 to 24, Source: U.S. Census Bureau; Pew Research Center (2009); and College Board (2010).
[2] Graduating High School Students, Source: *The Condition of Education 2007*, U.S. Department of Education (2007)

By misunderstanding Millennials, many employers are oblivious to the wave of positive youth trends. What's worse is that they also misunderstand the new array of problems and challenges facing today's young workers. On the flip side of each of this generation's strengths, in other words, can be found a corresponding vulnerability.

So pressured are Millennials to meet adult expectations that many fear taking creative risks. They know the stakes are high, and they perceive that the price of any mistake, whether a poor performance review or a misguided career move, is more consequential than it used to be. Managers report that it is harder to get young people to take creative risks and think outside the box.

So team oriented are Millennials that many would rather seek consensus and the approval of the group than express a divisive or controversial opinion. Managers struggle to bring out Millennials' go-it-alone leadership qualities because young employees are afraid to assert themselves and stand out from the crowd.

So special do Millennials feel that many have trouble facing criticism, coping with failure, and sticking with any activity that may at first prove disappointing—including the rote tasks that are common in entry-level jobs.

So trusting are Millennials of the institutions in their lives that they face particularly bitter disappointment when the system does not deliver success for everyone. This is of rising concern in an economy in which jobs are scarcer, and layoffs more common, than any time in since the Great Depression.

So sheltered are Millennials by their parents that many have trouble developing strong independent coping skills. Youth obesity is on the rise as kids spend more time in sedentary activities and less time playing independently out of doors. Overly involved and intrusive parents are creating new hassles for employers as they hover over young workers' job search and early employment.

The purpose of this book is to familiarize teachers, managers, and policy makers with both the new strengths and new vulnerabilities of today's young workers. Once you know their strengths, you can harness them. Once you know their vulnerabilities, you can overcome them. Yet to know either, you first need to abandon all of your assumptions about Boomer youth trends or Gen-X youth trends. The Millennials are arriving as a surprise, a corner-turner, a trend-changer.

This is why we steadfastly avoid calling Millennials "Generation Y." It is not only a name that today's youth don't much like (because the letter doesn't evoke anything about their collective experience). It also perpetuates the assumption that one generation linearly follows another, as Y after X. But that has never happened for any new generation. And it's certainly not happening for this one.

Understanding Generations

Now it's time to pause and address a couple of basic questions. We've been talking a lot about generations. But just what is a generation, anyway? And what is known about them?

The word *generation*—meaning an entire peer group—is ancient. It goes back at least as far as Homer and the Old Testament. In the century and a half following the French Revolution, the concept was much discussed by the most famous philosophers and social scientists (the likes of John Stuart Mill, Wilhelm Dilthey, José Ortega y Gasset, and Karl Mannheim). These thinkers often talked about "social generations" to distinguish them from other types of generations (like "family generations"). The concept has been so heavily used in postwar America, especially when discussing the pop culture, that the adjective "social" is no longer needed. Just say "generation" and everyone knows what you have in mind.

Now for a definition. A generation consists of everyone born over the span of a single phase of life, or roughly twenty years. Members of a generation share a collective peer personality that is defined by three basic attributes: a common sense of growing up at the same moment in history, a common set of attitudes and behaviors, and a common collective identity. The sense of collective identity enables members of a generation to identify with labels like "Boomer" or "Gen Xer." By this definition, Millennials clearly comprise a generation. And so do earlier-born Americans, who all belong to generations of their own, each with boundaries that are just as firmly drawn by when they came along, by who they are, and by how they see themselves.

What does it means to belong to a generation? It does not mean that we necessarily get along with or even like most of our peers. But it does mean that our bedrock beliefs, our assumptions about life, our daily habits, and our collective sense of self are strongly shaped by our formative years, and thus by our generational membership.

Like any social category that helps define who one is (such as race, class, or nationality), a generation can allow plenty of individual exceptions and be fuzzy at the edges. Yet unlike most other categories, it possesses its own biography. You can tell a lifelong story about the shared experiences of the Silent

Generation in ways you never could for all women, all African Americans, or all Californians. The reason, wrote Ortega y Gasset, is that a generation is "a species of biological missile hurled into space at a given instant, with a certain velocity and direction," which gives it a "pre-established vital trajectory." A generation can feel nostalgia for a unique past, express urgency about a future of limited duration, and comprehend its own mortality.

Understanding the concept of generations can help to correct many of the errors and misunderstandings currently being spread about generational differences in the workplace. Most management and HR consultants don't really understand these differences, so they ignore them, distort them, trivialize them, sensationalize them, attribute them mistakenly to age differences, or use them as a crude weapon to heap criticism on the young.

Workplace blogs are filled with comments by managers who do all of the above. Reading them, you learn that Millennials are different in the workplace because video games have reprogrammed their brains, or because liberals have force-fed them on self-esteem, or because conservatives have made them fearful to speak out, or simply because they're younger (that is, give them some time and they'll be just like Xers or Boomers are today). You may even learn that this whole fuss about Millennials is a pop-culture excuse for the young just not being able to measure up to older folks, despite having had it so much easier as kids.

But once you understand generations, you'll know all of these comments are mistaken—or at least, grossly inadequate.

Before concluding this chapter, let's clarify what generations are and how to analyze them usefully, by offering a few simple dos and don'ts.

* *DO appreciate that generations are a fundamental and timeless unit of social history.*

Tired of hearing about the "MTV Generation" or the "iPod Generation"? So are we. The media often imply that belonging to a generation involves nothing deeper than pop music tastes and familiarity with a new gadget. This is wrong. Empirical data confirm that generations, throughout their lives, differ from each other in the very deepest of their attitudes and behav-

Six Generations of Americans

The G.I. Generation (Born 1901–24) enjoyed a "good kid" reputation as the beneficiaries of new playgrounds, scouting clubs, vitamins, and child-labor restrictions. They came of age with the sharpest rise in schooling ever recorded. As young adults, their uniformed corps patiently endured the Depression and heroically conquered foreign enemies. In a midlife subsidized by the G.I. Bill, they built suburbs, invented vaccines, plugged missile gaps, and launched moon rockets. Their unprecedented grip on the Presidency (1961 through '92) began with the New Frontier, Great Society, and Model Cities, but wore down through Vietnam, Watergate, and budget deficits. As senior citizens, they safeguarded their "entitlements" but had little influence over culture and values.

Famous People: Walt Disney, Judy Garland, John Wayne, Katharine Hepburn, John F. Kennedy, Ray Kroc, Ann Landers, Walter Cronkite, Ronald Reagan, John Steinbeck

Workplace Reputation: Constructive team player ("technocrats" or "power elite"). As workers, G.I.s were known for promoting peer solidarity through unions, trusting large, hierarchical organizations, and socializing worker risks, often through new government programs. Their civic achievements and institutional trust were rewarded with generous benefits and entitlements in old age.

The Silent Generation (Born 1925–42) grew up as the suffocated children of war and Depression. They came of age just too late to be war heroes and just too early to be youthful free spirits. Instead, this early-marrying "lonely crowd" became the risk-averse technicians and professionals as well as the sensitive rock 'n' rollers and civil-rights advocates of a post-Crisis era—an era in which conformity seemed to be a sure ticket to success. Midlife was an anxious passage for a generation torn between stolid elders and passionate juniors. Their surge to power coincided with fragmenting families, cultural diversity, institutional complexity, and too much litigation. As elders, they have a hip style and a reputation for indecision. Most are abandoning the G.I. "senior citizen" label.

Famous People: Shirley Temple, Bill Cosby, John McCain, Warren Buffet, Nancy Pelosi, Martin Luther King, Jr., Elvis Presley, Sandra Day O'Connor, Paul Simon

Workplace Reputation: Credentialed expert ("organization man"). The Silent launched long-term, stable careers at a very young age, but adjusted course in midlife, when many learned to take risks and made major career changes. As today's senior workers, the Silent are known for their friendly professionalism, habitual reliability, and good interpersonal relationships with coworkers and customers.

| 1901 | G.I. | 1924 | 1925 | SILENT | 1942 | 1943 | BOOM |

The Boom Generation (Born 1943–60) grew up as indulged youth during an era of community-spirited progress. As kids, they were the proud creation of postwar optimism, Dr. Spock rationalism, and "Father Knows Best" family order. Coming of age, however, Boomers loudly proclaimed their antipathy to the secular blueprints of their parents; they demanded inner visions over outer and self-perfection over thing-making or team-playing. The Boom "Awakening" climaxed with Vietnam War protests, the 1967 "summer of love," inner-city riots, the first Earth Day, and Kent State. In the aftermath, Boomers appointed themselves arbiter of the nation's values and crowded into such "culture careers" as teaching, religion, journalism, marketing, and the arts. During the 1990s and '00s, they have trumpeted values, touted a "politics of meaning," and waged scorched-earth culture wars—amid growing complaints about their reckless and unaccountable leadership style.

Famous People: Bill and Hillary Clinton, George W. and Laura Bush, Oprah Winfrey, Bill Gates, Al Sharpton, Tom Hanks, Meryl Streep, Rush Limbaugh, Katie Couric, Donald Trump.

Workplace Reputation: Assertive visionary ("yuppie" or "cultural elite"). Boomers pioneered a new ethic of individualism and self-sufficiency in the workplace—becoming, for example, the first-ever generation of economically independent women. As today's midlife workers, they are known for their obsessive work ethic, their declining institutional trust, and their need to infuse their careers with values, mission, and meaning.

Except for many Boomers (who assume they've got the landscape mapped), when you talk generations, the first thing most folks want to know is: *Where do I fit?* This table puts the Millennials, their four predecessor generations, and the generation following them, into perspective. Think about your own family—your parents, your favorite aunt or uncle, your youngest brother, your kids. When were they born, and how did their generational membership shape them? Then think about some individuals who have inspired you—movie stars, great writers, even political leaders—and speculate whether they have ended up carrying out a key part of their own generation's "script."

Generation X (Born 1961–81) survived a hurried childhood of divorce, latchkeys, open classrooms, and devil-child movies. They came of age curtailing the earlier rise in youth crime and fall in test scores—yet heard themselves denounced as so wild and stupid as to put *The Nation At Risk*. As young adults navigating a sexual battlescape of AIDS and blighted courtship rituals, they dated and married cautiously. From grunge to hip-hop, their culture has revealed a hardened edge. Politically, they have leaned toward pragmatism and non-affiliation, and many would rather volunteer than vote. Widely criticized as "slackers," and facing a *Reality Bites* economy of declining young-adult living standards, they have embodied the "resilience" of post-9/11 America. They have matured into one of the most dynamic generations of entrepreneurs in U.S. history, and the most protective generation of parents.

Famous People: Barack Obama, Sarah Palin, Jeff Bezos, Tiger Woods, Jon Stewart, Jodie Foster, Michael Jordan, Tom Cruise, Michael Dell, Kurt Cobain, Ann Coulter.

Workplace Reputation: Get-it-done contractor ("free agent"). Economically hard pressed by policies favoring their elders, Gen Xers run their careers like small businesses, prioritizing the time, money, and tasks each individual needs to get by. As today's thirty- and forty-something workers, they are known for embracing risk, responding to incentives, and using a "whatever-works" pragmatism to get them to the bottom line.

| 1960 1961 | GENERATION X | 1981 1982 | MILLENNIAL | 2004 2005 | HOMELAND |

The Millennial Generation (Born 1982–2004) first arrived when "Baby on Board" signs appeared on minivan windows. As abortion and divorce rates ebbed, the popular culture began stigmatizing hands-off parental styles and recasting babies as special. Child abuse and child safety became hot topics, while books teaching virtues and values became bestsellers. By the mid-1990s, politicians were defining adult issues (from tax cuts to welfare reform to Internet access) in terms of their effects on children. Hollywood has replaced cinematic child devils with child angels; the media has cordoned off child-friendly havens; educators speak of standards and cooperative learning. As this generation graduates from college and carefully starts careers under the wings of protective parents, rates of community service and voting among young adults are surging.

Famous People: Michael Phelps, Miley Cyrus, Mark Zuckerberg, LeBron James, Taylor Swift, the Jonas Brothers, Christopher Paolini.

Workplace Reputation: net-centric team player ("organization kids"). As today's entry-level workers, Millennials are known for their confidence, teachability, and strong team skills. Many older workers also regard them as coddled, risk averse, and lacking in initiative. With their rising institutional trust, they are placing new focus on stable, long-term career paths.

The Homeland Generation (Born 2005–?) is arriving in today's nurseries. These will be the babies born roughly through the mid-2020s, and their first wave is just beginning to fill kindergarten classrooms. Their nurturing style—super-protected and programmed, with a new focus on sociability—is now being set by Gen Xers, but half of their parents will be Millennials.

iors—everything from risk-taking, self-esteem, and family life to gender roles, optimism, and institutional trust.

Some workplace consultants exclaim excitedly that "generational diversity" is a new workplace problem, or that Americans have never before had "four generations in the workplace." This too is wrong. Awareness of generational differences, both in and out of work, goes back to the beginning of recorded history. "Our civilization is doomed if the unheard-of actions of the younger generation are allowed to continue": So reads a four thousand year-old cuneiform tablet unearthed in the Sumerian city of Ur. In American history, the peers of Benjamin Franklin, and those of Thomas Edison, knew and wrote about generational differences.

If generational change were superficial, it would be unimportant. If it were entirely new, it would be unintelligible. The premise of this book is that generational change is deep and enduring, which is why so many workplace managers worry about it and hope they can do something about it. Even when the immediate cause of their complaints about young workers seem trivial—dress that's too casual or parents who are too close—most managers suspect, rightly, that something deeper is going on.

* *DON'T confuse generations with phases of life (that is, with age). Both are important, but different.*

A generation is a group of people, born over a certain period, who grow older with time. A phase of life is a socially and biologically defined age range, like childhood. The two are not the same. Some workplace consultants refer to "the Mature Generation." This is absurd: These folks are "mature" only due to their age, not their generation.

For many kinds of behavior, of course, age matters. For example, it is usually true that, whatever their generation, people over age 50 are likely to take fewer personal risks, worry more about their health, change jobs less frequently, vote more often, and have more trouble with new technology than people of under age 30. Yet generational membership may strongly affect the *relative* strength of these kinds of behavior. Examples:

* The G.I. Generation (born 1901–1924) has shown relatively high voting rates throughout its collective lifetime. Both as "junior citizens" in their youth and as "senior citizens" in old age, G.I.s voted more often than other generations did (or do) in the same age bracket.

* Boomers (born 1943–1960) obsess more than other generations about finding "meaning and purpose" in their lives and careers. Opinion surveys have consistently shown these worries peaking in whatever age bracket Boomers occupy. Today, workers in their fifties are more likely to display "work-centric" behaviors than workers in other age brackets.

* Millennials (born 1982–2004) are less likely to want to job hop than Boomers or Gen Xers were at the same age. By some measures, in fact, twenty-something Millennials are less likely to want to job hop than forty-something Gen Xers are today. In this case, Millennials are not only *relatively* less inclined to change jobs, but *absolutely* less inclined—a striking fact still unrecognized by most employers.

In this book, we avoid making timeless assertions about any age group—such as "young workers do this" or "midlife CEOs think that." To us, a phase of life is like an empty hotel room, with new generations checking in and checking out every couple of decades. Most of the time, you need to identify both the room and the occupant. It is not enough to say that Millennial workers are often put off by the ruthless workaholism of senior managers. It is more informative to say, of their *Boomer* senior managers.

* *DO think generationally backwards or forwards when assessing why people of a certain age behave the way they do, or how they will behave in the future.*
  Say for example you want to explain why workers in their fifties are now suffering rapidly rising rates of drug addictions and drug-related hospitalizations. Where do you look for answers? You could look *straight* backwards at workers in their fifties going back to the 1970s. But that probably won't tell you much. Or you could look *generationally* backwards at these workers

33

when they were 20-year olds in 1970—and find some answers in Woodstock or Vietnam.

Or say you want to anticipate the long-term consequences of strong team skills among today's twenty-something recruits. Now you know what to do. You look forward *generationally* and hypothesize (maybe on the basis of historical parallels) that forty-something managers in the 2020s will get rid of cubicles or adopt team compensation plans or favor unionization.

In both of these examples, the secret is to project *the same group of people* forward or backward through time. You will notice that we do a lot of that in this book.

✳ *DON'T assume that generations are only shaped by history. They also shape history.*

Of course generations are shaped by big events and social trends ("history"). That's how generations are formed. Yet generations also shape history—both in young adulthood and as they mature into parents, entrepreneurs, and public leaders.

Consider, for example, information technology. Boomers were shaped as children by the top-down mainframe computers and centralized databanks of the 1950s and 1960s. But as adults, Boomers reacted against this monolithic mindset by inventing (Bill Gates, Steve Jobs) the personal computer—a creative think station for each individual—which proved, according to the famous Apple ad, that "1984 won't be like 1984." Boomers changed the direction of IT to match their own anti-establishment personality.

And today? Millennials have been shaped as children over the last twenty years by the individualized, market-oriented tech innovations of Gen Xers. Yet as consumers and innovators, they too are beginning to shape—and not just be shape by—the direction of IT. So far, they are rejecting their elders' obsession with ever-more individualism and privacy, and are starting to lead IT (Mark Zuckerberg, Chris Hughes) toward community, friendship, and civic activity in a sort of electronic group hug via IM and Facebook.

Technology, of course, is just one piece of the picture. As they come of age, Millennials are beginning to shape social trends to reflect their pri-

Workplace Reputations

The 2008 *Randstad World at Work* survey tracks generational reputations in the workplace. When employees of all ages were surveyed, they identified the following positive qualities in coworkers of other generations:

Perceived Positive Qualities			
Millennials	Generation X	Boomers	Silent
Confident	Independent thinker	Strong work ethic	Committed to the company
Sociable	Seeks creative challenges	Willing to take on responsibility	Ethical
Ambitious	Open to new ideas	Demanding	Friendly

orities in areas as diverse as pop culture, family life, and the workplace. To all those workplace futurists predicting that today's young workers will eventually "adapt" to Boomer and Xer trends: The record of history shows something else—that it's the older generations who will ultimately have to adapt to many of the new attitudes of the rising generation.

To say that a generation puts its own stamp on history is to say that it comes of age with collective desires and aspirations that may not match those of any older generation. This is why one must never forget, above all, that every generation arrives as a surprise. That includes the Millennials. We now turn to their story.

02
Why Millennials Happened

"It's no accident that the psychology of entire generations is shaped by the milieu in which they grew up; economic research tells us that our lifelong behaviors are determined in large part by the seismic events—good or bad—of our youth."

— *NEWSWEEK* (2010)

"Echo boomers are a reflection of the sweeping changes in American life over the past twenty years…. From when they were toddlers, they have been belted into car seats and driven off to some form of organized group activity. After graduating from "Gymboree" and "Mommy and Me," they have been shuttled to play dates and soccer practice, with barely a day off, by parents who've felt their kids needed structure and a sense of mission."

— *CBS NEWS* (2004)

Why Millennials Happened

Millennials are emerging as a surprise for one simple reason: They have grown up in a very different social and cultural setting than the ones today's older generations may recall from their youth. Every generation is shaped by this kind of "location in history."

Why did the Silent Generation emerge as risk-averse, rule-abiding "organization men"? Because they grew up as the overprotected children of war and Depression and defined young adulthood in an era dominated by large, conformity-seeking institutions (the mid-1940s through mid-1960s).

Why did Boomers emerge as argumentative, values-obsessed individualists? Because they grew up as indulged postwar children and defined young adulthood in an era of social turmoil, youth anger, and rising distrust of big institutions (the mid-1960s through the mid-1980s).

Why did Gen Xers emerge as pragmatic, survivalist "free agents"? Because they grew up as the ignored children of the Consciousness Revolution and defined young adulthood in an individualistic era of market-driven free agency, risk-taking, and entrepreneurialism (the 1980s and '90s).

Now let's turn to the Millennial Generation.

The Millennial Generation's Location in History

Recall the last three decades of American family life. The change came in 1982. The February 22, 1982 issue of *Time* magazine offered a cover story about an array of thirty-something Boomers choosing (finally) to become moms and dads. That same year, bright yellow "Baby on Board" signs began popping up in station wagon windows.

Around Christmas of 1983, adult America fell in love with Cabbage Patch Kids—a precious new doll, harvested pure from nature, so wrinkly and cuddly-cute that millions of Boomers wanted to take one home to love. Better yet, why not a genuine, live Millennial? Over the next twenty years, as the U.S. birth rate boomed, businesses rediscovered children and began showing images of them in the ads of practically everything they marketed—cars, TVs, vacations, homes.

The era of the wanted child had begun.

In September 1982, the first Tylenol scare led to parental panic over trick-or-treating. Halloween suddenly found itself encased in hotlines, advisories, and statutes—a fate that would soon befall many pastimes once deemed innocent, from bicycle riding to BB guns. A few months later came national hysteria over the sexual abuse of toddlers, leading to dozens of adult convictions after what skeptics would liken to Salem-style trials.

All the while, new books (*The Disappearance of Childhood, Children without Childhood, Our Endangered Children*) assailed the "anything goes" parental treatment of the previous generation of children. Those days were ending as the family, school, and neighborhood wagons began circling.

Thereafter, year after year, state and federal legislators enacted an ever-more draconian battery of laws to protect children from harm. Americans were determined that nothing bad should happen to these wonderful kids.

The era of the protected child had begun.

From the late 1950s through the late 1970s, the national rates for most behaviors damaging to children—divorce, abortion, violent crime, alcohol intake, and drug abuse—had been rising. In the early 1980s, they reached their postwar peak, began to decline, and have been declining ever since. The wellbeing of children started to dominate the national debate over most family issues: welfare, latchkey households, drugs, and pornography.

In 1983, the federal *Nation at Risk* report on education blasted grade school students as "a rising tide of mediocrity," prompting editorialists to implore teachers and adults to do better by America's next batch of kids. By the end of the decade, school reform rose to the top of the nation's agenda.

In 1984, *Children of the Corn* and *Firestarter* failed at the box office. Hollywood was astonished, since these were merely the latest installments in a child-horror film genre that had been popular and profitable for nearly two decades, ever since *Rosemary's Baby* and *The Exorcist*. But parents were beginning to prefer a new kind of movie, about adorable babies (*Baby Boom, Parenthood, Three Men and a Baby*). Ten years later, by the early 1990s, they preferred movies about sweet, helpful older kids, who actually inspired their parents to become better people (*Sleepless in Seattle, Angels in the Outfield*).

The era of the worthy child had begun.

In 1990, the *Wall Street Journal* and *New York Times* had headlines—"The '60s Generation, Once High on Drugs, Warns Its Children" and "Do As I Say, Not As I Did"—that would have been unimaginable a decade earlier. Polls showed that Boomer parents did not want their own children to have the same freedom with drugs, alcohol, and sex that they once enjoyed.

Between 1986 and '91, the number of periodicals offered to young children doubled. In tot-TV fare, "Barney and Friends" (featuring teamwork and what kids share in common) stole the limelight from "Sesame Street" (featuring individualism and what makes each kid unique).

During 1996, major-party presidential nominees Dole and Clinton dueled for the presidency in a campaign full of talk about the middle school children of "soccer moms."

The next year, Millennials began to make an impression on the pop culture. Thanks to the Spice Girls, Hanson, Backstreet Boys, and others, 1997 ushered in a whole new musical sound. It was happier, brighter, less desperate, and more choreographed. In the years that followed, as Disney staged successive youth frenzies over Hilary Duff, *High School Musical*, "Hannah Montana," and the Jonas Brothers, the pop music center of gravity moved away from grunge and gangsta rap—toward R&B, dance, synthpop, and "hip pop."

From 1997 to 2000, just as Millennials flooded into their teen years, Duke University's *Index of Child & Youth Well-Being*—focusing heavily on teens— jumped upward. From crime, drugs, alcohol, and suicide to test scores and high school graduation, all the child wellbeing indicators were improving.

The era of the well-adjusted child had begun.

Through the late 1990s, the first wave of these much-watched children passed through high school, accompanied by enormous parental, educational, and media fascination. Americans of all ages responded to the Columbine and 9/11 tragedies by tightening family bonds and securing family perimeters. The adult absorption with Millennial safety, achievement, and conduct was reaching a fever pitch.

At the turn of the millennium, the first 1982-born cohort of this new generation began graduating from high school, amidst great media fanfare over the "high school class of 2000." Employers and postsecondary

Figure 5 ▶

Index of Child & Youth Well-Being: Duke University's Index of 28 Key Youth Indicators*, 1975 to 2008

* The 28 youth indicators track poverty, mortality, disease, violent crime, suicide, alcohol consumption, drug abuse, educational achievement, dropping out, church attendance, presence of two-parent family, and many other trends

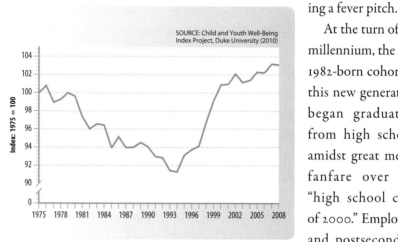

SOURCE: Child and Youth Well-Being Index Project, Duke University (2010)

schools began noticing a host of new trends: an influx of "helicopter" moms, over-programmed kids, the rising achievement of young women, the rising share of young people making long-term career plans, and intensifying competition to enter favorite companies and colleges.

Ever since, Americans born since 1982 have been entering the workplace in successive waves. In 2002 and 2003, the first Millennial summer college interns arrived. In 2004, the first four-year college graduates with BAs. In 2006, the first MAs and MBAs. In 2008, the first MDs and PhDs. Allowing for the usual time off their formal educational track, many of these first-wave Millennials are still tumbling into their entry-level career positions. And behind those born in 1982 come year after year of subsequent Millennial cohorts.

Workplaces are therefore just beginning to feel the full impact of this rising generation. The media attention that, for the last ten years, has focused on the college experience of youth in their late teens is now beginning to focus on the workplace experience of young adults in their mid-twenties. Managers are noticing a host of surprising new trends, from young applicants whose parents submit their résumés to young hires who expect weekly performance reviews to a rising media spotlight on youth in the workplace.

How can employers understand these new Millennial hires?

In the broadest terms, they can start by understanding how different Millennials' formative experiences have been from their own.

Millennials have grown up in a world that has taken trends Boomers recall from their childhood and turned them upside down. Boomers started out as the objects of loosening child standards in an era of conformist adults. Millennials started out as the objects of tightening child standards in an era of nonconformist adults. Boomers can recall growing up with a homogenous popular culture in an era when community came first and family stability was strong (though starting to weaken). Millennials have grown up with a fragmented pop culture in an era when individuals came first and when family stability was weak (though starting to strengthen).

Such reversals reflect a fundamental difference in the two generations' location in history.

Millennials also represent a sharp break from Generation X. Gen Xers can recall growing up as children during one of the most passionate eras of social dissent and cultural upheaval in American history, an era in which the needs of children were often overlooked or discounted. This has left a deep impression on most of today's Gen-X adults. But Millennials can recall none of it. Nor do they have any personal memory of the ordered Cold War world (when only large and powerful governments had weapons of mass destruction). They only know about a post-Cold War era of multilateral confusion and power vacuums (when terrorists and rogue states are seeking these weapons).

The Millennials have been shaped by such formative collective experiences as Columbine, the 2000 election, 9/11, Hurricane Katrina, and the wars in Afghanistan and Iraq. In all of these instances, the real danger seems to come not from out-of-control institutions, but mostly from out-of-control individuals, or small groups of conspirators, who have become a menace to humanity because national or global institutions are not strong enough even to monitor them.

The Millennials' response to their formative experience is following a pattern we have seen throughout U.S. history. Each new youth generation breaks with the styles and attitudes of the young-adult generation (today, Generation X), which no longer function well in the new era. They correct for what they perceive as the excesses of the current midlife generation (today, Boomers), which includes their parents and the nation's political leaders. And they fill the social role being vacated by the departing elder generation (today, G.I.s), a role that now feels fresh, functional, desirable, and even necessary for society's wellbeing.

The bottom line? Today's youth are bringing a fundamentally new outlook to America's workplaces. The new Millennial trends, both welcome and unwelcome, are here to stay—and they will require broad changes in management.

03

Who They Are— The Demographic Numbers

"However they might turn out, one thing is certain: By the sheer weight of numbers, the Millennials will shape the nation in profound ways."

— NEW GEOGRAPHY (2008)

"This group of young people is more ethnically and racially diverse than the generations that preceded it…. The number of Millennials currently in college or hoping to attend one is higher than ever."

— PBS NEWSHOUR (2010)

Who They Are—The Demographic Numbers

To the social scientist, each new generation brings with it a new batch of numbers and trend lines. One good test of whether we are drawing an accurate qualitative profile of a generation is whether this profile matches the numbers. Let's take a new look at Millennials by the numbers: their sheer size; their diversity by race, ethnicity, and gender; what they do with their time; and how they are leaving home and facing up to "adulthood."

Baby Boomlet (population)

The best-known single fact about the Millennial Generation is that it is large. As of 2010, America has just over 96 million Americans born between 1982 and 2004, with an average of 3.5 native births per year. Already larger than both the Boom Generation and Generation X, the Millennial Generation will almost certainly exceed 100 million members by the time future immigrants join their U.S.-born peers.

Since most Millennials born in the 1980s are the children of Baby Boomers, the media often refer to them as America's new "Baby Boomlet" or

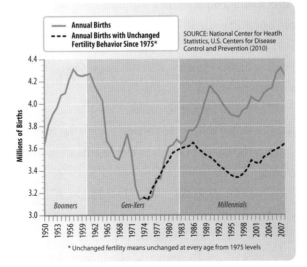

◄ **Figure 6**

Total U.S. Births, in Millions, 1950 to 2008

47

"Echo Boom" generation. In two key ways, these terms are misleading. First, Millennials born after the early 1990s—the larger half of the generation—are primarily the children of Gen Xers, not Boomers. Secondly, these terms imply that the large number of Millennials is mainly a matter of arithmetic, as though a "Baby Boomlet" mechanically had to issue from "Baby Boom" parents. In fact, the echo effect accounts for only a small part of the rise. For the most part, what led to the large number of Millennials was the passionate desire of their parents to bear and raise more of them.

The larger-than-expected size of this generation is an extension of the early-1980s shift in adult attitudes toward children. In the early '60s, the arrival of the first Gen Xers coincided with a sharp decline in the U.S. fertility rate and a society-wide aversion to children. And so it remained for the following twenty years, as young children seldom received positive media, while adults complained to pollsters about how family duties hindered their self discovery. Children became linked to new adjectives: unwanted, at risk, throwaway, homeless, latchkey.

All of this began to change with a surge in new births during the late 1970s and early '80s. Most experts at the time explained this as a delayed echo from the large number of Boomer women entering their prime child-bearing age—and they predicted the echo would be short lived. They were in for a surprise. After leveling off at about 3.6 million from 1980 to 1983, the national birth rate did not drift back down. Instead it rose—to 3.8 million in 1987, 4.0 million in 1989, and 4.2 million in 1990. Overall, Millennial births have been roughly 20 percent higher than if the fertility of women at each age had remained steady at mid-1970s rates.

What's important about this "baby boomlet" is how sustained it became and how it has reflected a resurgent adult desire to have kids. During the 1960s and '70s, the era of Gen-X babies, adults went to great efforts *not* to produce children, driving up the demand for contraceptive technologies and for sterilization and abortion clinics. During the Millennial baby era, by contrast, adults went to great efforts to conceive and adopt babies. Sterilization rates, which rose sharply during the 1960s and '70s, plateaued in the mid-'80s and have since fallen. The annual abortion rate, after ramping up during the Gen-X baby era, hit a peak in 1980 and has gradually declined ever since. The rate is now about a third lower than it was in 1980. Meanwhile, the share of all births declared to be "unwanted" by their mothers has also declined—with an especially sharp drop in unwantedness by African-American mothers.

Demographically, Millennials have two birth peaks with a shallow valley in between. The first (mainly Boomer-parented) 1990 peak of the Millennial birth bulge has just graduated from high school and is beginning to enter colleges and the workforce. The second (mainly Gen-X-parented) post-2000 peak is still pushing its way through elementary schools. These later-wave Millennials won't begin entering the workforce until 2018, and will comprise the bulk of young entry-level employees throughout the 2020s.

The final birth year of the Millennial Generation is probably 2004. This is the last cohort old enough to have any memory of America before the watershed public events of 2008: the global financial market crash, the beginning of the "great recession," and the election of President Barack Obama. The next batch of children, born 2005 and after—we call them the "Homeland Generation"—will include children of both Gen-X and Millennial parents.

Colors of the World (race, ethnicity)

Millennials are the least white and most racially and ethnically diverse generation in U.S. history. As of 2010, nonwhites and Latinos account for just over 41 percent of the population age 5 to 27, nearly two-thirds larger than the share for Boomers, and more than double the share for today's seniors.

Millennials also have a much greater range of global diversity than Boomers did when they entered the workforce. The issue of color can no longer be defined in clear black-white (or even black-white-Latino) terms. A cross section of Millennial employees, even when one looks just at American citizens, can include young women and men whose ancestors come from nearly every society on earth, including regions that were far less represented among the youth of the 1960s.

To this point, Millennials are less often immigrants themselves than the children of immigrants. In 2009, just over 7 percent of Millennials were immigrants themselves, versus 18 percent of Gen Xers and 12 percent of Boomers.

49

Yet Millennials contain more second-generation immigrants than any earlier twenty-year cohort group in U.S. history: one in five have at least one immigrant parent, and one in ten have at least one non-citizen parent.

In time, with further immigration, will Millennials eventually acquire the same foreign-born share as Generation X? Perhaps not. Net immigration to the United States (both legal and illegal) has decelerated over the decade since 9/11—and has fallen very sharply since 2007, due to the global recession. If the U.S. labor market continues to attract relatively few immigrants over the next decade, Millennials will forever remain more native born than their parents. Today, the foreign-born share of (Millennial) workers in their early twenties, at 12 percent, is less than half of the foreign-born share of (Gen-X) workers in their late thirties and early forties, at 29 percent. Boomers and Gen Xers have spent a lifetime looking up to older workers who were more native born than themselves. With Millennials, it may be the reverse.

Thanks to the Cold War's end, satellite news, porous national borders, and the Internet, Millennials are becoming the world's first generation to grow up thinking of itself, from childhood forward, as global. This, combined with the growing diversity of their geographical and racial family origins, makes the old black-and-white divisions seem far less relevant to this generation. The presidential election of 2008, in which Millennials supported Barack Obama by large margins, indicates a growing comfort among youth with mixed race and ethnicity. Indeed, on U.S. Census surveys, a rapidly growing share of Millennials decline to say that they belong to any one race or ethnicity. Millennials are moving away from the idea of a *multiracial* society, with a fixed number of separate minority groups, and towards the idea of a *transracial* society in which infinite gradations of racial identity come together into one community.

Surveys confirm the declining divisiveness of race among Millennials. When they are asked for the most important characteristic that defines their identity, "religion," "ethnicity," "race," and "sexual orientation" clock in distantly behind "music or fashion preference." From the late 1980s to today, the share of youth age 18 to 25 who "completely agree" that "it's alright for blacks and whites to date each other" has risen from 20 percent to 64 percent. Millennials are twice as likely as Xer youth were in the late 1980s to disagree with the statement "I don't have much in common with people of other races." A 2009 Pew survey found that Americans of all ages agree, by a large margin, that Millennials are "more racially tolerant" than older generations (even if, among minorities, Boomer parents are sometimes miffed that their grown children refuse to "stick up" for their own group).

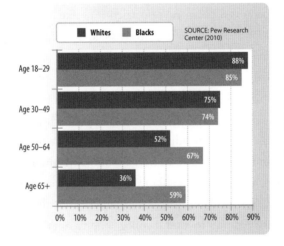

◀ **Figure 8**

Interracial Marriage? Percent who would be "fine" with a family member's marriage to someone of another race/ ethnicity, in 2009

America's Millennial workforce also marks the leading edge of a rising worldwide generation. Since World War II, new European generations have arrived roughly five to ten years after those in America. The leading-edge European Millennials were born in the late 1980s—and within the last few years, some observers in both Europe and Asia have been describing the emergence of a Millennial-style shift among young teens. In Germany, these new kids have been called the *Null Zoff* ("no problem") generation—in Sweden, *Generation Ordning* ("ordered generation"). China has started to notice a pampered yet civically engaged "Little Emperor" generation of youth: The Chinese public watched in astonishment as students organized rescue efforts and mobilized themselves into aid groups in response to the Sichuan Earthquake in 2008.

Millennials are the first American generation in which Latinos clearly outnumber African Americans. With over half having at least one immigrant parent, many Latino youth face a future full of hard challenges: Between one-quarter and one-third live in poverty, in substandard housing, and without health insurance. In high school, the share of Latinos who drop out each year (9 percent) is twice the share of non-Latinos (5 percent). Yet most young Latinos know that they are doing much better than their parents did in the 1980s or 1990s. By overwhelming margins, they believe they will do better financially than their parents did. Latino pop celebrities like America Ferrera, Selena Gomez, and Mark Sanchez reflect this upbeat attitude. With parents even more attached to "family values" than the white adult majority, the Latino youth culture is helping to set the new Millennial tone—positive, team playing, community-minded—in schools and neighborhoods from Boston to San Diego.

Asian youth are also a rapidly growing presence. Propelled by cultures that honor filial duty and credentialed achievement, teens from Chinese and Indian families have won a reputation among Millennials as stellar academic achievers—especially in math, science, and engineering. According to the U.S. Census Bureau, Asian-American women are the most likely among all Millennials to attend college and to obtain a college degree. Most Asians of both genders are entering the workforce with high Millennial expectations and impressive educational track records.

Dating back to Emancipation, African Americans have been an outsized cultural contributor to generational currents. In recent decades, this has been seen in civil rights (Silent), black power (Boomers), and hip hop (Gen Xers). That contribution continues today. To be sure, inner-city minority students face some of the toughest challenges in launching successful careers, from high dropout rates to substance abuse to poor test score achievement. Yet urban nonwhite youths—especially African Americans—are in many respects bigger contributors to this generation's emerging positive persona than white youths. Ask yourself these questions: Which public school kids are more likely to be wearing uniforms? Urban nonwhites. Whose schools are moving fastest on back-to-basics drilling and achievement standards? Urban nonwhites. Whose neighborhoods are producing the swiftest percentage decline in youth murder, teen drug use, child poverty, teen pregnancy, and school violence—and the swiftest percentage rise in test scores? Urban nonwhites. Which students have shown the highest rate of improvement in entering higher education and the workforce? Urban nonwhites.

Duke University social scientists combine twenty-five key indicators of adolescent wellbeing (from child poverty to teen crime to drug use) into an "*Index of Youth & Child Well-being.*" The index not only shows a dramatic upward thrust starting in 1994—just when Millennials began occupying adolescence—it also shows that the improvement for Latino and African-American minorities has been considerably steeper than for the white majority.

Regionally, the (mostly minority) urban areas have shown the steepest gains. The (mostly white) suburbs have shown average gains. If there is an area that is lagging behind the average, it would be the (mostly white) rural areas, which have shown the slowest gains, with the least decline—and in certain areas a continued rise—in many negative indicators, especially substance abuse. The youth of rural America were the last to start consuming more drugs back in the 1970s. Forty years later they show a similar lag, and appear to be the last to stop.

Power Girls (gender)

"Boys are stupid. Throw rocks at them." This declaration on a popular T-shirt worn by high schools girls in 2004 (and later affixed to many other novelty items, even becoming the title of a book), touched off a minor media stir. It also threw sardonic light on a youth trend that puzzles many older Americans: The energetic, even aggressive self-confidence of Millennial girls and young women.

Millennials may be the first generation in American history whose desire to achieve, lead, and build is being driven more by the female side than the male. Just think of a positive trend associated with the Millennial Generation. Whatever it is, young women are probably way out in front of young men in spearheading that trend. This explains why these "power girls" are thus far singlehandedly defining the media image of their generation. Boys, meanwhile, have been struggling as best they can to follow the girls' lead.

Over the last fifteen years, both boys and girls have been spending more time planning their future lives and are expressing more confidence that they will succeed. Yet Millennial girls are clearly outperforming Millennial boys on these fronts. Compared to boys, surveys show girls now schedule more of their daily time, spend more time planning for the future, start planning at an earlier age, and consult more with counselors and other trusted adults while they plan. Rates of depression and attempted suicide are often used as proxies for self-esteem. These rates are still higher for adolescent girls, but have fallen further for girls than for boys over the last decade and a half.

Over the last fifteen years, both boys and girls have been trying harder to serve their communities, get civically engaged, and gain institutional credentials and approval. Yet here again, Millennial girls are way out in front. Compared to boys, girls are more likely to volunteer for community service, to say it's important to make the world a better place, to vote and give to charities (if age 18 or over), or to say they will vote and give to charities (if under age 18). Among grade school children, according to a 2008 study by the Girl Scouts of America, a larger share of girls than boys say they "want to be a leader." This is true within every race and ethnicity, and the gap between girls and boys widens with age. Girls now dominate extracurricular activities and student governments at the high school and college levels. They are also more likely to seek official recognition of their accomplishments, from awards and certificates to membership in clubs and honors societies.

In academic achievement as well, both boys and girls are improving. But here girls' advantage over boys in effort and outcome has grown so large that it shows up in nearly every academic indicator. Compared to boys, girls in grade school have better attendance, participate more in class, do more homework, say they like school more, and get a much larger share of the As and a much smaller share of the Ds and Fs. In high school, they are less likely to drop out or be held back a grade—and more likely to take honors and AP classes, to take achievement and aptitude tests like the AP and SAT, and to graduate on time. The Horatio Alger Association's *State of Our Nation's Youth* observes that, among high school students, "females challenged themselves more frequently to take the most difficult courses available... and worked harder at their course work and received better grades than males."

Once out of high school, girls continue to forge ahead of boys. They are more likely to apply to college, to enter college, to stay in college, and to complete college with a degree. As a result, young women dominate in the race for academic credentials.

They now account for four out of seven (57 percent) of all college undergraduates and annual BAs awarded. To be sure, most of this margin was obtained in the Gen-X college era—that is, during the 1980s and 1990s—

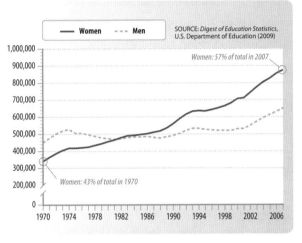

◄ Figure 9

Bachelor's Degrees Conferred by Gender, Yearly from 1970 to 2007

but Millennial women have maintained their outsized share despite surging enrollment by Millennial men since 2000. A newer trend is in the women's share of annual professional degrees (such as law or medicine) and doctorates awarded, which has now reached virtual parity with men. Women are even making inroads in such traditional male bastions as the tech sector. In 2007, for the first time, girls won both the team and individual categories of the Siemens Competition for high school students in math, science, and technology.

Meanwhile, future salary expectations of teenage girls have now risen to match those of boys. And once these girls get jobs, their earnings are much closer to equal—despite the fact they tell pollster they care less about "money" than boys. Among full-time, year-round workers their twenties, the average pay for women over the last few years has been about 90 percent of the average for men—higher than it has ever been before. Words like "smart," "driven," and even "nerd" have lost most of their negative connotations for girls. Remarkably, according to UCLA's 2009 survey *The American Freshman*, a slightly larger share of freshman women than men rank themselves in "the highest 10 percent" in their "drive to achieve."

So where do all these power girls come from? They are the product of profound changes in the gender landscape that began just before Millennials arrived and that reshaped their childhood the 1980s and 1990s. An older (Silent) generation of legislators made sure that girls had equal opportunities in the classroom, in the workplace, and (thanks to Title IX, mandating gender equality in sports funding) on the playing field. Boomer moms and dads rooted passionately for their daughters' ambitions without regard for gender stereotypes. And to inspire these girls, Gen-X pop-culture artists dreamed up plenty of heroines who weren't afraid to compete with men on their own terms, from Powerpuff Girls, Sailor Moon, and Mulan to Buffy, Xena, and Nikita.

Like a giant slingshot, all three of these older generations (more or less coinciding with three generations of feminism) have propelled today's young women into an energized life trajectory.

The cultural repercussions have been profound. Just as first-wave Millennials entered their teenage years, the public image of boys versus girls underwent a dramatic reversal. Back in the mid-1990s, girls were still deemed to be the gender "in crisis," with serious deficits relative to boys in self-esteem and life development. Today, the tables are turned. It's boys who are deemed to be in trouble relative to girls. According to such recent bestsellers as *Real Boys*, *The War Against Boys*, and *Hear Our Cry: Boys in Crisis*, boys have been left adrift in a hostile culture. Meanwhile, the media and entertainment focus has broadly shifted to reflect girls' interests over the last decade—favoring family networks like Disney, diva contests like "American Idol," and "relationship software" like Facebook. Young female celebrities today vastly outnumber their male counterparts. Meanwhile, what boys do to have fun (watch "South Park," play *Halo 3*, listen to Linkin Park) is increasingly regarded as controversial and even dangerous.

To be sure, some of the new gender hysteria is overwrought. Not everything is going better for Millennial girls. In some respects, they are having a harder time than ever—more often feeling "overwhelmed" by the pressure to achieve, for example, and troubled more by body-image fears. As for Millennial boys, they are hardly as dumb and directionless as some people think. Even though boys don't try as hard in school, they still score higher on average than girls on nearly all of the standardized tests (the SAT, ACT, GRE, GMAT, and MCAT) and, among the very top scorers on these exams (top ten percent, five percent, and one percent), boys outdo girls by progressively larger margins.

More importantly, Millennial boys get little credit for their own improving behavior. Over the last fifteen years, they have brought down rates of violent crime and of alcohol and tobacco use faster, perhaps, than any other generation of boys in American history. Yet hardly anyone notices. Because boys still do these things a lot more than girls, they are still deemed "troubled"—a defective version of the more rule-abiding girls, who are responsible for only 10 percent of the violent crime, only 20 percent of the ADHD diagnoses, only 25 percent of the dropouts, and only 30 percent of the special education students. Millennial boys struggle more in a generation that is commended mainly for the risks it avoids, the consensus it forges, and the rules it follows, with every "i" dotted and "t" crossed.

Given the track record of earlier generations, we can offer a couple of safe predictions about the future of Millennial gender roles.

First, generations often get defined early by one gender. When that happens, the other gender soon merges to give their generation a common shape. Among Boomers, for example, risk-taking and outspoken young men defined the defiant media image of their generation in the late 1960s. Young women joined a bit later, in the 1970s. During the coming decade, Millennial men are due to join the women. Some of the men, especially the underachievers who have thus far avoided recognition for their talents, may even leapfrog past many of the women. The new generational image that young men and women jointly create will probably be somewhat more masculinized than the Millennial image is today.

Second, Millennial women will almost certainly revise and even reject some of the "supermom" feminism of their own mothers—just as Boomer men revised and rejected much of the "superman" macho fixation of their dads back in the 1960s. For Millennial women, being a super achiever is a life starting point rather than a life aspiration. This means that talented young women in the workplace typically aspire to promotion and a leadership role every bit as much as male coworkers. (An employer who assumes otherwise is in for a rude awakening.) But it also means that they feel less need than their mothers to prove themselves in the workplace to the exclusion of other life pursuits. According to a 2010 Accenture survey, Millennial women with full-time jobs agree by more than two to one (66 percent to 29 percent) that "family life" is more important to them than "career success." To attain non-career goals, they may be more willing than their moms were to welcome the initiative of others (even men) who can help bear some of the achievement burden.

Because Millennial women don't see men as a collective threat, fewer of them are attracted to the politics of gender identity—a fact which shocked many Boomer moms when their Millennials daughters overwhelmingly chose Barack Obama over Hillary Clinton in the 2008 Democratic primary. Remarkably, in the Accenture survey, only one in five reported that more women in C-suite or director positions would help them professionally. These young women don't feel the need to seek power. They believe they already have it. They're just waiting for the guys to catch up.

Busy Around the Clock (use of time)

Millennials may be America's busiest people. No matter what they're doing, today's youth are always trying to squeeze more activities into a limited time frame. When asked how much time they spend during the average workday on email, Internet browsers, Microsoft Office, and instant messaging, Millennial employees report a total of twenty-three combined hours across all these applications—nearly triple the standard eight-hour workday, and far more than the ten hours logged by Boomers. And it's not just at work that Millennials are multitasking to get it all done. Managers are noticing a surge in stressed-out young employees juggling graduate school applications, family commitments, and a range of organized after-work activities.

What employers may not realize is that today's young people have been busy and activity-oriented their entire lives—and not in ways that today's older adults can recall from their own youth.

When this generation came along as children, the old days of Boomer kids being shooed outside to invent their own games—or of Xer kids being left "home alone" with a "self-care" guide—were long gone. By the time these first-wave Millennials were in grade school, the child environment was turning decisively toward structure, planning, and supervision.

In 1998, hard evidence of this shift first showed up in a study by University of Michigan researchers, who compared time diaries kept by eighth and tenth graders in the 1981–82 school year (Gen-X kids, who today are in their late thirties and early forties) with similar diaries kept in the 1997–98 year (first-wave Millennials now filling the young-adult workforce). The researchers observed sharp reductions in the share of those who engage "every day" or "at least once a week" in such open-ended youth activities as going to movies, cruising in cars and motorcycles, or walking around shopping malls. During the 1990s, the sale of student day planners soared from one million to fifty million. As 10-year old Stephanie Mazzamaro told *Time* magazine at the time: "I don't have time to be a kid."

In 2004, the Michigan team redid their study, updating the data to compare the 1981–82 group with a 2002–03 group (slightly later-wave Millennials). The results were remarkable. From the first group to the second:

* Time spent in school classrooms increased from twenty-six to thirty-two hours a week—due to longer school days, longer school years, more sessions after school, and more summer school. This six extra hours per week was the largest absolute increase in any activity.

* Weekly hours working for employers outside the home declined, but this was roughly compensated by more time working (for parents) inside the home.

* Time watching TV declined, but this was more than made up by time interacting with computers, which rose from zero to 2:45 hours per week.

* Time spent in unstructured activities outdoors and in sports and personal hobbies declined sharply, by two to three hours per week.

* Time spent reading, studying, and (especially) visiting with friends each increased by two to three hours per week.

These shifts point to many distinctive Millennial trends. More time at school and studying tracks Millennials' rising academic achievement, as measured by standardized tests. More time socializing is linked to the greater impor-

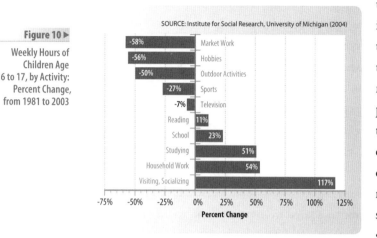

Figure 10 ▶

Weekly Hours of Children Age 6 to 17, by Activity: Percent Change, from 1981 to 2003

tance of group activity in their lives. Less time working outside the home reflects the new consensus among parents and counselors that such work can be dangerous and is in any case a poorer investment than time spent studying. Less time spent outdoors just running around and more time spent in sedentary activities indoors certainly contributes to this generation's high and rising incidence of obesity.

Another important trend is in parent-child time, which has increased steadily from late-wave Gen-X kids to late-wave Millennial kids (with a slightly steeper increase for African Americans, for girls, and for college-educated families). In spite of the long-term shift toward single-parent families and working mothers, parents are prioritizing time with their children—for example, by spending less time on house cleaning and meal preparation. This reflects the growing importance of parents in Millennials' lives, monitoring, directing, and even stage-managing their many activities.

Much of the Millennial time crunch can be attributed to the growing perceived importance of a college degree and the growing competition among parents to prep their children to qualify for the best colleges. College competition, declared the American Academy of Pediatrics in a 2007 report, is directly responsible for the unhealthy overscheduling of today's children.

Entrance into college by no means puts an end to the time pressure. Once they arrive on campus, Millennials are busier than ever. A recent MIT study found that college students today spend significantly more time in extracurricular activities, clubs, and athletics than students did in the 1990s. Multiple majors are on the rise for college students, as is paid employment. The same students who are putting more effort into college activities, both inside and outside the classroom, are also struggling harder to make ends meet in the face of rising college tuition.

What's more, Millennials are flooding into colleges at a greater rate than any earlier generation in American history. In 2008, the shares of 18- to 24-year olds enrolled in a two-year college (12 percent) or in a four-year college (28 percent) both reached record highs. Meanwhile, the share of this age group that is neither working nor in school (8 percent) has dropped to a record low. So has the share that has dropped out of high school (9 percent). Quite simply, today's young people are more directed and engaged than any earlier youth generation in living memory. The *American Use of Time Survey* directed by the U.S. Bureau of Labor Statistics corroborates this picture. From 2003 to 2008, among Americans age 15 to 24, time spent on work and education were up and time spent on leisure, sports, and shopping were down.

Employers should pay attention. The young people now entering the labor force, and the work habits they bring with them, are the product of a very special life story. As small children, they spent less time than previous generations lying on their backs imagining stories as the clouds rolled by and more time learning how to excel at directed activities and standardized tests. As adolescents, they spent less time playing self-invented games and more time playing adult-supervised games with teams, rules, and referees. In college, they have been less likely to experiment with creative lifestyles and more likely to join clubs, scholarship societies, and student government. On the job, they are less comfortable delving into free-form conceptual thinking about where the organization should go—and more comfortable juggling a myriad of tasks in order to move the organization towards a goal defined by others.

Beyond "Emerging Adulthood" (growing up and moving out)

In the 2006 movie *Failure to Launch*, actor Matthew McConaughey plays a thirty-something slacker who lives so comfortably with mom and dad that they have to concoct fantastic schemes to persuade him to move out. Most viewers over age 50 nodded in agreement. They see a lot more young adults living with their parents than when they were that age, including possibly their own son or daughter, and wonder if it's a healthy trend. More broadly, they worry about so many young people avoiding the "normal" steps that once led to adulthood—not just leaving home, but getting married, having kids, and being serious about a career.

Older Americans are certainly on to something. Social scientists have been monitoring a broad trend toward delayed or dependent young adulthood for over forty years. Many have even coined labels for a whole new phase of life: "emerging adulthood," "adultalescence," or "odyssey years." The youth themselves have been called "twixters," "boomerangers," or "threshholders." Popular and thoughtful books have been written about young adults who move in with their parents (*Boomerang Nation*) or avoid marriage and other commitments (*Urban Tribes*).

So what do these trends have to do with Millennials? The answer may surprise you. In fact, Millennials are beginning to reverse many of them—and to replace the old image of young-adult aimlessness with a new definition of this phase of life as a time of preparation and deliberate planning. Even when Millennials continue to delay "adulthood" as conventionally defined (and that still happens a lot), they do so for new reasons that older generations often don't understand.

To get some perspective, let's look at the numbers. For most of American history until the end of World War II, young people lived with parents at a much higher rate than they do today. Housing was scarce and living standards were lower, forcing everyone to economize. (Recall all those Frank Capra movies from the Great Depression, with houses full of people of all ages.) In the years after the war ended, the building of suburbs and highways unleashed young couples yearning to start nuclear families. These Silent Generation young adults were pleased to conform to the prevailing ideal of adulthood—and with very high incomes relative to older Americans at the time, they were easily able to do so. Rates of co-residence plummeted as the Silent got married and started households at a younger age than any other generation before or since, reaching an all-time low by the early 1960s.

Over the next two decades, young Boomers came along and began pushing rates of co-residence back up, pioneering a new lifestyle then known as "extended adolescence." From 1960 to the early 1980s, the share of 18- to 24-year olds living at home (or in college dorms, which the Census treats as "in parents' home") grew from 43 to 54 percent. Late-wave Boomers were less

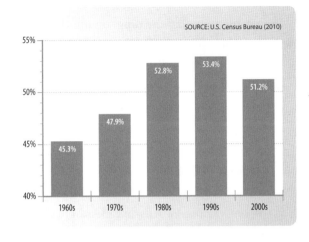

SOURCE: U.S. Census Bureau (2010)

◀ **Figure 11**

Youth Age 18 to 24 Living with Parents, Annual Average by Decade*

* Average for 2000s includes an estimate for 2009.

willing to conform to the norms of "adulthood," said so loudly, and started looking for alternative ideals. They also got hit hard by stagflation in the 1970s, making it harder for them to set up their own homes.

Then young Gen Xers came along and pushed co-residence to its postwar peak, where it hovered (around 55 percent) through the late 1980s and '90s. Xer young adults traded convention for pragmatism, looking for any living arrangement that "works for me." Today, late-wave Xers are still pushing up the co-residence rate in the 25 to 34 age bracket—which explains why Hollywood appropriately chose McConaughey (born in 1969) as the live-at-home poster boy.

Since 2000, however, the rate of 18- to 24-year olds living with their parents has fallen to just over 50 percent, just as Millennials have entered this age bracket. Why the change? In a striking shift from the Boomer or Gen-X youth trend, Millennials feel more pressure to plan and organize their future in ways that lead to earlier independence. That's why they're so busy. According to an annual MonsterTRAK survey, the share of college grads living at home a year after graduation was actually *lower* in 2009—despite the terrible job market—than it was earlier in the decade. Some indicators do show a rise in co-residence during the recent recession. But even when Millennials live at home, out of choice or necessity, they are more likely to regard their stay as a way to invest more money or time into their future independence (into their own education or ultimate home purchase, for example).

An urgent sense that the rungs on life's ladder must be crossed by certain deadlines is affecting other Millennial life decisions as well:

* A record-high share of Americans in their mid-twenties now possess four-year college degrees, two-year college degrees, and other postsecondary credentials certifying them as capable of economic independence. This is true of both men and (especially) of women.

* A record-low share of college freshmen say they may change their career choice or will require an extra year of college. Though average college completion times remain high, a growing share of undergrads are completing their AAs, ABs, and BAs in fewer than the normal number of years (for example, getting a BA after three years in college).

* A record-high share of college freshmen (75 percent) believe that raising a family is an "essential" or "very important" life objective. A growing share of young women say that having a career is no reason to delay child bearing—and don't want to worry (like many of their mothers did) about their "biological clock" ticking down. The average age of first-time mothers, which rose for decades, has leveled off since 2000 and actually declined in 2006, for the first time since 1968. The decline was led by Millennial women age 20 to 24.

The Millennials' close relationship with parents, supported by much survey evidence, is also affecting their life decisions. The Millennials got along better with their parents when they were kids, and today keep in touch with them more frequently, than older generations did at the same age. Retiring Boomers are seeking out active-adult housing with extra rooms and facilities for their grown Millennial children. Young adults increasingly say they want to live "near" their Boomer parents and no longer see the "multigenerational" household as stigmatizing.

As a result, when Millennials do live with their parents, it feels like the seamless continuation of a tight relationship. There is less of the awkwardness or shame that young Boomers and Gen Xers (and their parents) felt upon "boomeranging" back home. With Millennials, the decision to live with parents is even losing some of its age-old connection with economic necessity. A growing share of young adults who live with their parents are economically self-sufficient—yet choose to live with affluent parents in spacious homes where everyone can benefit by sharing expenses and chores. When young unmarried job applicants check the "location matters" box, there is a good chance they live with their parents and that using their new salary to move out just isn't a priority.

When Millennials don't live with their parents, most want to move to places where they can jumpstart their careers. For the best and the brightest, that means moving to the big bicoastal cities. Young Boomers idealized rural or wilderness locales. Young Gen Xers popularized the edgy urban street where self-starters can take risks and make deals. Young Millennials are also attracted to cities—but to dense urban beehives where they can form active peer communities, network, socialize, stay relatively safe (thanks to the recent decline in crime rates), and join the cutting-edge brand names in business, government, media, or hi-tech. Their favorite destination is New York City. Also near the top of their list are Seattle, San Francisco, Atlanta, Boston, Los Angeles, Denver, Portland, Austin, San Diego, and Washington, DC. Compared to young Gen Xers, Millennials are a bit more drawn to the urban West Coast and Northeast, a bit less to Sun-Belt cities. They typically cope with the high cost of housing by crowding several-at-a-time into single units and sharing expenses—or by reconsidering second-tier cities that are less expensive.

Whether Millennials stay near their parents' homes or go to an urban hub, they are not relocating as often. They tend to make one move and stick with it. Here Millennials are leading a remarkable national trend: a steepening decline in geographic mobility at all ages. In 2008, only 12 percent of Americans moved their residence, the lowest figure since World War II and a large drop from the 20 percent annual figure in the 1950s, 1960s, and 1970s. Because young adults are always the biggest movers, they are driving the numbers: The annual share of twenty-somethings who are now moving from one state to another is *less than half* of what it was three decades ago. Geographic lifestyle expert Joel Kotkin observes a growing movement he calls the "new localism." It reflects a new attachment to family, friends, and community—and also a new aversion to drastic life disruption. All Americans are participating in this trend, but Millennials are at its cutting edge.

Educators and employers need to resist the influence of the Hollywood image of youth. According to that image, today's young adults (the young men, especially) are self-centered, commitment-avoiding, live-for-today nomads who mooch off mom and dad and don't much care about growing up. The image is not entirely wrong: In any generation, being young is about testing limits and trying things out. Yet enough of the image is wrong—or at best outdated—that it obscures what is different and interesting about the young men and women now entering professional schools and starting careers.

04
Who They Are—
The Dollar Numbers

"Not long ago, the economy seemed poised not only to embrace the Millennials but to start taking orders from them…. But that was before the financial crisis. The recession is hitting younger job seekers hard."

— **GREGORY RODRIGUEZ**, SENIOR FELLOW AT THE NEW AMERICA FOUNDATION (2009)

"As a generation, Millennials are still optimistic and ambitious, but the pressures of the current economy are reshaping our approach and our outlook on relationships with our employers."

— **LAUREN BEGLEY**, MILLENNIAL AND SENIOR ACCOUNT EXECUTIVE AT PEPPERCOM (2009)

Who They Are—The Dollar Numbers

How a generation feels about the workplace is necessarily connected to how it feels about economic and lifestyle choices. In its youth, a generation grows accustomed to a certain level and type of affluence. As it grows older, it develops life goals (leisure, starting a family) that require a certain level of income and the job skills to match. In this chapter, we look at Millennials from an economic perspective. What do they think about consumption? Why do they spend so much to go to college? How affluent are they as young adults? How do they handle debt and economic adversity? When did they first learn about paid employment? And what are their biggest fears and hopes about their careers?

Kids "R" Us (consumption)

A 2008 TV ad for Chevy Malibu showed a baby girl being showered with gifts and toys and love while moving along a hi-tech factory conveyor belt. As she moves, she gradually grows older. A college-age young woman by the time she reaches the factory door, she is buckled into her brand-new car while her parents wave goodbye. The ad was irresistible, and many viewers felt they wanted to wave as well. It seemed natural that a growing child so special, protected, and cared for should be surrounded by nice things—which are not so much chosen by the child as carefully chosen for her by parents and experts.

Welcome to the story of Millennial consumption. It is the story not just of vast growth in the goods and services consumed by youth, but also of the public's new-found obsession with everything that targets youth—as though every American has a strong opinion about what young people should and should not be consuming.

There is no question that inflation-adjusted expenditures on young people have vastly increased over the last twenty-five years, as anyone who has recently visited a typical teen bedroom can attest. The first wave of this generation grew up during an era of surging prosperity—from the early 1980s through the year 2000—when there was only one mild recession and the Dow Jones Index rose almost every year. The poverty rate for all children fell by a quarter and for minority children by even more. Families in every income quintile had more to spend, and proved just how special Millennials are by allocating much of that extra income to their kids.

During the 1990s, purchases by and for children age 4 to 12 tripled. Amid talk of a new "golden age" in cartoon movies for children (from *An American Tail* and *Land Before Time* to *Lion King* and *Aladdin*—all with commercial tie-ins), entire TV networks devoted to kids' programming (Nickelodeon, Disney, Cartoon Network) became stunningly profitable. Digital gaming moved from the arcades into every home with the Gameboy and PlayStation. The market for child literature exploded, thanks in part to the appearance in 1997 of a fictional boy named Harry Potter. Meanwhile, major corporations started rebranding their new product lines for the Millennial child: from Aquafresh for Kids, L'Oreal Kids, and Ozark Spring Water for Kids to Colgate SpongeBob SquarePants, TicTalk cell phones, and Sports Illustrated for Kids. A new fashion trend appeared in branded clothes lines just for kids, such as Gap Kids, Eddie Bauer Kids, and now even Sheen Kidz and Kidtoure t-shirts.

Beyond its exuberant growth, spending on Millennial kids has been notable for the enhanced role played by parents and other adults (such as doting grandparents) in directing that spending. Regular weekly "allowances" that let kids spend money as they wish have been marginalized in favor of direct ad hoc payments from parent to child, often for specific purchases on which parent and child confer. While parents often pay in full for major teen purchases that in times past were financed by youth work and savings, they are also doing more to influence teen purchases through rules, advice, and earmarked cash. At the same time, teens are influencing parental purchase decisions on big-ticket items like cars, houses, and vacations (by voicing their opinion), and on small-ticket items like groceries and takeout food (by saving their parents time).

Thus has emerged the parent-child "co-purchase," a democratic mode of family purchasing in which everyone participates. Twenty-five years ago, the big new trend in youth marketing was the independent child buyer. Back in the mid-1980s, Nickelodeon pioneered the theme of a "parent-free zone," in effect trying to attract (Gen-X) kids to a place where parents weren't welcome. A few years later, after focus groups showed that new (Millennial) viewers missed the presence of parents, the network dropped the slogan. Over the last decade, nearly all of the youth networks (especially Nickelodeon and Disney) have been pushing the "family" togetherness image so heavily that programmers now assume hardly any distance at all between the preferences of kids and the preferences of parents.

After 2000, as the media glare followed first-wave Millennials into college and the workplace, advertisers turned increasing attention to the lifestyle dreams of twenty-somethings. These are now featured on such newly profitable TV networks as WB/CW, Comedy Central, Adult Swim, Bravo, Spike, G4, Fuse, and Mun2. The strong family focus remains, with sitcoms that increasingly script parents into the same scene as their grown children and commercial messages that show them vacationing together, shopping together, and choosing careers together.

The 2000s decade—rocked as it was by severe economic shocks—curtailed the heady consumption binge that so many Millennials had enjoyed earlier in their childhood. Most indicators of teen consumption (several are published by youth marketing firms) show that total spending per teen rose rapidly during the 1990s, zigzagged up and down from 2001 until about 2005 or 2006, and then plunged along an accelerating downward trajectory at the decade's end. By most accounts, inflation-adjusted spending per teen by 2009 was well below where it was a decade earlier, in 1999. College-age consumption likely declined just as steeply.

As they mature—and as they learn to economize—Millennials are beginning reshape youth attitudes toward consumption in a new direction. When choosing products, they are listening more to their parents and friends and less to celebrities and marketers. They are opting more for long-term "value" (up in youth surveys over the past decade) and less for transitory "cool" (down over the past decade). They are finding the standard big brands more appealing and the edgy niche brands less appealing. Aided by their digital networks, Millennials pay keen attention to what's happening at the gravitational center of their peer group. Mass fads, mainstream stores, group focus, and a lower-profile commercial style are making a comeback. Meanwhile, "the edge" is losing its appeal—along with weak product loyalties, hypercommercialism, and the focus on risk and self.

Successful marketers have taken advantage of this shift. While edgy youth brands like Calvin Klein and Abercrombie & Fitch have taken a beating over the past decade, bright and friendly "middle class" chains like Target have developed an unexpected youth following. Young people are spending less on cars so they can spend more on college—and less on fashion so they can spend more on cell phones and laptops. According to JWT, a growing share of teens are distinguishing between brands that have "value" and brands that are "cool" (between Microsoft and Apple, for example, or the PSP and the XBox).

Politicians are also detecting a new youth sensitivity to the growing inequalities in income and consumption. Growing up, Millennials noticed these inequalities in the gap between the kids whose parents had fancy houses, vacations, and cars and the kids whose parents didn't. Now as voters, they notice them in the gap between young adults who can afford or will soon inherit the houses, vacations, and cars, and those who know they can't or won't. Political programs intending to restore or reward a "middle class" lifestyle have a fresh appeal to Millennials that they never had to other recent youth generations.

Economic challenges tend to reveal more than shape the consumer style of a coming-of-age generation. During the early '90s recession (which was severe for young adults), youthful Gen Xers responded with torn-flannel grunge, heroin chic, guerilla marketing, a wave of body piercings, and slacker jokes. Millennials are responding very differently. Is this because it's a different challenge? No, just a very different generation.

College for Everyone (cost of higher education)

In his first joint address to Congress, President Obama called for every American to pursue some form of education beyond high school. His goal was greeted enthusiastically by Millennials, who overwhelmingly agree that being "smart" and having a "college degree" are tickets to success in life—and who, with their high collective self-esteem, surely believe they are well worth the investment.

The numbers are remarkable. Over 90 percent of today's high school students say they want to pursue some sort of education after graduation. Roughly 80 percent say they intend to do so immediately after graduation. Two-thirds actually enroll in a two- or four-year college within a year of graduation. And well over 50 percent of all 18- to 24-year olds are enrolled in some type of college or proprietary school. Including trade schools and apprenticeships, it is closer to 60 percent. Never before in American history has such a large share of young adults dedicated themselves to credentialed self-betterment.

So is America well on our way to President Obama's 100 percent? Regrettably, no. Of the large share of the young adults now in postsecondary school, nearly half will drop out before they earn a degree. To some extent, high drop-out rates can be attributed to inferior K–12 school systems,

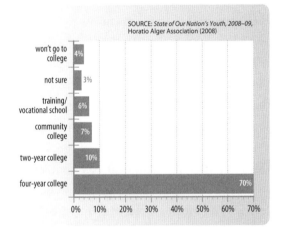

SOURCE: *State of Our Nation's Youth, 2008–09,* Horatio Alger Association (2008)

won't go to college — 4%
not sure — 3%
training/ vocational school — 6%
community college — 7%
two-year college — 10%
four-year college — 70%

◄ **Figure 12**

Asked of high school students in 2008: *Do you plan to go to college sometime after high school?*

whose graduates are not (though they are often told they are) "college ready." Overwhelmed with remedial courses in their freshman year, some of them give up. Yet a far more important driver of high drop-out rates is the staggering and still-growing cost of postsecondary education—combined with inadequate career counseling that allows too many bad program choices and wasted tuition years. In a 2009 Public Agenda survey, adults age 22 to 30 who had quit college overwhelmingly reported that they did so because they couldn't afford it, they had to work full time, their parents couldn't help out, they felt "left on their own," or they had other family commitments. Relatively few said that the coursework was too difficult or that college just wasn't worth the effort.

Millennials are still on track to overtake every earlier generation in educational attainment—but the failure of many of these programmed-to-achieve young people to get a college degree, whether due to the high price tag or simply an unwillingness to assume large student debts, will come as a heavy blow. A handful are taking to the streets, as did U.C. Berkeley students in the fall of 2009 after the University of California announced a 30 percent tuition hike (note that, unlike Boomer collegians, they were protesting over dollars, not ideals). Many students are now exploring alternatives to the expensive, brand-name four-year degree package. These alternatives include accelerated degrees, two-year degrees, community college transfers, and targeted training programs, mainly offered by for-profit colleges that focus on credentials that lead directly to specific careers. Paying a lot of money for schools that offer no clear "pipeline" to employment is a growing Millennial complaint.

College wasn't always so expensive. Back when the Boomer parents of today's collegians were themselves in college, price was not a big problem. In 1965—in dollars inflation-adjusted to 2009—tuition and fees averaged $2,000 for a four-year public college and $7,000 for an equivalent private college. Over the next fifteen years, the prices didn't change much in real terms. In an era when the real median family income grew from around $40,000 to $50,000, this was a very affordable deal—and not just for the median family. Because incomes were more tightly packed around a "middle class," four-fifths of all families had incomes greater than twice the average private college tuition. The vast number of Boomer students put a strain on demand, to be sure, but older voters in many states agreed to pay higher taxes in order to fund enormous expansions in public university systems without placing larger tuition burdens on students.

This era of price stability came to an end just as the first Gen Xers filled America's colleges. From the early 1980s on, tuitions began to rise faster than inflation year after year.

A new mood hit America that encouraged every institution—not just in business, but in higher education as well—to seek profitability and respond to market signals. Many colleges figured they could push families closer to the brink of affordability and use the proceeds to enhance their quality and competitive reputation. Ambitious Gen Xers and their parents took a hard look at the erosion of the non-college middle class and gladly paid up. An expensive degree seemed a small price to pay for being able to jump to the upper end of life's income distribution. The public sector, meanwhile, did little to restrain tuition hikes by expanding the capacity of state colleges, many of which suffered budget cuts in the 1990s and needed to raise tuitions to make ends meet.

A familiar refrain during the Gen-X college era was that the "college earnings premium" made college a bargain at any price. As Millennials reached campuses in 2000, a new catchword—"globalization"—summed up family fears that without a brand-name degree their kids would be fated to compete against low-wage foreign workers for the rest of their lives. As the cost of higher education shifted inexorably from taxpayers to the students themselves, parents felt they had no realistic alternative but to pay the price.

The end result? From 1980 to 2009, on average, private four-year tuitions rose 3.6 percent faster than inflation every year. Public four-year tuitions rose even faster (about 4.3 percent above inflation annually). By 2009, the average private four-year tuition had grown to $26,273 and the average public four-year tuition to $7,020— in both cases roughly 350 percent higher in real dollars than

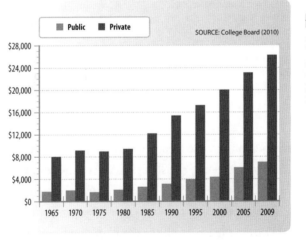

◄ **Figure 13**

Average Yearly Tuition and Fees at Four-Year Colleges, 1965 to 2009, in Constant 2009 Dollars

they were back in 1965. Over the same period, the real income of the median household only rose by 30 percent and incomes below the median rose more slowly than incomes above it. Today, only half of all households earn more than double the tuition for a private four-year college, down sharply from the 1960s. The average income of the lowest quarter of all families today barely equals

For-Profit Colleges on the Rise

As complaints mount about the high cost, inflexibility, and inadequate career focus of many traditional colleges, a rising number of Millennials are turning to for-profit colleges, whose rapid growth has both surprised educators and ignited heated controversy. These colleges are lowering standards, stealing student loan money, and turning education into a commodity, say defenders of old-school academe. Nonsense, say the new for-profits, we're simply focusing more of our resources on what students really want: job skills, career success, and bottom-line customer service.

Twenty years ago, "going to college" meant attending a regionally accredited non-profit or state institution, period. For-profit colleges were small, little known, focused primarily on older adults (often through "correspondence courses"), and accounted for barely 1 percent of students enrolled in degree-granting institutions. Today all that has changed, thanks in part to the rapid expansion of such for-profit giants as the Apollo Group (University of Phoenix), DeVry, ITT Educational Services, and Kaplan Higher Education. For-profits now account for over 7 percent of degreed enrollment at any one time—or over 10 percent, adjusting for the fact that for-profits run year round. That translates into roughly two million students educated on three thousand campuses.

Non-degreed training institutes (which don't offer at least an associate's degree) have also been growing rapidly, but no one knows how much, since no public agency tracks all of them. By some estimates, for-profits account for one-quarter or even one-third of everyone enrolled in a postsecondary institution granting an educational or training credential.

Whether degreed or not, for-profits come in all shapes and sizes. Some have remained very small, including elite art or design academies with less than one hundred students. Others are enormous, like the University of Phoenix, whose undergraduate enrollment of half a million easily exceeds that of the entire Big Ten combined. Some of the smaller schools remain entirely bricks and mortar. The larger schools either "blend" online learning with on-site classrooms or (like Capella University, whose Minneapolis headquarters few students ever visit) do virtually everything online.

Some for-profits, including Kaplan, Walden, American Intercontinental, and Phoenix, offer a liberal-arts education and

regionally accredited bachelor's degrees or even graduate degrees. Their course credits are recognized by other colleges and are eligible for funding by career-development programs at companies like Google or Microsoft. Other nonprofits focus on shorter-term programs with little or no educational accreditation. Their goal is to train students in specific career skills—from nursing, home health, accounting, and project management to electronics, cuisine, cosmetology, and truck driving.

Yet most for-profits share certain elements in common, which explain their rapidly growing market:

■ **Exclusive dedication to student learning.** For-profits don't use tuition revenue to cross-subsidize research or athletics. They spend little or nothing on residences, libraries, museums, or cultural events. The curriculum is centralized. The faculty (who do not have

the cost of one year at a private four-year college. Just since 2000, according to Public Agenda, the share of Americans who believe that most qualified, motivated students have the opportunity to attend college has fallen from 45 to 28 percent.

During the era of Millennial undergraduates, the impact of rising tuitions has been compounded by two serious recessions, which have hammered the wealth and income families can draw upon to pay for college. The second recession, beginning in 2008, has also hammered the wealth and income of colleges, forcing many to curtail "need-blind" admission policies and focus more on special types of students (out-of-state, foreign, or "developmental admits") tenure) are on contract and are evaluated on their ability to teach rather than to publish. Compared to community-college students, for-profit students receive more academic support and career services, are less likely to drop out, and are more likely to attend full time and complete their degrees.

■ **Cost-effective teaching methods.** For-profits excel at the applied-learning teaching style prized by employers. Also, by minimizing physical infrastructure and in-person lecture time in favor of online classes, podcasts, DVDs, and e-texts, for-profits are able to leverage high-quality teaching materials at a low marginal cost. With digital tools, they can scale up quickly to handle more students—giving them an edge over many state colleges that have to turn applicants away due to overflowing classrooms.

■ **Flexibility.** With their strong consumer orientation, for-profits go out of their way to serve busy young (and older) adults with jobs or families, who would be unable to attend a traditional college. Online work can be completed at night, and exams taken on weekends.

■ **Strong focus on finding students jobs.** According to surveys, for-profits do a better job than traditional colleges in counseling students about careers, helping them find first jobs, and tracking their success after graduation. By most accounts, they maintain closer relationships with employers and retool their curriculum faster in response to changing employer demand.

■ **Proven track record with minorities.** Compared to traditional colleges, the for-profits graduate a greater share of minority students (both black and Latino) as well as students from first-generation college families.

To be sure, for-profit colleges are not without their problems. The murky complexity of accreditation systems invites confusion and misrepresentation. Some for-profits, by promising jobs that don't exist, have been guilty of outright fraud. And the price, while often reasonable, is not exactly cheap. The average annual tuition for a degree-granting for-profit is around $14,000.

Yet traditional colleges clearly perceive that the for-profits must be getting something right, since they have been rushing to adopt many of their innovations. Most nonprofit liberal-arts colleges are rapidly shoring up their career counseling, experimenting with online degree programs, and adding professional programs in business or nursing. The share of degrees issued strictly in the arts and sciences has steadily dropped in recent years in all but the most elite liberal-arts colleges. Community colleges, which compete most directly with the for-profits, are working harder to reach out to the local business community and (for the first time ever) launching marketing campaigns to establish a brand among local K–12 students and their parents.

For-profit colleges have succeeded because the traditional colleges grew complacent—too accustomed to measuring their success by self-serving input measures (our prestige, our facilities, our credit hours) rather than student-serving output measures (their education, their skills, their careers). In a well-known Kaplan ad, a tweedy-looking professor looks at the camera and says, "The system has failed you. I have failed you." The message hit home. No one wants the rising Millennial Generation to march off to an institution that is likely to fail them. For-profit colleges are far from perfect—but they are good enough to deliver an important message to traditional colleges: It's time to wake up. Over time, a friendly competition may help to improve accountability and effectiveness on both sides.

who can pay more. The old question was: Can you afford your dream college? Now add a new question: Can your dream college afford you?

Contrary to the stereotype, higher education for most Millennials does not mean residing on campus and studying full time for a four-year degree. Many study for two-year degrees or for job-specific credentials in fields like health care, electronics, or personal services. Many live at home or on their own. Many already have jobs, have kids, are married, or care for a parent. Many who have completed or dropped out of one type of school are now enrolled in another. While Millennials often dream about well-planned straight lines to a perfect future, most understand that real life is full of complications and tradeoffs.

As four-year colleges become increasingly unaffordable, their supposed monopoly on access to desirable careers is coming under attack—and a rising number of Millennials and their parents are trying to evade it. They are insisting on the right to transfer from community colleges to more expensive four-year schools. They are attracted to online or blended classroom formats that can reduce the cost of instruction and increase scheduling flexibility. They are combining cheaper and more practical two-year degrees with entry-level jobs that offer ample room for advancement. Some are rejecting the whole logic of the college earnings premium and setting out to master a craft or trade, a set of skills that don't require formal education. The college earnings premium stopped growing around 2000. If it starts shrinking, Millennials with a craft or trade could do very well indeed.

Thus far, the challenge of rising college prices is affecting Millennials in ways characteristic of their generation. It is adding to the pressure they feel about the future and the need to plan ahead (like figuring out how to repay large student loans with entry-level salaries). It is bringing them even closer to their families, to the extent that most college youth hardly bother to distinguish anymore between their own housing and financial resources and those of their parents. It is further sensitizing them to the widening class and income gaps within their generation, fissures that threaten their hopes for a more cohesive national community.

Tuition and student borrowing started growing in the Gen-X youth era, long before Millennials showed up on campus. But Gen Xers seldom responded in any of these ways. Once again, it is not just new circumstances—but rather a new generational response to these circumstances—that is putting today's youth on a different life course.

Generation Debt (standard of living)

When today's young adults first set up their own household on their own income, the experience can come as a surprise. They may have spent years growing up in a big home with nice clothes, family-funded amenities, and vacations. They have probably planned and discussed with their parents some of the great careers they could launch. They have almost certainly watched

TV shows featuring young celebrities with designer lifestyles and tricked-out apartments. Then, with college, comes the sticker shock and the debt. After that comes the paycheck that delivers less than they expected and the rent that costs more, along with the group living, the used cars, the second jobs, the skipped health insurance, and the craigslist.org hand-me-downs.

How are they handling this surprise? On the whole, rather well. They are making checklists, huddling with friends, staying in close touch with relatives—and keeping their hopes high. Most surveys confirm that young adults are much more optimistic about their economic future than older Americans.

The stagnation of young-adult living standards in recent decades—and their obvious decline relative to the rising affluence of older Americans—is not a new trend. First

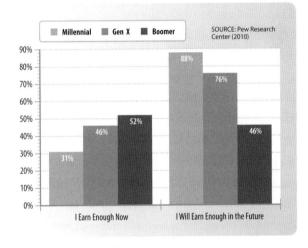

noticed way back in the stagflation years of Jimmy Carter's presidency, it later helped shape the trademark fatalism and minimalism of young Gen Xers. In the early 1990s, it was the premise for movies like *Reality Bites* and *Wayne's World*, about the lives of twenty-somethings. A decade later, it was the subject of hard-hitting books like *Generation Broke* and *Busted*, about the lives of thirty-somethings. Yet even if the trend itself is not new, the emerging Millennial response to it is. Young Gen Xers typically viewed economic adversity as a reason to take risks, go it alone, and distrust the system. Millennials are more likely to view it as a reason to plan ahead, start saving, stay close to your family, and get civically active. Remarkably, this more upbeat attitude has been emerging during the aftermath to the worst youth recession since the Great Depression.

To gain perspective, let's look at the numbers. According to the U.S. Census Bureau, personal income for young adults started to grow more slowly than older-adult income in the mid-1970s. In other words, youth began to fall behind just when late-wave Boomers reached their twenties, or about the same time when young adults were beginning to move back home with their parents. Over the years, this divergence has been considerable—though of course it has widened more in some years (usually recessions) than in others. Consider: From 1974 to 2008, the inflation-adjusted median income of Americans of all ages has risen by about one-quarter, but it has actually fallen slightly for Americans age 25 to 34. The median real income of young men has actually fallen considerably, by a negative 23 percent, though this has mostly been made up by gains for young women.

Changes in net worth tell a similar story. Household net worth means all of your assets (including your home) minus all of your liabilities and debts. Here again, according to the Federal Reserve, younger households have been lagging behind older households for nearly forty years. In 1983, for example, the median net worth of a household age 55 to 64 was just under 10 times larger than the median net worth of a household under age 35. In 2007, it was 22 times larger, at $254,100 and $11,800, respectively. A growing (if still small) share of young adults have been buying their own homes. Yet as a group they've been gathering debt far faster than they've been gathering assets.

Debt, in fact, has become the new reality for today's youth—mostly in a flood of student-loans they take out to get degrees that (they hope) will boost their future incomes. Total federal lending to students, now at $84 billion per year, has exactly doubled over the past decade. Private college lenders, almost unheard of in 1990, grew to $22 billion in 2008 before imploding after the financial crash to a still-hefty $11 billion in 2009. Of the 72 percent of 2007–08 graduates from four-year private college who have student loans, half have borrowed more than $22,000; one-fifth have borrowed more than $40,000. Of the 62 percent from four-year public colleges, half have borrowed more than $18,000; one-tenth more than $40,000. These are just undergraduate averages, and don't include the large numbers of Millennials leaving college with debts of over $50,000, or those graduating medical or law school with debts of well over $100,000. Debt-service payments often amount to 10 or even 20 percent of the after-tax earnings of an entry-level employee.

Even these numbers do not include the extra credit card debt racked up by an estimated quarter of all students to help pay tuition and fees. (Credit cards are heavily promoted by most colleges, which receive a kickback from the banks.) Or the extra home-equity loans or 401(k) loans taken out by Boomer parents, some of whom are paying for their kids' college out of their own retirement. According to the *LifeCourse-Chartwells College Student Survey*, 41 percent of Millennial undergrads say that paying for college will be a "very" or "extremely" difficult financial burden. Fifty-one percent say their college debt will affect their career choices.

Older Americans are inclined to believe that the economic challenges facing young people are largely the result of their own improvidence. Millennials themselves are the first to admit that they often don't make the best financial choices. In 2007, nearly half of all households under age 35 had unpaid credit card balances (average amount: $5,100) and it wasn't all for investments like college. Even Millennials who struggle with debt may find it hard to resist regular amenities like the daily "Starbucks" break—especially if they tend to regard their family's budget, and not their own, as the one that really matters.

Yet the evidence suggests that most Millennials are trying to do their best under tough circumstances. Several recent studies (one was published in the *Journal of Consumer Affairs* and another by the research firm Yankelovich) have concluded that, despite their lower income, today's young adults save at the same rate as older Americans, are just as likely to be "bargain hunters," and are even as likely to worry about their future retirement income. Like younger teens, today's young adults are willing to cut back. A 2009 JWT survey found that roughly half of 18- to 29-year olds were prepared if necessary to "stop entirely" drinking alcohol, eating out, attending sporting events, and watching most media. A 2008 study published in the *Monthly Labor Review* looked at singles living alone, age 21 to 29, and compared their actual per-capita consumer spending behavior in two different years: 1985 and 2005. The results were revealing:

* Annual spending in 2005 ($22,744) was slightly below inflation-adjusted spending in 1985 ($23,866).

* From 1985 to 2005, the largest single rise in spending was on shelter and utilities (up 8.2 percent as a share of total spending). The next largest rise was on education (up 3.5 percent).
* All the declines were in areas usually associated with youth extravagance: clothing and services (down 2.9 percent), travel and trips (down 1.9 percent), eating out (down 1.4 percent), and entertainment (down 0.4 percent).
* Daily transportation was also down (2.3 percent), mostly due to less spending on new cars and trucks. Between 1985 and 2005, the number of vehicles per capita used by these singles declined by roughly one-quarter.

In light of these stagnating consumption trends, you might marvel at Millennials' optimism about their economic future. Consider that, over the next several years, youth employment and youth wages are likely to be tightly constrained by a slow-to-recover economy. Consider as well that, further into the future, fiscal Armageddon looms: The publicly held federal debt is likely to reach $20 trillion by 2020, and unfunded liabilities for federal retirement benefits amount to roughly $100 trillion—all of which, nearly everyone knows, must eventually translate into higher taxes or broken benefit promises. Few Millennials believe that they will not number among the affected taxpayers or that their Boomer parents will not number among the affected retirees.

So what explains the Millennials' optimism? It comes from their refusal to accept the pessimistic assumptions of older generations. More than their parents, Millennials believe that new technologies can revive productivity growth, international coordination can revive global demand, bipartisan deals can pull the budget out of deficits, and an alliance between working-age and retirement-age Americans can put an end to unfunded red ink. It is likely that this optimism will be put to a severe test by lingering recessionary riptides that will require Millennials to sacrifice much more before a better future is attained. Yet Millennials can take some satisfaction that, with each passing year, their generation of workers and voters will call more of the shots. And as that happens, they will be able to put ever-more pressure on business and political leaders to rotate the economy's balance sheet back in favor of their future.

Organization Kids (employment)

Millennial attitudes toward jobs and careers have been defined by several extreme phase-of-life trends that set this generation apart from Gen Xers or Boomers at the same age—from declining teen employment and the aging of "temp" work to a weak entry-level job market and the rise of government service careers.

Ever since Millennials began to enter middle and high school, the share of teens wanting to work (or allowed to work) outside the home has been sinking to postwar lows. This is a measure of the extra sheltering and structure in their lives. Employers in their forties and fifties should keep this in mind the next time they are baffled at the workplace awkwardness of young Millennial interns or hires and their deficiency in "soft skills" (such as punctuality, proper dress, and polite communication). By age 18, today's midlife employer probably had a couple of years of work experience after school and over summers. By the same age, most of today's newbies have had only a few months or none at all.

Declining youth work experience shows up clearly in the historical employment data. Year to year, teen employment usually tracks the patterns of adult employment, but over the longer term, it often does not. For example, you would think the stagflationary 1970s would have been a shakeout time for teen workers, and the roaring 1990s a growth time. But very much the opposite occurred. From one generation to the next, shifting parental and youth attitudes have played key roles in pushing teen employment up or down.

For Boomer teens, the "right" to work was a newly won youth freedom. Then first-wave Gen Xers came along and pushed teen workloads higher. Summer and after-school teen work grew strongly and almost continuously from the mid-'60s to the early '80s, when late-wave Boomers and first-wave Gen Xers (girls especially) pushed paid teen employment to a postwar peak. Xers kept it at high levels for the rest of the 1980s.

Throughout the Gen-X youth era (from the mid-1970s through mid-'90s), the purpose of teen work shifted away from supporting families in favor of personal spending money, career-building, or self-fulfillment. One out of every six 15-year olds held an after-school job, one of every three a paid summer job, and, for the first time ever, employed girls outnumbered employed boys. Later in the Gen-X youth era, as adult immigrants began moving into the service sector, teen employment began to ebb slightly. By the late '80s, employment rates for 16- and 17-year olds were roughly 5 percent below those of the late '70s. Rates for 15-year olds were 20 percent lower.

In the Millennial youth era, employment has continued to fall among teens, especially younger teens, despite an economy that, through the year 2000, desperately wanted young workers and was willing to pay plenty for them. Then came the dual recessions of the next decade, each of which pushed teen employment lower with practically no recovery in between. Between 1979 and 2000, the share of employed teens age 16 to 19 drifted down from 49 percent to

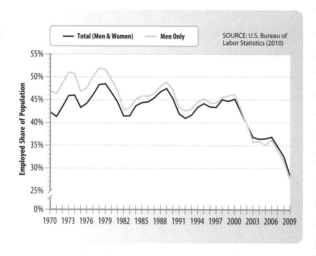

Figure 15 ▶

Employment Rates for Youth Age 16 to 19, 1970 to 2009

45 percent—but by 2003 it had plunged to 37 percent (the lowest rate since records were first kept in 1948). By 2009, the rate had dropped still further to 28 percent. To be sure, the unemployment rate for these teens in 2009 was very high, with one teen looking for work for every three having a job. But even if every teen looking for a job had one, teen employment would still be hitting all-time lows.

What accounts for the ebbing popularity of paid work among teenagers? One reason, accounting for about half of the decline, is that teens are spending more time in grade school (longer days and more summer school). Another reason is the growing competition for low-skilled jobs from recent adult immigrants. Finally, and perhaps most importantly, social attitudes have changed. During the '90s, educators, parents, and teens themselves began to suspect that too many teens were wrapping tacos when they ought to be wrestling with math. Families started paying attention to the college wage premium.

When the only road to a good career runs through a good college, time spent on select soccer, community service, or SAT prep courses seems more valuable, long-term, than time spent on mere money making. Families also began worrying about workplace dangers such as accidents, hazing, drugs, and crime—especially when teens work alongside wilder (Gen-X) young adults.

By the time Millennials become adults, this aversion to paid work disappears. Adjusted for the business cycle, the employment rate of youths age 20 to 24 has been basically flat over the past twenty-five years, with no downward trend after 2000. More young adults are enrolled in school, but among those in colleges or trade schools, employment was actually higher in the mid-2000s than it was in the late 1970s. Clearly, many Millennial collegians who never worked in grade school are now eagerly seeking employment in college to help cover the high cost of tuition, ease the burden on parents, or pay for their living expenses.

With teens working less and college-age youths focusing on longer-term career positions, much of the high-turnover and temp-work service sector is aging with Generation X. Older adults in their late twenties, thirties, and even forties are now filling positions (in hospitality, construction, and high-end retail, for example) that used to be held by younger adults. Millennials in their early twenties are likewise taking positions (in fast food, cleaning, and low-end retail) that used to be held by teens—especially as they struggle with the high price of college. Back in the 1980s, half of all McDonald's employees were teens; today, less than a third. In 1985, according to the Bureau of Labor Statistics, 29 percent of all contract workers were age 18 to 24, a share that declined to 17 percent by 2005.

Whereas Gen Xers have always been attracted to the flexibility and open-ended variety of high-turnover jobs, Millennials are more likely to associate them with perpetual insecurity and low wages. As young children, most Millennials grew up seeing entire industries (from personal services to construction) dominated by an unlimited supply of low-skill adults who can immigrate here from any corner of the globe. As teens and young adults, many Millennials today stay away from such industries and even categorically avoid tasks involving, say, cleaning or food preparation. While the significance of race and ethnicity is certainly declining with Millennials, the significance of class and income—and its dependence upon lifelong occupational success—is still strong and indeed may be rising.

Ever since this generation began to embark on steady careers in their mid-twenties, the economy has been buffeted by the weakest demand for entry-level workers, and the highest youth unemployment rates, since the Great Depression. Thus far, most Millennials have responded without panic and by keeping their eyes firmly fixed on their long-term goals. This is a measure of their achievement orientation. A generation raised to be special is not about to be distracted from a step-by-step life plan with a special destination.

Both the challenging economy and the Millennials' new generational sensibility have created marked shifts in the career priorities of young adults over the past few years. Employers have been noticing that this generation is more averse to life risks. Fewer of them want to become startup entrepreneurs (unless they are fully backed by family and friends) or independent consultants (unless they are just waiting for a full-time position). In JWT's *Millennials at Work* survey, only 2 percent of working people in their twenties call themselves "free lance"—versus 5 percent in their thirties and 7 percent over age 40.

Most Millennials find high-income careers attractive, of course. Yet they show a rising reluctance to enter very high-income professions in which the time commitment or drop-out risk is extreme. A rising share of Millennials (even the most talented) are looking for middle or upper-middle income careers that also offer some degree of security and work-life balance. They want challenging work with the possibility of advancement, but only as a sustainable long-term proposition—not a quick burnout deal in which this many years of abuse are traded for that many dollars of reward.

Career appeal by field is also shifting. The popularity of government service is broadly rising among Millennials, including everything from education and the environment to intelligence and national security. This popularity spills over into allied public-service specialties such as forensics and public health. Interest in finance, marketing, and media is down. Among the professions, medicine is up and law is down. In the pursuit of grad school degrees, STEM (science, technology, engineering, and math) fields show a rising trend,

The Graying of the Public Sector

Boomers dominate today's public-sector workforce. Because of generous and often early retirement benefits, older Silent Generation workers have virtually disappeared. And because Generation X never gravitated as heavily into public service—and was often put off by big bureaucracies—younger post-

Boomers never joined in comparable numbers. At the federal level, where the civil service has hardly grown at all for the last thirty years, there was little need to hire many Gen Xers to begin with, and those that were hired often found themselves termi-nated through "reduction-in-force" orders starting with the last hired.

The result? The public sector is graying. Only one-quarter of the federal workforce is under age forty—versus half of the private-sector workforce. Fully 56 percent of all federal workers (and 64 percent at the Department of Energy) are age 45 to 64, while the share of the total U.S. economy is only 39 percent. State and local government work-forces are also graying, especially in professional, technical, and admin-istrative personnel.

With such a vast number of Boomer public employees due to retire over the next decade, most public agencies will have no choice but to hire large numbers of Mil-lennials to replace them—creating what some are calling a government-wide "succession crisis" in the 2010s. How well senior public servants can attract, train, mentor, and energize the best and brightest of today's rising generation may determine how effectively America governs itself over the next half-century.

▼ **Figure 16:** Distribution of Total U.S. and Federal Employment, by Age in 2006

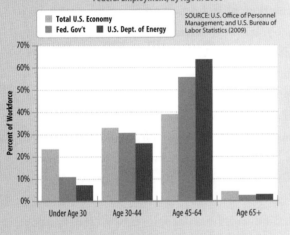

SOURCE: U.S. Office of Personnel Management; and U.S. Bureau of Labor Statistics (2009)

along with the behavioral sciences, while most of the humanities and qualita-tive social sciences show a declining trend. When surveyed about the size of their ideal employer, Millennials express a bimodal preference. They are very attracted to elite global brands like Google or Disney, yet also to small close-knit firms with elite clientele. Employers that can offer both the secure big brand and the family-like feel will find it easy attract Millennial recruits.

Demographic trends are reinforcing many of these preferences. Most public-sector agencies currently employ a disproportionately large share of Boomers, nearly all of whom will soon be leaving due to early and generous retirement benefits. The same is true of many large, old-line private-sector corporations, especially in manufacturing, utilities, energy, and mining. These agencies and companies have no other choice than to hire vast numbers of entry-level Millennials over the coming ten or fifteen years. Companies and departments that are top-heavy with Gen Xers, including those specializing in media, marketing, sales, and financial services, will feel less pressure to hire Millennials. Meanwhile, in many academic, professional, and service sectors (such as business consulting) where 401(k)-style defined-contribution retirement plans are the norm, many Boomers with shrunken pension savings are deferring retirement. By preventing Gen Xers from advancing, their deferral will likewise suppress the hiring of entry-level Millennials.

Millennials have been entering the full-time workforce with high school degrees since 2000, with four-year college degrees since 2004, and with graduate and professional degrees since 2006. Already, businesses are beginning to take stock of the opportunities and challenges this generation presents. On the plus side, employers report that they excel in group work, crave approval, are very teachable, like to plan their futures, and take a genuine interest in the overall purpose of the organization. On the minus side, employers report that they require a lot of oversight, avoid creative risks, are unfamiliar with the bottom-line demands of paid employment, and are overly attached to their parents and families.

Few would have reported similar pluses or minuses when talking about Generation X (or Boomers) at the same entry-level age. Why the contrast? Why do Millennials behave differently, even when responding to similar challenges? And what can employers do about it? To find the answer, we need to dig deeper—and examine this generation's core traits.

05

Seven Core Traits

"Generations, like people, have personalities, and Millennials—the American teens and twenty-somethings who are making the passage into adulthood at the start of a new millennium—have begun to forge theirs: confident, self-expressive, liberal, upbeat, and open to change."

— PEW RESEARCH CENTER (2010)

"With their emphasis on teamwork, achievement, modesty, and respect for authority, today's high school graduates bear little resemblance to their more nihilistic Gen-X siblings and even less to their self-indulgent Baby Boomer parents."

— MILWAUKEE JOURNAL SENTINEL (2005)

Seven Core Traits

Every generation contains all kinds of people. But each generation has a group persona, with core traits. Not all members of that generation will share those traits, and many will personally resist those traits, but—like it or not—those core traits will substantially define the world inhabited by every member of that generation.

The following are the seven core traits of the Millennial Generation.

* **Special.** From precious-baby movies of the mid-1980s to the media glare surrounding today's young workers, older generations have inculcated in Millennials the sense that they are, collectively, vital to the nation and to their parents' sense of purpose.

* **Sheltered.** From the surge in child-safety rules and devices to the post-Columbine lockdown of public schools to the hotel-style security of today's college dorm rooms, Millennials have been the focus of the most sweeping youth-protection movement in American history.

* **Confident.** With high levels of collective optimism and a focus on positive solutions for big problems, this generation is striking an upbeat new tone about their own—and the nation's—future.

* **Team oriented.** From youth soccer and social networking to collaborative learning and community service, Millennials are developing strong team instincts, tight peer bonds, and a rising sense of civic engagement.

* **Conventional.** Taking pride in their improving behavior and comfortable with their parents' values, Millennials provide a modern twist to the traditional belief that social rules and standards can make life easier.

* **Pressured.** Pushed to work hard, plan for the long term, and take full advantage of the opportunities offered them, Millennials feel a "trophy kid" pressure to excel, both in the classroom and in the workplace.
* **Achieving.** As accountability and higher school standards have risen to the top of America's political agenda, Millennials have become a generation focused on achievement—and are on track to become the best-educated young adults in U.S. history.

On the whole, these are not traits one would have associated with Silent, Boomers, or Gen Xers in youth—though many are remembered from the days of G.I. Generation teens.

Millennials and Specialness

Millennials first arrived in the early 1980s as the offspring of "yuppie" parents touting "family values": of Boomer supermoms opting to have in vitro babies (a historical first) and Boomer dads demanding to be to be present at childbirth (another historical first). When this first Millennial wave entered grade school in 1989, America suddenly mobilized around a national school reform movement. With the end of the Cold War a few years later, the fate of children became the central focus of political speeches, new legislation, and a gathering culture war. By 1998, more than half of all Americans (a record share) said that "getting kids off to the right start" ought to be America's top priority. National issues having nothing directly to do with children—Social Security, the War on Terror, unemployment—began to be discussed in terms of their impact on children.

As children, Millennials absorbed the adult message that they dominate America's agenda. As young adults, they now come easily to the belief that their future is the nation's future, their problems are the nation's problems and, by extension, everyone in America will naturally be inclined to help them solve those problems.

Many Boomer and Gen-X parents have thrown heart and soul into raising, nurturing, and helping these special Millennials—and they are remaining hands-on every step of the way. K–12 schools have been grappling with hovering "helicopter parents" who monitor every aspect of their students' lives and intervene at the slightest hint of a life problem. Ten or fifteen years ago, parents were conspicuously absent from TV shows about teens and young adults (recall "Beverly Hills 90210" or "Party of Five"). But today's popular teen shows reflect a young-adult world full of highly involved parents, with shows such as "Gilmore Girls," "The O.C.," and "My Super Sweet Sixteen."

Even as Millennials grow up and leave home, parents remain very involved in their lives. On college campuses, administrators are expanding their "empty nest" orientation programs for doting moms and dads (complete with teddy bears for them to hug) designed to assure them that the colleges are merely adding the final touches on their wonderful progeny. Parents agree by a three-to-one margin that they are more involved in helping their children succeed in college than their own parents were with them. Hovering parents are also following Millennials into the workplace. Employers report rising numbers of parents requesting company information for their children, showing up for interviews, advising their children on whether to take a job offer, and even calling up managers to protest poor performance reviews.

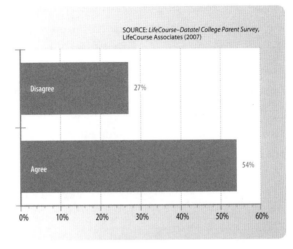

SOURCE: *LifeCourse–Datatel College Parent Survey,* *LifeCourse Associates (2007)*

Disagree — 27%

Agree — 54%

◄ **Figure 17**

Asked of Parents of Millennials: *You spend more time with your children than your parents spent with you at the same age. Agree or Disagree?*

Older generations of teachers and managers are often surprised to find that Millennials don't see their parents' involvement in their lives as intrusive. From cradle to career, they have come to accept and even expect the very special attention that parents shower upon them. According to College Board surveys, most college freshmen agree that their parents are "very involved"—and they also agree more than four to one that they want more involvement from their parents, not less. First-generation and minority college students (whose parents may be less likely to intervene) are even more likely to agree that they would prefer more involvement.

Millennials and Sheltering

Americans have been tightening the security perimeters around Millennials ever since this generation began arriving over twenty years ago. Images of the Columbine and Virginia Tech shootings, of 9/11 and the War on Terror, of AMBER alerts and Code Adams have alarmed Americans of all ages about the dangers threatening youth. Worried parents have become avid consumers for a childproofing industry that has snapped up new patents for everything from stove-knob covers to safety mirrors. Ever since the early 1980s, adults have been gradually pulling down the divorce rate, the abortion rate, alcohol consumption per capita, and other hardships to children.

Today's youth look up at a castle-like edifice of parental care that keeps getting new bricks added—V-chips and "smart lockers" last month, campus underage drinking monitors this month, wellness seminars and life-counseling in workplaces next month. The older '80s-born Millennials recall more open sky, while the younger ones born in the '90s look up at the growing walls, unable to imagine what could be seen in their absence.

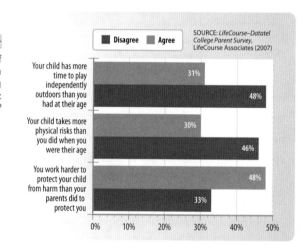

Figure 18 ▶

Parents of
Millennials on
Protecting
their Kids:
Agree or Disagree?

This new sheltering movement has reversed the trends that today's older generations recall from their own youth eras, when adult protectiveness was being dismantled (for Boomers) or not really there at all (for Gen Xers). According to the *LifeCourse-Datatel Parent Survey*, parents of today's college students overwhelmingly agree that they have worked harder to protect their kids from harm than their own parents did with them. This

Examples of Child Protection Policies Since 1982

- child restraint & helmet rules
- child-proof homes
- blanket Medicaid coverage
- school vaccination checks
- "youth rules" in the workplace
- V-Chips

- social-host liability laws
- video-game ratings
- Megan laws
- Amber Alerts
- graduated auto licenses
- "cops in shops"

- dragnets for "dead-beat" dads
- urban curfews
- "safe-place" havens for kids
- drug-free zones near schools

majority is larger for younger Gen-X parents than for older Boomer parents—which helps explain why the sheltering is rising for each passing birth cohort, from the first-born Millennials to the last-born.

Far from rebelling against the barrage of adult protections, today's youth accept it as just another sign that they are a special generation. Throughout their childhood and teen years, the Millennials came to expect authoritative security and rule enforcement for their protection. Today's teens rarely resist uniform dress codes, locker searches, see-through backpacks, or cell phone GPS once they understand that these policies enhance their safety. Compared to Gen Xers, surveys show that they are more comfortable with "zero tolerance" for even minor infractions in schools, are more likely to say that enforcement does not go far enough, and are somewhat more inclined to report infractions to adults in charge.

Millennials also try hard to protect themselves and stay on track by taking fewer lifestyle risks. As already noted, this generation is smoking less, drinking less, and getting pregnant less in their teen years. Of the forty "youth risk indicators" that have been continuously monitored by the CDC from 1995 to 2007, 35 have fallen, 4 have remained unchanged, and only one (related to obesity) has risen. Three-quarters of all teens agree that there is nothing embarrassing about saying you are a virgin—to the amazement of older Americans, who imagine that a much smaller share of teens would agree. When asked which of all "issues" concerns them most, Millennials say their number one concern is "personal safety" (81 percent). A rising share of college students say they want to pursue careers in public health, forensics, and law enforcement.

All this sheltering and risk aversion has created a youth generation that has been, on the whole, much healthier and less prone to injury and predation than any earlier generation in American history. Infant mortality and death rates from disease, violence, and accidents are all down by at least a third from what they were for Gen Xers at the same age. Thanks in part to more aggressive law enforcement and social service intervention, federal data show that, between 1988 and 1999, rates of child abduction fell by 23 percent, runaways by 25 percent, substantiated child abuse by 43 percent, and missing children by 51 percent.

Yet the urge to shelter has also been responsible for some new health problems among Millennials. Consider, for example, the dramatic decline in their physical activity—especially unstructured activity outdoors. In 1969, half of all 18-year olds walked or rode a bike to school. Today, hardly any do that, making youth six times more likely to play a video game than ride a bike on a typical day. Just since 1995, bike riding is down by one-third—as is the share of children ages 7 to 11 who swim, fish, canoe, or play touch football. Since 1997, baseball playing is down 28 percent. Meanwhile, physical education classes at schools are being cut back to make room for more academics. Most experts agree that this decline in physical activity has contributed to the quadrupling (from 4 to 16 percent) in the share of children and teens classified by the CDC as "pre-obese"—and perhaps also to the rising incidence of ADD and ADHD. Increasing body mass indices (along with a new emphasis on cleanliness) may also be pushing the rising incidence of asthma among kids.

True to the wishes of adult America, Millennials are protected, feel protected, and expect to be protected—even, some might say, overprotected.

Millennials and Confidence

Millennials have arrived with a sunny outlook, confidence that they can achieve great things, and faith that America's big problems really can be solved. While Boomers, according to the Pew Research Center, have infused a new pessimism into every phase of life they have entered, Millennials are thus far infusing a new optimism. For over thirty years, until the mid-1990s, the teen suicide rate marched relentlessly upward. Over the last decade, it has declined by 30 percent. In a striking turnaround, the share of K–12 students who think growing up now is harder than it was for their parents is actually going down, from 50 percent in 1989 to 39 percent today. In 2005, 67 percent of 15- to 22-year olds rated themselves as happy or very happy most of the time. Nearly nine out of ten of today's high school students say they would use the word "confident" to describe themselves.

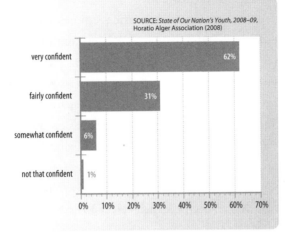

SOURCE: *State of Our Nation's Youth, 2008–09,* Horatio Alger Association (2008)

◂ **Figure 19**

Asked of high-school students in 2008: *How confident are you that you will reach your career goal?*

Pushed by the high expectations of parents and raised on "self-esteem" movement injunctions to believe in themselves and reach for the stars, the Millennials are coming of age with a firm new faith in their futures. A rising share of teens (including overwhelming majorities of Latinos and African Americans) believe they will someday be financially more successful than their parents. Among youth age 10 to 17, 95 percent say they "have goals that I want to reach in my life," 92 percent agree that "my success depends on how hard I work," and 88 percent agree that "I'm confident that I'll be able to find a good-paying job when I'm an adult." According to Pew, young adults overwhelmingly believe they have better educational opportunities and access to higher-paying jobs than young adults did twenty years ago.

Young Xers often felt like they were in a high-stakes gamble for success. Though most in their generation might not go far, they figured that individually, with a bit of luck and nerve, they could buck the trend. What differentiates Millennials is their strong collective assurance: A rising share believe that their entire peer group will be successful and that, with enough hard work and planning, they will all come together to solve some of the world's toughest problems. When asked which groups will be most likely to help America toward a better future, Millennials rank "young people" second, behind only "scientists." In a recent survey, 18- to 29-year olds were the most optimistic group in assessing whether today's children would grow up better or worse off than people are now.

Older generations sometimes criticize today's youth for unrealistic "over-confidence," and there is some truth to this: Millennials have a harder time rebounding from personal failures than Xers—with their "abort, fail, retry" philosophy—did in their youth. Yet Millennials' collective confidence and team outlook makes them better prepared to face society-wide challenges. This is one reason why the severe recession that began in 2008 has not shaken this generation's confidence. After all, why worry when everyone is in the same boat? Surely we can all pull together and get our future back on track. Surveys show that, in spite of being hit hard by job losses, Millennials remain confident that they will achieve their career goals.

Millennial girls and young women are leading the confidence trend and are pulling ahead of boys in a number of measures of success, including choosing challenging courses, getting good grades in high school, and enrolling in and graduating from college. Many Millennial males remain personally confident, and young men are more likely than young women to say they consider themselves "exceptionally talented." But Millennial males are less likely to participate in the sense of collective assurance and long-term mission that energizes their female peers.

Millennials and Team Orientation

From preschool through grad school, Millennials have been developing strong team instincts and tight peer bonds. In the Gen-X youth era, adults told kids to look after themselves and do everything they could to ensure their own success in life. In the Millennial youth era, adults have been telling kids to look after each other and do everything they can to help the community succeed. Through group projects, peer grading, student juries, honor systems, and the like, Boomer educators have encouraged Millennials to acquire the sorts of team habits and civic attitudes that Boomers never really acquired themselves.

The new team orientation has broadened Millennials' search for peer friendships and given rise to a more inclusive, collaborative style. During the 1990s, there was a sharp decline in the share of eighth and tenth graders who felt lonely or wished they had more friends—and a growing desire to share the credit for winning. Today, only three teens in ten report that they usually socialize with only one or two friends, while two in three do so with groups of friends. Colleges have been adding common rooms and lounges to dorms so students can spend more time together in groups. In the workplace, as in schools and colleges, surveys show that Millennials favor collaboration and disapprove of cut-throat competition. Rising numbers of young adults entering the workplace report that the social environment in the office is very important and also that they want to socialize with coworkers outside of the office.

For Millennials, the use of information technology has

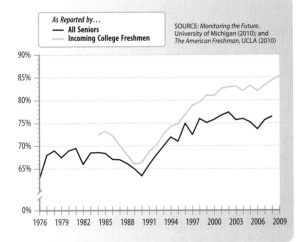

As Reported by...
— All Seniors
⸺ Incoming College Freshmen

SOURCE: *Monitoring the Future,*
University of Michigan (2010); and
The American Freshman, UCLA (2010)

◄ **Figure 20**

Share of High
School Seniors
Who Volunteer,
1976 to 2009*

* 2008 for seniors,
as reported by
Monitoring the Future

become a group activity. Today's young people power up their IM and email servers as soon as they touch a computer, making themselves the most 24/7 peer-to-peer "connected" generation in the human history. They're less interested in the anonymous freedom of the Internet and more interested in its ability to maintain their networks of friends. And they want to maintain those networks even while in the workplace: A majority of young workers admit to using personal email at work as well as accessing Web sites such as MySpace and Facebook.

On a broader level, Millennials' ethic of teamwork is driving a rising sense of civic and community obligation. A record-high 69 percent of college freshmen now say that it is "extremely important" to help others in need. The share of 16- to 24-year olds who volunteer in their community has doubled since 1989.

Since the presidential election of 1996, in which only 37 percent of Americans age 18 to 29 voted, the arrival of Millennials into this age bracket has pushed voter rates steadily higher: to 41 percent in 2000, 48 percent in 2004, and 52 percent in 2008—the highest rate in decades.

Service-oriented Millennials are showing a rising interest in pursuing government and nonprofit careers. They are also drawn to private companies that have built a brand for serving their local communities. Whatever kind of workplace they find themselves in, today's youth expect the opportunity to participate in community service activities, whether through company-sponsored activities, pro-bono work, or time off for personal volunteering.

Millennials and Convention

Boomer children felt overdosed on norms and rules and famously came of age assaulting them. Millennials show signs of trying to reestablish a regime of rules. A recent JWT study found that Millennials show a new respect for national institutions, traditions, and family values—including monogamy and parenthood (94 percent), marriage (84 percent), the U.S. Constitution (88 percent), and the military (84 percent).

Gallup surveys note a conventional shift in teen leanings on issues ranging from substance abuse to abstinence to divorce. As recently remarked by George Gallup, Jr.: "Teens today are decidedly more traditional than their elders were, in both lifestyles and attitudes. *Gallup Youth Survey* data from the past twenty-five years reveal that teens today are far less likely than their parents were to use alcohol, tobacco and marijuana. In addition, they are less likely than their parents even today to approve of sex before marriage and having children out of wedlock." According to a Boys & Girls Clubs of America national survey, the share of teens who agree that music, movies, and TV should be censored is as large as the share who disagree. Researchers would not have said anything similar about Boomers or Xers in their youth. Unlike these older generations, Millennials' rebellion lies in moving to the ordered center, rather than pushing the anarchic edge.

Why this Millennial move to the center? Having benefitted from a renorming of family life following the turbulent 1960s and '70s, today's young people no longer feel alienated from the older adults in their lives. Surveys by the National Association of Secondary School Principals (NASSP) show that eight in ten teens now say they have "no problems" with any family member—up from four in ten back in the early 1970s. Pew reports that twice as many of today's parents say they recall "often" having major disagreements with their own parents as say they now have them with their own kids. The share of teens reporting "very

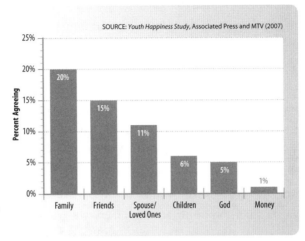

SOURCE: *Youth Happiness Study*, Associated Press and MTV (2007)

◀ **Figure 21**

Top Five Responses of Youth Age 13 to 24: *What makes you happy in life?*

different" values from their parents has fallen by roughly half since the 1970s and the share who say their values are "very or mostly similar" has hit an all-time high of 76 percent.

Behind these trends lies a deeper agreement between young adults and parents on cultural values—in fact, a virtual closing of the generational culture gap. Millennials trade advice easily with their parents about clothes, entertainment, and careers. They listen to (and perform) their parents' music, share songs with their parents on iPods, and watch remakes of their parents' old movies. Six in ten say it is "easy" to talk to parents about sex, drugs, and alcohol. The special relationship between Millennials and their parents is reflected everywhere in today's culture—even in a popular new line of Hallmark greeting cards that reads, "To my mother, my best friend."

Millennials remain so close with their parents that moving back home is losing its stigma. Young Xers largely viewed the move back home as a sign of failure, but Millennials see it as just another stage in a close relationship with parents and families, which they expect will last a lifetime. A recent Associated Press survey reports that teens and young adults rank "spending time with family" as the one thing that makes them the most happy. Seventy-three percent say their relationship with their parents makes them happy, and nearly half say their parents are their heroes. Back in the 1960s and '70s, when Boomers were coming of age, the extended family was dismissed as an old-fashioned and freedom-inhibiting convention. Now that the Boomers' children are coming of age, the extended family is again becoming a valued norm.

While Millennials are broadly willing to accept their parents' values, they also think they can someday apply these values a whole lot better. They agree by a two-to-one margin that "values and character" will matter more to their own generation than their parents'. Today's young people are also far more trusting of the capacity of large national institutions to do what's right for their generation and for the country. When they are asked who's going to improve the schools, clean up the environment, and cut the crime rate, they respond—without irony—that it will be teachers, government, and the police. Today's youth often complain about Boomers who get angry about their convictions and paranoid about politics. Most Millennials gravitate instead to leaders who are constructive, consensus-minded, and want to make the system to work better, not tear it down.

As they come of age, this generation wants to build stable careers that can be part of a conventional lifestyle. Unlike free-spirited young Boomers and entrepreneurial young Xers, they are carefully planning career ladders, seeking "big brand" employers with structured yet comfortable workplace environments, and prioritizing a new form of work-life balance (what we call work-life blending). Defiance, cynicism, and risk are out. Stability, trust, and life balance are in.

Millennials and Pressure

Stress has become a daily reality in Millennials' lives. Their new digital technologies place more demands on them. Schools and colleges place more demands on them. Most importantly, their own ambitions (and their parents' ambitions for them) place more demands on them. Today's youth watch classic goof-off Gen-X films like *Ferris Bueller's Day Off*, *Fast Times at Ridgemont High*, and *Wayne's World* with amusement, to be sure, but often with little or no self identification.

A Pressured Lifestyle

High School- and College-Age Youth: Trends Over the Last 15 Years

	Change
Unstructured free play, hours per week	▼
Sleep, hours per week	▼
Age at which career choices are made	▼
Temp work for pay, hours per week	▼
Homework, hours per week	▲
Share who want to go to four-year college	▲
Admission standards at typical college	▲
College tuition & debt relative to family income	▲
Share who get their first job via internship	▲

The new youth assumption that long-term success demands near-term organization and achievement sometimes overwhelms Millennials. What a high school junior does this week determines where she'll be five and ten years from now and that first full-time job can make or break a successful career. This, at least, is the new youth perception—and it's a reversal of a forty-year trend.

In the 1960s and '70s, Boomers felt decreasing pressure to achieve as they perceived their future growing more chaotic, less linked to credentials, and less subject to institutional rules. A common youth view was that you could do almost anything you wanted in high school or (especially) college and not expect that your life would be hugely affected by it. Twenty years later, young Gen Xers brought a new twist to this perception: Success seemed largely random in a fast-moving, risk-rewarding economy that offered a lot more opportunities than guarantees to young people. Long preparation often seemed like a waste of time; what mattered was street smarts, perfect timing, and a bit of luck.

For Millennials, the connection between today's behavior and tomorrow's payoff has been returning—driven both by pushy parents and by rising expectations for school achievement. Since the mid-1980s, "unstructured activity" has been the most rapidly declining use of time among American kids in primary grades. At the middle and high school level, record shares say they worry about their grades, want to go to college, and don't get enough sleep. Technology, with its incessant stream of emails, instant messages, and text messages, puts still more burdens on kids' time. To help themselves cope, students are multitasking like never before. An MTV survey of how much time teenagers spend on various activities added up to twenty-six hours each day—not including sleep. The growing flood of well credentialed high school seniors is increasing the competition for entrance into the best colleges and professional schools.

Raised in this pressured environment, it is no wonder that today's youth are fixated on long-term planning, which will (they hope) minimize the chance of missteps. The majority of today's high school students say they have detailed five- and ten-year plans for their future. Students often begin actively planning careers before the end of the ninth grade and seeking professional internships long before their junior year of college. Young employees are demanding tight cycles of feedback and redirection from managers so they can make minimize uncertainty and make sure that they are on track.

Millennials do well under pressure—but pressure (like sheltering) can sometimes be excessive, with negative health consequences. Time pressure prevents most Millennials from getting enough exercise, leading to the youth obesity epidemic, while some are pressured to overspecialize in a single sport, leading to the rise of repetitive stress injuries. Emotional distress that leads to life-threatening behaviors (suicide, violent crime, heavy substance abuse) is declining. But the frequency of eating disorders, sleep deprivation, "smart drug" use, and cutting is rising—as a rising share of youth try to cope with stress through obsessive rituals of self control.

To many Millennials, it's as though a giant generational train is leaving the station. Either they're on the platform, on time and with their ticket punched, or they'll miss the train and never be able to catch up.

Millennials and Achievement

Thirty years ago, many a Boomer had big plans. So does many a Millennial today—but that's where the similarity ends.

As Boomers moved through school—from the first "free speech" movement in 1964 to the widespread adoption of pass-fail systems in the late 1970s—students expressed a growing resistance to being graded, ranked, or categorized by the "system." Boomers preferred to be judged by who they were on the inside. As Millennials have moved through school, they have been pushing in the opposite direction. Today's young adults have spent far more time worrying about their grades, training for aptitude tests, and often even begging teachers to "evaluate" them before the score is due. Millennials prefer to be judged by what they do on the outside.

Today's youth strive to achieve according to the same adult-approved institutional exams and benchmarks that their parents rejected in their own youth. When Boomers were in school, most achievement test scores showed a decline at every age as each passing Boomer cohort reached that age—but for Millennials, most of the news on achievement tests has been positive. The average SAT score fell almost every year from the early 1960s to the late 1970s as Boomers passed through high school. Since the early 1990s, the SAT scores have risen steadily, thanks to late-wave Gen Xers and Millennials. In 2005, the average SAT score was higher than in any previous year since 1973. Average scores for nearly all of the graduate exams have been rising since the early 1990s, including the GRE (from 533 on the quantitative section in 1965 to 591 today) and the MCAT (from 23.4 in 1991 to 25.1 today). The LSAT and GMAT show a similar story.

Compared with earlier generations, Millennials have shown greater improvement in math than in verbal achievement. They have also shown greater improvement in younger than in older grades. According to the National Assessment of Educational Progress (NAEP), which tests students nationally at age 9, age 13, and age 17, math scores have improved from the 1970s and 1980s for all three ages. For age 9 and age 13, they are the highest they have ever been. Reading scores have risen for age 9 and held steady at older ages. The NAEP also shows a narrowing achievement gap between racial and ethnic groups—meaning that black and Latino kids have been improving their scores more than white kids.

In spite of Millennials' high achievement record, serious problems remain. High school dropout rates, while recently falling, remain distressingly high (especially for minorities). Even among students who graduate from high school with good grades, a large share remain academically underprepared. College professors—and employers—complain that young people come in lacking the basic skills they need to succeed. Yet most of the public alarm over these problems is driven by rising expectations about what the educational system should deliver to Millennials, not by objective evidence that it worked any better for earlier generations of youth.

Whatever the shortcomings of the education system, no one can blame them on Millennials, whose desire to achieve and succeed within the system exceeds that of any youth generation in living memory. This desire is reflected in the unprecedented and still-rising share of high school students who aspire to go to four-year colleges, who take Advanced Placement courses and exams, and who sign up for academic summer camps and non-remedial summer school. Cynicism about school is passé. According to the 2005–06 Horatio Alger survey, 79 percent of high school students feel motivated or inspired to work hard. According to the 2005 *High School Survey of Student Engagement*, two-thirds say they take pride in their school work and place a high value on learning.

Many Millennials (urban minority teens especially) feel that a major problem with the system is that it doesn't ask enough from them. Surveys show that students strongly support standardized testing and higher academic standards, and overwhelmingly agree that they would work harder if high school offered more demanding and interesting courses.

Whether in the classroom or the workplace, achievement-oriented Millennials hold both themselves and their institutions to very high standards. They are constantly striving to master their field, be at the forefront, and never accept second best—as is evident in their constant scrutiny of the quality of their teachers and professors (with Web sites like *ratemyprofessor.com*) and their oft-noted desire to work with professionals at the cutting edge of their field. Employers are noticing that today's young workers place rising value on professional development, demand measurable benchmarks for success, and want to work at the forefront of their profession.

PART TWO

MILLENNIALS **IN THE WORKPLACE**

06
Special

"They were raised by doting parents who told them they are special, played in little leagues with no winners or losers, or all winners. They are laden with trophies just for participating."

— **CBS 60 MINUTES REPORT**, "THE MILLENNIALS ARE COMING" (2007)

"Parents are a generational phenomenon, regularly advising their adult-age children about school, social life, and career. In extreme cases, helicopter parents will schedule job interviews and even talk to potential employers. It is a type of parental behavior that crosses socio-economic lines."

— **JUDY WOODRUFF**, *GENERATION NEXT* DOCUMENTARY (2007)

Special

Every manager has a favorite story illustrating just how special these Millennials feel. There's the young marketing assistant who is offended because her boss doesn't thank her after a routine project. Or the new law-firm associate who wants a partner to reassure his mom about his future. Or the auto tech apprentice who is crushed the first time she is criticized for an error. Or the interns who send a joint email to the CEO complaining that their supervisor is "too unfriendly."

As a generation, Millennials feel a specialness that began with devotion from parents and families and has since worked its way into schools, politics, the media, and most recently the workplace. Since birth, older generations have instilled in them the sense that they are central to their parents' sense of purpose and vital to the wellbeing of the nation. Through legislation like No Child Left Behind and principles like the Gates Foundation's commitment to make "every child" college ready, America has concentrated its attention on preparing a bright and secure future for each of them. Even college presidents are starting to hold open office hours for students, something unheard of before Millennials arrived. In the words of Bradley University President Joanne Glasser, "I want each and every student to say, 'I know my president. My president knows me.'"

Leading the cheers—even as Millennials enter the workplace—continue to be their own parents. Though many employers express surprise at today's rising parental involvement, they should have seen it coming. Highly involved parents have followed Millennials through every stage of life, attending "mommy and me" preschool classes, challenging poor grades, negotiating with coaches, and helping their children register for college classes. That attention isn't going away any time soon. A rising share of young adults are living with or near their parents—and talk to their parents daily.

Many busy managers, who suspect that "special" really means "spoiled," may wonder why they should give these entitled youngsters extra attention and good treatment. What they must understand is that, even if Millennials expect more from managers, managers can also expect more from them. Many Boomer or Gen-X supervisors are tempted to lecture Millennials about how they really aren't very special at all—a tactic that will surely fail. A much better approach is to leverage this generation's high self-regard by saying: *yes, you are special—and guess what, we expect special things from you.*

Sensible councilors, managers, and policymakers do not complain about the self-esteem of this rising generation. They use it as an energizing fuel. They invite Millennials to demonstrate their workplace potential, they offer parents a partnership role, and they understand how all Americans are rooting for their success.

Implications for Educators

The Millennials arrived in America's high schools and colleges accompanied by an entirely new approach to education: "student-centered learning." The idea is that the classroom should be restructured around the student's learning experience. In pursuit of that basic goal, educators have cut class sizes, fostered student collaboration, introduced contextual problem solving, and insisted on frequent and individualized feedback on student performance. Educators have tried to motivate this special generation by making the learning experience not just more rigorous, but also more efficient, enjoyable, personal, and tailored to student needs. Old-style vocational educators used to tell students what skills they needed and prescribe dreary drills to learn them. New-style career and technical educators now ask students what career clusters interest them and stage riveting simulations to bring them to life.

Career counselors need to keep these "student-centered" expectations in mind. When Millennials want help in planning their future, they expect career guidance to be as easy as a few clicks on their mouse and as comforting as a close friend—an approach that a National Association of Colleges and

Employers (NACE) survey calls a "blend of high tech and high touch." A one-on-one meeting can strike Millennials as too time consuming, and a simple email or Web page can strike them as too cold. What works best is both quick and personal, like a phone call or handwritten note to every student inviting them to use career counseling followed up with a variety of online discussion tools to sustain the connection. These include blogs, wikis, advice lines, live chats, or MySpace pages. Millennials also appreciate personnel who can guide them through the process and be on-call when they hit an obstacle or don't know the next step. AT&T's "personal coaches" program for at-risk college students has had an outstanding track record of success.

Since each Millennial is special in a special way, today's students expect the process of career guidance to be customized to their individual needs. One-size-fits-all career guidance is also no longer acceptable to today's parents (especially Gen-X parents), who want a career that will

Hire Your Own Career Counselor

As Millennials enter the workforce, a new trend is emerging: privately hired career counseling.

Career counselors for hire first appeared a decade ago at the high school level. As college admissions grow increasingly competitive, they are now becoming a popular tool for parents and students at the college and graduate levels. Associations of personal college admissions consultants report that their membership has tripled over the past ten years and now numbers about four thousand.

A myriad of businesses are also springing up to train Millennial college graduates in the rituals and formalities of the job search, from résumé writing and interview dress to the minutiae of handshakes and eye contact. Counseling firms like the New York-based Five O'Clock Club, which have traditionally focused on mid-career professionals, are developing "Career Starter" programs to cater to younger clients. These consultants often sell themselves by stressing the kind of customization, individual attention, and 360-degree guidance that today's youth have come to expect. The Boston-based firm Hayden-Wilder markets a four-phase program of individual career counseling, from a personal qualification assessment to assistance with salary negotiations.

be just the right "fit," a life path that will bring their Millennials both personal fulfillment and economic security. Now that the *Princeton Review* has added a new ranking for career services, colleges are trying harder than ever before.

Counselors are reporting a rising interest in personalized evaluations and psychological testing such as the Myers-Briggs Type Indicator, the Keirsey Temperament Sorter, the Kingdomality Personal Preference Profile, and the Strong Interest Inventory. To ensure that their children are getting individualized guidance of the highest quality, some parents look outside the school system and pay hundreds of dollars for sessions with independent counselors and psychologists. Large companies like Kaplan and dozens of small startup companies are beginning to move into this market as well. Some elite MBA programs offer weekly career strategy meetings for students during the school year and even "check-ins" during the summer.

Most high schools, trade schools, and colleges of course cannot afford to offer expensive counseling and individual coaching to every student. At many schools, career counselors are so underfunded and thinly staffed (with counselor-student ratios of 1:500 or even 1:1000) that they struggle to arrange one brief meeting with every student. Many colleges can barely cover broad-gauge "career counseling" for all of their graduates, much less hands-on "career placement." How can resource-strapped institutions meet the Millennial demand for special and personalized treatment?

The key is to leverage technology and third parties. By investing in Web-based tools offering blogs, live chats, and Q&A, counselors can scale up and converse "personally" with many students at once. By linking students to online self-evaluation exams and to the growing number of state and local sites offering career "pathways" advice, counselors can indirectly plug their students into 24/7 on-call expertise. They can also connect students with local employers, with recruiter chat rooms, with employer Web sites offering virtual tours or live chats with employees, and with professional alumni willing to offer advice and contacts. Many of these third parties will be highly motivated to help (or at least be seen as helping) a generation with a collectively "special" reputation.

When dealing with parents, educators must look constructively at the major role they play in Millennials' lives. Just as young people and their parents jointly participate in the purchase of the son's clothes and the daughter's car (or the mom's computer)—a phenomenon marketers call "co-purchasing"—so too are parents and students jointly making career decisions. In fact, a recent College Board study concludes that parents of Millennials in high schools are more highly involved in planning for their children's future, including college and career planning, than in any other area of their lives. Even when they leave home, most Millennials stay in nearly constant contact with parents—with an average of 9 phone, email, or IM conversations per week between college students and their parents (14 per week for freshmen), according to the *LifeCourse-Chartwells College Student Survey*. Overwhelmingly, today's parents agree that they are more involved in their children's career preparation than their own parents were with them.

Are parents *too* involved with their Millennial children? A rising number of educators certainly think so. Since 2000, according to an annual MetLife survey, K–12 teachers have identified parents as their number-one professional problem. College administrators have invented the term "helicopter moms" to describe these hovering parents. They tell horror stories about parents essentially "hijacking" the career-planning process, showing up at counseling sessions without their children or even writing the applications themselves. Most Millennials, however, seem comfortable with their parents' role. Data from the College Board show that a majority of college freshmen agree that their parents are "very involved" yet also that they are perfectly OK with that. Only 6 percent of freshmen want less involvement, while a much larger share, 28 percent, want *more*

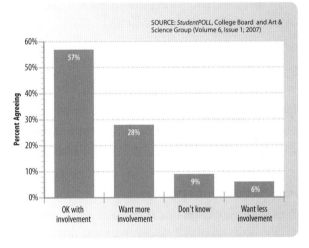

SOURCE: *StudentPOLL*, College Board and Art & Science Group (Volume 6, Issue 1; 2007)

◄ **Figure 22**

Student Satisfaction or Dissatisfaction with Parents' Level of Involvement in College Search

involvement. First-generation and minority students, whose own parents may lack the time or confidence to intervene, are especially likely to want more parental involvement.

Educators need to accommodate the new parental role by including parents in career planning as much as possible. Unless the student objects (and few will), send career information to parents along with the students, invite parents to attend students' career counseling sessions, and encourage joint research and discussion of educational and career options. Many colleges are already inviting parents to participate with targeted parent orientations and newsletters. Parents whose children are the first in the family to attend college often need extra encouragement to get more involved, perhaps through special early meetings that allow them to ask questions more freely and establish longer-term relationships with counselors.

To be sure, educators need to draw clear boundaries so that parents do not interfere with their school's core mission—which includes helping students to become independent adults and to follow their own (perhaps confidential) career aspirations. This is especially important when a student appears to be unduly swayed or intimidated by their parents' opinions. But the best way to draw boundaries is not to *block* parental participation—which will usually trigger hostility and suspicion—but rather to *channel* that participation in a helpful direction.

In effect, the best permanent solution to the interfering parent problem is to establish a formal division of labor between the school and the parents, in which the school welcomes parental participation in certain areas of career planning, but not in others. Many colleges now set these ground rules by having parents sign "contracts" or "covenants" during freshman orientation, which specify how parent are, and are not, expected to help to help their children succeed. By instructing parents in this model, counselors will also be helping them relate constructively to their adult children as they move forward in life.

Implications for Employers

Personalized, one-on-one recruiting techniques work as well for Millennials in their mid-twenties as they do for Millennials in their late teens. Popular colleges woo potential freshmen by sending articulate recruiters to high schools and by having alumni, faculty, and current students make phone calls or send friendly notes to applicants. Popular employers do the same. Enterprise Rent-A-Car sponsors job skill projects and presentations among high school students, getting to know individual students as they complete their work. Boeing connects promising candidates to employees who are alumni of the same college. Some senior executives of major companies, including JPMorgan Chase CEO Jamie Dimon, make college students feel special indeed by meeting with them personally on several campuses each year.

Successful employers also give students the chance to speak one on one with recruiters and recently hired employees in person (one reason career fairs remain popular) as well as through email, Web chats, or over the phone. These employers understand that, with job decisions as with purchasing decisions, Millennials tend to ignore the glossy ads and seek out the "customer reviews": the inside scoop from someone who's already experienced the product. PricewaterhouseCoopers (PwC) has former interns act as "student ambassadors" at their colleges, attending PwC campus recruiting events and career fairs and talking to students about their experience at the company.

Finally, when it's time to close the sale, popular employers know how to be nice—like the research systems company FactSet, which sends new hires gift baskets and personalized notes before they start work. They appeal to the Millennials' strong collective self-image by avoiding condescension and by welcoming them as if veterans should feel privileged to join with talented youth, not just the other way around. These employers vet their recruiting language and imagery to celebrate the arrival of today's rising generation, something no one would have bothered with for young Gen Xers.

A smart digital presence is of course essential to reach time-starved, menu-driven young recruits. But high-tech outreach should be used to enhance high-touch connections, never to replace them. Personalized emails, live online chats with recruiters, and day-in-the-life blogs by young employees are just a few ways that companies can attract prospective hires. Microsoft fields sites like "View My World" and "Hey Genius," where job seekers can read insider accounts to find out what it's really like to work for the company.

Prepare as well for new hires who seek a closer, more personal relationship with their employer. Kids who grew up with "attachment parenting" often look for "attachment managing." More than Gen Xers, Millennials want managers who act as trustworthy mentors with whom they can consult about personal challenges and career or life plans. According to a Hudson Highland Group survey, a steeply rising share of young workers say that it is important to work in the same office as their bosses, and that they want to socialize with their boss at least monthly. After a lifetime of relating confidently and informally with their own parents, they are puzzled and annoyed by the suggestion that they should always stay respectfully silent around senior personnel. Above all, Millennials want employers to see them as individuals with something special to contribute. In a globalizing labor market, they are well aware that a person possessing unique intangibles is much harder to downsize or outsource than a worker with replaceable skills.

Mentoring programs for Millennials work best when they are formalized, with standardized training for the mentors, so that young employees know the relationship will not be left to chance. Older generations tend to distrust mandated relationships, but Millennials actually prefer them. Many Xer managers may consider mentoring an unnecessary burden on their time—after all, they got along fine on their own when they entered the workplace. These managers need to understand that Millennial workers are very different than they were in their youth, and that investing individually in them generates bottom-line productivity results.

Mentoring programs also work best when mentors play the role of coach rather than taskmaster. The U.S. Army recently improved its basic training success rate by getting drill sergeants to make a better personal connection with recruits. Instead of barking orders and instilling fear, drill sergeants now do virtually everything they ask their soldiers to do, from navigating obstacle courses to marching with heavy backpacks. Recruits report that they were motivated to overcome difficulties by their drill-sergeant mentors, who showed that they cared about them and believed in them.

Mentoring can also help companies fill the skills gap left behind by waves of departing retirees. Many Boomers nearing retirement age are not very interested in passing on their skills and knowledge except in a one-on-one, personalized setting. Employers ranging from PricewaterhouseCoopers to KPMG to Abbott Laboratories have already reported very favorable results using mentoring as part of an overall succession strategy—and also using job shadowing, in which an older and younger employee partner through every aspect of the job.

Parents, the Millennials' number-one mentors, are an entirely new challenge for most employers. Educators have already experienced—and have started adapting to—the new parental presence. Now it's the employers' turn. According to a 2007 Michigan State University survey, nearly a quarter of all employers have "sometimes" to "very often" seen parents involved in the recruitment and employment of recent college graduates. This involvement ranges from casual helping out (parents gathering employment information on behalf of their children, reported by 40 percent of employers) to intrusive coaching (parents showing up at the job interview, reported by 4 percent of employers). Mothers are more likely to collect information on the companies and arrange for visits and interviews, while fathers are more likely to intervene when a son

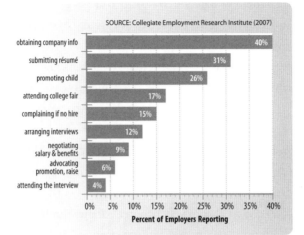

SOURCE: Collegiate Employment Research Institute (2007)

Type of Parental Involvement, as Reported by Employers in 2007

or daughter is not hired or is disciplined by an employer.

Many employers express annoyance at this new parental presence and respond by doing everything they can to avoid encountering these parents. That's a mistake. Employers who avoid hiring recruits whose parents seem "pushy," for example, are ruling out some of the best prospects. According to data from the *National Survey of Student Engagement*, college students whose parents frequently contact them and intervene on their behalf report higher levels of engagement and more frequent use of "deep" learning activities, such as intensive writing and independent research, than students with less-involved parents. As survey director George D. Kuh puts it, helicopter-parented students "trumped their peers on every measure we use." Employers who hire such young people but then try to push their parents away don't fare much better. They aren't making their problem go away (such parents will typically get more frustrated and continue to interfere) and meanwhile they undermine the morale of these new employees and worsen the odds of retaining them.

Employers can learn from institutions that have already figured out how to work with the parents of Millennials. In the mid-1990s, K–12 schools found themselves bombarded by hyper-involved parents. After years of inaction, schools eventually responded by establishing closer ties with parents and by building online systems that let parents monitor their children's performance in real time. Educators now report that the best way to handle parents is to keep them in the loop. By 2000, colleges noticed a sudden tide of interfering parents who, again, refused to be deterred by official notices telling them to get lost. Ultimately, most colleges decided to meet their demands by developing special orientations, newsletters, Web cams, and "liaisons" just for parents. The same story unfolded for the U.S. armed forces. They too initially responded to helicopter parents by ignoring them. After missing quotas, the armed forces totally recast their approach. Today, they co-market extensively to parents and have instituted protocols requiring recruiting officers to meet early and often with parents. Thanks in part to these measures, recruitment rates have dramatically risen.

Handled properly, helicopter parents can in fact be an enormous asset to employers' goals of recruitment, productivity, and retention. But like schools, colleges, and the military, employers will have to change tactics: Accept that parents will remain actively involved in Millennials' lives and offer them avenues for *constructive* involvement. Instead of considering them as awkward liabilities, employers should consider involved parents (who often give their kids sound advice about perseverance and long-term goal setting) as potentially valuable assets.

So how can employers enlist parents as workplace allies? They can start by co-marketing employment opportunities to parents. NACE reports that 73 percent of college seniors review a job offer with parents before accepting or rejecting it. Even among 21- to 28-year olds who already have a college degree and are working full time, one in four (according to Robert Half International) still consult parents before any employment decision. As long as Millennials are sharing their decision with parents, employers may as well start the conversation themselves—and on their own terms. Develop slogans and pamphlets telling parents that you'll take extra good care of their very special children, and tailor portions of your Web site for parents of applicants. Develop orientation materials specifically for the parents.

Which Employers Attract the Most Helicopter Parents?

A 2007 Michigan State University survey found that certain types of employers notice higher levels of parental involvement with their young employees:

- Large employers with regional and national brand recognition. Parents may feel that their children could get lost at a large, brand name company, while a small, intimate workplace is more likely to provide the personal mentoring they want for their children. Smaller companies are also more likely to be local, so the parents of employees may know them personally and not need to seek out information and get involved.

- Employers with strong internship programs and those who recruit heavily on campuses. Large companies with national brand recognition often have internship programs, so these categories likely overlap. Because parents know that many companies use their internship programs to develop long-term relationships with prospective employees, they want to know how that relationship will affect their children's future.

- Employers in the Northeast and Northwest. Companies in the Northeast and Northwest may attract more job candidates from affluent backgrounds, whose parents may have invested large sums of money in their children's education and feel entitled to make sure their investment pays off. Also, because urban areas are ahead of rural areas in many Millennial trends, the more urbanized Northeast and Northwest may be leading the helicopter-parent trend.

- Employers filling positions in marketing, human resources, and sales. Parents whose children work in these positions intervene more because these careers have a relatively high outcome uncertainty. By contrast, positions in fields like accounting and engineering have more direct and specific educational requirements and a narrower range of salaries. Marketing and sales careers also tend to attract alpha-personality careerists, who are often pushed into those fields by alpha-personality moms and dads—exactly the kinds of moms and dads who are likely to intervene with employers.

Once Millennials are on board, keep parents up to date. Employers can send them a regular e-letter or prepare a parent section of the company Web site with general information on what the company is doing and any structural or policy changes that may affect employees. The message should be that the employer cares personally about the experience of each employee's family. Though some employers may fear that keeping parents in the loop only encourages more time-wasting interference, experience shows the opposite—that better-informed and less-anxious parents are actually less likely to bother managers with emails or phone calls.

How Some Employers are Responding to Parents

Offerings	Companies
Package employer info for parents	Ernst & Young, U.S. Army, EchoStar, Enterprise Rent-A-Car
Offer a Web site for parents	Office Depot, Enterprise Rent-A-Car, Southwestern
Send job offer letter to parents	Enterprise Rent-A-Car, Stockamp, Ferguson, Vanguard
Invite parents for office visits	Merrill Lynch
Stage event for parents of interns	PNC Financial Services

Upon occasion, engage personally with parents. From kindergarten through college, parents of Millennials are accustomed to visiting and examining their offspring's daily environment. This parental habit will not end when the sons and daughters graduate. Employers can give their companies a personal, family-friendly touch by inviting parents to visit their children's workplace and engage with managers. They can give parents of new hires a tour of the company, hold a yearly event when young employees bring their parents to work, or have a dinner where employees can invite parents and other family members.

Be creative about tapping parental energy, especially on behalf of company efforts to help the community, influence public opinion, or provide special services to employees. Many K–12 school districts have zealous parents of young teachers donate their time to extracurricular activities. Similarly, some businesses invite parents to help organize their community service activities, chat up their company mission on Web sites, or offer comfort or informal assistance to employees in stressful situations or remote locations. Many retired parents have ample time for these kinds of activities and some will have expertise that companies can use to their advantage.

Finally, keep in mind that a large number of young employees will soon need to care for their parents as they age. A growing share of young-adult Millennials are living with or near their parents. Meanwhile, a growing share of newly retiring Boomers lack any kind of nest egg or safety net. As they try to plan their lives, Millennials are certain to seek help in preparing for this burden. Employers should start thinking now of innovative ways to support these employees, including flex time for elder care and financial counseling on acute care insurance, reverse mortgages, and long-term care.

Implications for the Public Sector

In many ways, public-sector employment seems like the perfect fit for Millennials, from the structured environment to the community focus to the career tenure. If the rising generation wants a special career path, this one has their name written on it. That's the view from a distance, at least. Once Millennials actually start applying for jobs, they quickly notice drawbacks. Four in ten college students say working in "public service" appeals to them—but only two in ten say the same about working in "government or politics."

The sheer process of being hired by a government agency carries an unequivocal message to any job seeker: You are *not* special. With its standardized forms and months of waiting to be contacted, the hiring system makes bright-eyed young applicants feel like insignificant cogs in a bureaucratic machine. A recent Partnership for Public Service survey found that perceptions of red tape and "too much bureaucracy" are one of students' top reasons for not pursuing a government career.

To counteract this image, public-sector employers should stress personalized, one-on-one recruiting. Seven out of ten college juniors and seniors said they were more likely to consider a career in the federal government after talking individually with a recruiter. Agencies such as the U.S. Department of State have recently begun to use high-tech methods to spread a high-touch message. The State Department's retooled recruitment site personally welcomes visitors with a pop-up video of the Secretary of State, offers videos of staff members recounting their experiences, and provides tailored job searches based on visitors' interests and qualifications.

The glacial pace of hiring at most government agencies also sends an antispecial message. Over half of graduating seniors report that finding a job with the government is "confusing" or "slow." Managers should look for system loopholes that may allow faster hiring. For example, the Office of Personnel Management (OPM) recently expanded the scope of the Direct-Hire Authority program, which allows civilian agencies with candidate shortages to hire directly, rather than going through the full federal application process. High-security jobs with a drawn-out security clearance process face the greatest hurdles in fast-tracking hires.

Agencies that cannot expedite hiring should call in-process applicants regularly to update them and see if they have any questions. Once a new employee is finally brought on board, emphasize that they are not just another badge and number. The Office of the Comptroller of the Currency sends a gift basket to welcome new bank examiners. That's a good start. In time, perhaps, public agencies will adopt a more substantive and intensive "onboarding" protocol—including agency tours, personal interviews, and team-building orientations.

Like their private-sector competitors, government employers should prepare for young workers who want managers to be trustworthy mentors. The public workplace is having trouble here. Thirty-three percent of all federal workers think their immediate supervisors are not doing a good job, 8 percent more than private-sector workers. Managers who are skeptical about giving young workers more attention should consider the potential payoff in higher morale, elevated productivity, and lower turnover. All of the U.S. armed services (most recently the National Guard) are implementing formal mentorship programs.

Boomer and Gen-X parents often have a more negative image of government than their Millennial children, which makes co-marketing to parents especially important. The U.S. Army is leading the way with ads that show recruits discussing with parents the decision to join and with its new parent-targeted slogan, "You made them strong, we'll make them army strong." But most public employers have yet to harness parental involvement for their benefit. They should take their cue from the growing number of parent-friendly private-sector employers.

Millennials' sense of specialness will also have important implications for public policy.

Over the past four decades, legislators have paid special attention to issues that affect older workers, from eligibility for Medicare and disability benefits to the solvency of pension plans. Over the next decade, policy interest will shift to the issues that affect younger workers, such as high youth unemployment, mounting student debt burdens, and rising government entitlement outlays due to demographic aging. Accustomed to the nation's lifelong fixation on Millennials, most older Americans will go along with new policies that tilt more to interests of the Millennials and less to their own. Indeed, the majority of voters in some states are already demanding changes in laws that prevent any reductions in public-employee retirement formulas—while school budgets are frozen, state college funding is slashed, and the salaries of new public employees are cut. In the years to come, electoral reversals of this kind will become common place.

Policy makers should also expect growing media attention to any news, surveys, or reports on the economic condition of young adults. During the Millennials childhood and teen years, the public took steadily greater interest in indicators of how well kids were doing, from the *Nation's Report Card* to the *Index of Child & Youth Well-being*. As Millennials push further into young adulthood, expect similar indicators on how young adults are doing. Imagine a "national report card" on the state of young workers driving a policy discussion on the challenges facing this special generation. Ten years ago, most Americans wouldn't have paid much attention to such a report. Over the next decade, they will.

07
Sheltered

"The young workers are totally in agreement about greater security. We just added security guards to the building and the Boomers are all complaining, but the young workers all say they like it."

— **JANE WULF**, CHIEF ADMINISTRATIVE OFFICER, SCOTTRADE (2008)

"They're inheriting an economy in which many of the things their parents took for granted are evaporating: company-provided health insurance, attainable housing, Social Security, affordable education, well-paying jobs… No wonder this generation is so obsessed with structure, savings, and security."

— *BUSINESSWEEK* (2008)

Sheltered

A chain of convenience stores recently instituted a new safety policy: Managers issue young employees different colored smocks, based on age, to let supervisors know at a glance who is not allowed to operate the electric meat slicer. One fast-food chain has developed a computerized tracking system to make sure that teens aren't scheduled for too many hours during school weeks. A California zoo assigns each new intern a "buddy" or mentor who gives them hands-on training and safety tips.

Such creative workplace safety practices are on the rise—which is perhaps no surprise, now that a watched-over youth generation is entering the workforce. Over the last twenty-five years, Millennials have grown up as the focus of one of the most intense child-protection movements in American history, a crusade that has given us drug-free zones and child-proof homes, school uniforms and bicycle helmets, V-chips and urban curfews, AMBER alerts, and a revival of the *in loco parentis* school and college.

Today's 20-year olds have grown up seeing perimeters rise around every aspects of their lives. They cannot recall a time when there weren't video cameras in the nursery, metal detectors in the high school, or "smart keys" in the college dorm. Millennials have come to expect protections that prior generations at the same age would have assailed as unnecessary and intrusive. Most Gen-X youths would have distrusted these measures, suspected the motives of the authorities implementing them, and perhaps would have been disappointed that young people weren't seen as resilient enough to take care of themselves. Millennial youths react differently. Most accept the protections showered on them with polite acquiescence and sometimes even gratitude.

To them, it's logical: Older people think we're special and therefore want to protect us. We're OK with that.

This new consensus about youth safety will transform tomorrow's workplaces. Educators will be called upon to train young people to avoid a wide range of bad career and workplace outcomes. Employee safety measures will be more strictly enforced, and any mishaps that do occur will be far more likely to attract lawsuits, media attention, and public outrage. Meanwhile Millennials—and their parents—will expect employers to protect young workers not just against physical injury but against threats to everything from their emotional health to their financial security. Can you imagine the company of tomorrow offering a complete menu of career planning and life guidance services? If you're over 40, you probably can't. But if you're under 30, you probably can.

States are enacting ever-stricter social host liability laws (which hold parents responsible for any crimes committed by minors on their premises, regardless of the parents' knowledge). States may soon decide that any mishap to young workers will similarly be deemed the responsibility of whoever is in charge, regardless of fault. Managers prepare: The era of the *in loco parentis* employer is on its way.

Implications for Educators

With Millennials filling high schools, the media are paying more attention to safety in summer and after-school jobs. Recent surveys, including the National Consumer League's *Five Worst Jobs for Teens*, have spotlighted improper training, hazardous conditions, and the abuse or molestation of teen employees. Fear of workplace danger is contributing to the steep recent decline in paid employment for teens, especially in service industries with a reputation for small establishment size and minimal supervision. Companies in these industries—like food processing, restaurants, hospitality, personal services, and auto and appliance repair—must go out of their way to explain how they differ from these negative expectations.

High schools can help both Millennials and the surrounding business community by offering to compile a list of local establishments that have excellent safety records. Most parents and students would be eager to consult a list of safe employers with a strong record of collaboration with local schools. High schools should also offer workshops or require modules on how to deal with potential hazards in summer and after-school jobs such as sexual harassment, lifting injuries, and fatal accidents due to falling asleep while driving or operating machinery. Encourage parents by explaining that, so long as it is safe, paid work experience enables their children to acquire important workplace skills that (complain many employers) this sheltered generation often lacks.

Within their own vocational programs, instructors should emphasize to parents that their children are supervised every minute when working with chain saws, shielded from contagion during hospital internships, and protected from dangerous fumes when working in an automotive shop. Market these programs as a place where students can develop hands-on career skills in a supervised, zero-risk environment.

Across all school programs, educators need to persuade both students and parents that their curriculum is tested, their faculty is experienced, and their learning environment is tight, structured, integrated, and personal. Ideally, it should be organized around small groups and teams in which no student can possibly fall through the cracks.

No educator should be surprised by the new emphasis on smallness: The appeal of intimate teamwork has been following Millennials throughout their schooling. When they entered elementary school, small classrooms were the rage. When they moved into middle school, educators introduced block scheduling, looped teaching assignments, and team teaching. When Millennials moved into high school, principals welcomed them with freshman "houses" and "academies." Most recently, as Millennials have moved into college, freshman academies are multiplying there as well—along with "living-learning communities" where teams of students actually live with their classmates and with certain faculty.

What do all these innovations have in common? They provide learning environments in which all students feel they belong and no student can easily become lost, disoriented, or disengaged. For secondary and postsecondary students—and especially for young men in career and technical education programs—"small-school" environments, "career academies," and workshop-sized instruction units now demonstrate a large and growing advantage in retention, conduct, achievement, and salary outcomes.

As today's risk-averse students plan for their futures, both high schools and colleges should offer them (and their protective parents) information on the safety of potential long-term careers. Schools could easily put together helpful guides with written job descriptions and links to national safety data sites (such as "Matching Yourself with the World of Work," a U.S. Department of Labor publication that includes detailed occupational safety ratings).

Beyond the risk of physical injury, educators will be expected to help Millennials avoid the more general risk of a bad life outcome, such as ending up in a dead-end career or with ruinous personal debt. This kind of "sheltering" was hardly known when Milllennials' parents were students. Young Boomers were famous for throwing themselves into ambitious pursuits like becoming a world-class musician or NBA star without worrying about the odds—confident that, if things didn't work out, they could step effortlessly back into the American Dream. Young Gen Xers were less optimistic about their career options but embraced job-market risks with entrepreneurial savvy. To Gen Xers, "going bust" just made you tougher and better prepared for life's next challenge. Millennials, by contrast, are accustomed to a strong safety net and find no romance in failure. They assume there must always be a best-practice method for making safe life choices, from no-risk online dating to no-risk apartment hunting.

As Millennials reach the end of their formal education and confront the vagaries of a globalized job market, most would welcome a formal curriculum (perhaps a course or half-semester module) offering a systematic understanding of career risks. It would explain the basic dynamics of the labor market, how fields expand and contract, how earnings and benefits are determined, how recessions start and stop, and which jobs are most secure and why. By helping Millennials learn how to assess career risks, educators can teach them how to take on just the level of risk they are willing to accept.

Handling finances involves another set of risk management skills of intense interest to Millennials and their parents. Few young adults know how to weigh the time value of money. A record share are entering their first full-time jobs heavily burdened by educational and credit card debt. Most face a wide variety of salary, health-benefit, and pension options; many have relatives and friends who have lost their jobs or most of their assets during the current economic weakness; and some are looking forward to buying houses and starting families.

Despite the obvious need, grade schools do little to impart financial literacy and, in college, the typical financial aid office is much better designed to help students get further into debt than to educate them about how to get out of it. According to a recent Harris Interactive study, more than half of young workers born after 1979 admit they have little knowledge of financial planning. As of 2007, only 17 states required students to take a personal finance course before graduating from high school. Postsecondary schools should make elementary financial literacy mandatory—and they should do so before Congress orders them to do so. (Congress has already issued this order for students receiving certain types of federally funded support services.) Parents, especially the new crop of Gen-X parents, will love a financial literacy requirement even when the students themselves don't. No institution need be deterred by cost, thanks to the plethora of quality online training aids and innovative multimedia courses offered by nonprofit groups like Decision Partners.

As the glare of the media focuses increasingly on young people's debts and job woes, educators will face rising pressure to teach students how to protect themselves. Even if courses in job markets or financial literacy were not required, most students (judging from the rising share who take economics when offered) would probably take it. The curriculum could be billed as an overall "Life Skills 101: How to Climb the Ladders and Avoid the Chutes."

Implications for Employers

With Millennials coming on board, safety has now become an essential dimension of any employer brand. Companies should learn from colleges, which have discovered that a great safety record generates an aura of public goodwill while any serious lapse triggers negative publicity, expensive lawsuits, and political outrage. Colleges have also learned that a credible reputation for safety requires accountability and transparency. Increasingly, colleges are letting applicants (and their parents) know which individuals are in charge of preventing accidents and injury—and responding to public demands that safety data be made easily available. Parents and students can now easily track campus crime, thanks to the federal Campus Security Statistics Web site, and campus fires, thanks to the 2008 Campus Fire Safety Right-To-Know Act.

Smart employers should follow suit. They too should let job applicants and the public at large know that they have high-level managers whose sole mission is safety. They too should offer easy access to safety records—before the federal government requires it, which (again) is likely to be soon. Many companies are already demonstrating their commitment to safety by teaching it through workshops and role-playing. One retail clothing chain with a high concentration of young employees has monthly "safety meetings" where workers act out the best way to handle health or safety problems. Instead of simply handing out safety manuals, UPS has begun implementing hands-on safety seminars in which employees practice responding to scenarios in staged neighborhoods.

When the work involves repetitive tasks, employers may want to introduce detailed protocol training as a method of reducing injury. Federal Express employees now undergo a comprehensive training regimen in which each motion in the delivery process, from getting out of the vehicle to placing a package on a doorstep, is meticulously planned and memorized. With Millennials on board, this kind of detailed training—in which every situation is planned, every risk is foreseen, and protocol responses are ingrained in each employee—will gain new popularity.

Employers in high-risk occupations can set themselves apart by guaranteeing zero risk in every aspect of the job under their control. The military services and many emergency agencies, for example, have recently gone to extraordinary lengths to prevent injury or death during training. With a little creativity, these employers may find innovative ways to give their entire profession a pro-safety spin. The U.S. Marine Corps, for example, may be able to claim that that longevity benefits due to a structured lifestyle and physical fitness far outweigh the risk of death on the battlefield—making this a "low-risk" career when viewed from a lifetime perspective. To most young Gen Xers, such an

Millennial Magnets

Each year, *Fortune* magazine and the Great Place to Work Institute conduct a nationwide employer survey to find the *100 Best Companies to Work For*. In 2008, *Human Resource Executive* magazine asked the Institute to sort the rankings by age of the respondents, and created a *Millennial Magnets* list of the companies ranked best in America by employees under age 25. Millennial Magnet companies range from state banks to multinational corporations, from energy and gas companies to hotel chains. What do they have in common?

- **Personal-Touch Recruiting.** Many of the companies take an extremely active and personal role in the recruitment of young employees. FactSet, a software company based in Connecticut, sends new hires who are college seniors a gift basket and "good-luck" note before they take their finals.

- **Work-Life Balance.** These companies offer employees flexible schedules that allow them to have a balanced life. Marriott Hotels has instituted a "Teamwork-Innovations" program in which employees can increase efficiency by working together and scheduling their own hours.

- **Group Socializing.** Millennial Magnets understand that this generation enjoys working and socializing in groups. Kimley-Horn and Associates, an engineering firm in North Carolina, holds regular lunchtime forums in which employees get together to network, share advice, and plan social get-togethers.

- **Recognition.** The chosen companies know how to motivate Millennials through positive feedback. Scottrade, a Millennial Magnet firm based in St. Louis, has implemented an "Above-and-Beyond" program in which any employee can nominate another for recognition.

Several of the Magnets make employees eligible for rewards such as jewelry and iPods.

- **Casual but Professional Environment.** Many Millennial Magnet companies are crafting a "Google-style" corporate environment that is friendly, comfortable, and cutting edge. Umpqua Bank in Oregon has outfitted its branches with cafes and couches, and often provides recreational activities in the office for its employees. In a livable workplace, long hours—when necessary—will hardly be noticed.

argument would have seemed bizarre. To Millennials, with their longer time horizons and penchant for quantitative planning, it may make sense.

Employers should expect rising attention to sexual harassment of Millennials, especially teen Millennials. Having learned all about proper and improper behavior and speech from K–12 teachers and counselors who now follow strict "touching" guidelines, even the shiest Millennials are more likely to know their rights and less hesitant to speak out when those rights are violated. The number of EEOC sexual harassment complaints involving teens has risen sharply as a share of total complaints over the past decade. Companies should remind all employees of the gravity of the offense and show young workers and their parents that they take harassment seriously—following up on any complaints and providing prevention training when necessary.

Beyond avoiding physical injury and harassment, Millennials and their parents are increasingly looking for a much broader array of protective safeguards, including health insurance, wellness policies, disability accommodation, emotional counseling, "life-resource" assistance, and a wholesome business culture with special emphasis on small work groups.

Millennial attitudes toward health insurance represent a clear break with Gen-X trends. From the early 1980s until quite recently, the share of young employees covered by insurance has steadily fallen—a trend driven in part by the rising cost of coverage to employers, but also by the willingness of young Gen Xers to take the chance, "go bare," and cash out the benefit. Young Millennial workers are already beginning to reverse this decline, pushing up the employer-based coverage rate among workers age 19 to 24 since 2004. Young Millennial voters are broadly supportive of health-care reform (like the legislation enacted in 2010) pushing in the direction of universal coverage. Attitude surveys confirm this shift. On a recent NACE survey, students ranked medical insurance as the number one job benefit. According to a MonsterTRAK and Michigan State University survey, 84 percent of today's young job seekers rate "good benefits, e.g., health insurance" as among the most important characteristics in choosing a job.

For most Millennials, an ideal employee-protection plan should include more than just acute-care insurance. It should include a wellness policy that may, for example, feature guidelines and incentives for proper diet and sufficient exercise. More endangered than any other generation by obesity, Millennials will welcome institutional nudges to slim down. Better accommodations must also be made for disabilities. When they were in grade school and college, most Millennials diagnosed with physical and learning disabilities expected educators to give them the tools and training to join the mainstream classroom. That won't change once they become employees. They will expect to be invited to join the mainstream workplace.

An ideal protection plan should include emotional counseling. By objective standards, today's young people show fewer signs of serious emotional distress

What Young People Want in a Job, Then and Now

How Graduating College Seniors Ranked Job Attributes, by Importance

	Ranking...		
	in 1982	in 2008	Change
job security	5	1	⬆
quality of insurance/benefits package	7	2	⬆
friendly coworkers	4	3	⬌
job location	8	4	⬆
opportunity for personal development	1	5	⬇
high starting salary	7	6	⬌
recognition	2	7	⬇
opportunity for creativity	3	8	⬇

SOURCE: National Association of Colleges and Employers (2008)

than prior generations: For the first time in decades, the rate of youth suicide and self-reported depression is trending down. Nevertheless, Millennials are proving to be enthusiastic users of counseling. Unlike Gen Xers, who wanted to be seen as self-sufficient and who often regarded a visit to a counselor as a form of punishment, Millennials welcome the special attention and the opportunity to get expert feedback on how they are performing. Already, Millennial undergrads have been making major new demands on college counseling services. Those demands will carry over onto their first employers.

Accustomed to trusting the advice of experts-in-charge, many Millennials will be attracted to a comprehensive envelope of support, protection, and guidance on life basics, from relocating to a new city to filling out tax forms to finding the best health-care provider. Large employers, who often already offer some of these benefits, may even want to designate a "life resources" manager to give young workers guidance on these issues and direct them to the best external assistance. With only a modest investment, most employers can set up an impressive umbrella of employee protection. They can create a digital bulletin board where young recruits can exchange advice and information. They can expand their relocation assistance to include all new hires, offer transition housing, and provide information on regional transportation and activities. Young Gen Xers, who took pride in figuring things out themselves, would never have wanted this degree of institutional support and guidance. Yet many Millennials will expect and value it.

One form of life-resource assistance that Millennials will find especially attractive is a guarantee against sudden job loss—and, if job loss itself cannot be avoided, assistance in transitioning to a new employer. Employers largely underestimate the importance of job security in attracting young workers. According to a recent MonsterTRAK and Michigan State University survey, 82 percent of young adults ranked "job security" as one of the most important characteristics they look for in a job—far above a "high salary." When corporate recruiters were given the same survey, they mistakenly supposed that young adults would rate job security and benefits far lower, while overestimating characteristics like pay and prestige.

Above all, Millennials feel protected in a workplace that embodies a wholesome business culture. This is a workplace in which managers are mentors who take an interest in the lives of younger workers and whose lifestyles exemplify (outwardly, at least) stability and good judgment. The connection between business culture and personal risk will be instantly recognizable to parents— and has been repeatedly confirmed by research. A recent study published in *Occupational and Environmental Medicine*, for example, shows that the attitudes of managers and supervisors toward drinking have a major impact on employees' drinking habits outside of work. Companies should emphasize to parents and the media that they promote an overall culture of safe life practices and prudent life choices.

One important indicator of a wholesome and protective workplace culture is a small-team work environment where leadership is personal and everyone is looked after. Companies of all sizes can find ways to benefit from the Millennial need for group connections. Small and midsize firms should emphasize that their employees can enjoy a more personal work experience as members of a more intimate group. In a recent survey of young college graduates, 70 percent said that (all other things being equal) they would prefer working for a medium or small employer, while only 30 percent said they would prefer to work for a large international company. With a record share of Millennials saying they'd like to work for a family business, many smaller companies should be able to use the imagery of "family" to their advantage.

Large companies, on the other hand, must take care to complement the advantages of size that Millennials will certainly find appealing—such as the security of a big brand and abundant opportunities for advancement—with assurances that each recruit will still be able to join a close-knit team. Maureen Crawford Hentz, a recruiter for Osram Sylvana, explains, "It's a whole new ball game in terms of landing our top candidates. We spend a lot of time emphasizing our smaller working groups" as well as "individual professional development and the ability to move up within the company." As schools have done with the highly successful "small learning community" model, large companies should stress how their workforce is organized into small work units, each with its own personality and traditions.

Much like K–12 schools and colleges before them, employers will be expected to take official, institutional responsibility for protecting young employees across all aspects of their lives. This doctrine of *in loco parentis*, thrown over by rebellious Boomers forty years ago, virtually disappeared for young Gen Xers—but it has reemerged in full force for their Millennial children.

Implications for the Public Sector

The good news is that government agencies are ahead of the curve when it comes to job safety. In 2004, the federal government ramped up efforts to reduce injuries and illnesses in public workplaces by launching the successful Safety, Health and Return-to-Employment (SHARE) Initiative, which reduced workplace injuries by 17 percent overall. Public employees themselves agree that they have good job safety. According to a 2008 OPM survey, federal employees agree by 76 percent to 10 percent that employees are protected from health and safety hazards on the job, and by 74 percent to 9 percent that they have been prepared for potential security threats.

The bad news is that government employers have failed to communicate their good safety records either to the general public or to potential new employees. This is a major oversight with a safety-conscious Millennial workforce. Given the media attention to high-risk public occupations such as law enforcement, firefighting, and the armed services, Millennials may assume that government jobs are a lot more dangerous than they are. Public employers should showcase zero-risk policies and publicize statistics on their safety records to demonstrate that even these high-risk occupations are a relatively safe life choice.

As health insurance rises in importance for young job seekers, agencies with top-notch health plans should showcase them in recruitment materials. Young workers will expect public employers to take on the same guiding *in loco parentis* role as private companies. According to North Carolina's 2008 *Young Employees Project Report*, young state employees want onboarding to include not only an explanation of what benefits are available, but also hands-on guidance on how to use them. Millennial state employees also report that they value wellness incentives and peer resource groups.

Recruiters worried about competing with high private-sector salaries should rejoice at the new evidence that Millennials rate job security far more highly than starting salary. Two of the top five reasons offered by college students for wanting to work for the federal government are "job security" and "good benefits." According to North Carolina's study, these were also the top two reason young employees accepted a job with state government. Government recruiters should regard protection from sudden job loss as a key competitive advantage in their campaigns to attract talented Millennials. It is not a footnote. It is a major attractor.

Local government employers should emphasize a small-team, family-style work environment, while national agencies can complement their big-brand feel with the promise of close-knit work teams. Large, bureaucratic public employers tend to be less effective than their large, private-sector competitors in projecting this feeling of the friendly platoon. A recent Partnership for Public Service report found that efforts to integrate young workers into an agency's group culture break down as early as first-day orientation, which usually consists of little more than paperwork. Only a few federal agencies, notably the FDIC and the Department of the Treasury, have developed structured, team-oriented onboarding programs for each new cohort of young employees.

Millennials' desire for sheltering will also have important implications for public policy.

Millennial voters will expect aggressive regulation and government safety nets to protect them from every variety of workplace risk. Surveys show that this generation favors policies that, for example, guarantee them a minimal level of health-care insurance or protect them against catastrophic loss of their pension benefits. (Particularly welcome was the 2010 healthcare reform provision that allows young people to remain on their parents' policies until the age of 26.) Millennials also broadly support tough enforcement of fraud or safety regulations and rules that encourage risk-free behaviors and healthy lifestyles, like incentives to quit smoking.

Policy makers should keep in mind that Millennials (along with their parents) will want to continue monitoring their own workplace safety as they grow older using real-time digital tools. Just as the federal government now informs teens and their parents about regulations through *youthrules.gov*, tomorrow's new programs will be focused on young people in their twenties or even thirties—and they will be customizable and interactive. This could have a dramatic impact on high-risk sectors that rely on young workers, from fire and police departments to food processing.

Protecting Young Workers—No Longer Optional
Additional workplace regulations may be coming soon in the following areas: ■ Mental-health counseling ■ Toxic chemicals/Hazardous materials ■ Ergonomics ■ Workplace inspections ■ Teen employment/Child labor ■ Longer COBRA eligibility ■ Minimum termination notice ■ Outplacement assistance

In addition to protecting this generation's physical health and safety, voters will focus on sheltering them from broader workplace-related hazards, such as absence of health insurance or pension coverage and job termination without notification. Risks that never bothered voters when Gen Xers were young adults will now seem intolerable.

08
Confident

"In large part as a result of their protected, structured, and positively reinforced upbringing, the Millennials are an exceptionally accomplished, positive, upbeat, and optimistic generation."

— **MORLEY WINOGRAD AND MICHAEL D. HAIS**,
IN *MILLENNIAL MAKEOVER* (2008)

"In spite of these hard economic times, they are far more optimistic than older adults about their own economic future. And they feel better about the state of the country. This is a very confident generation."

— **PAUL TAYLOR**, PEW RESEARCH CENTER, IN *MILLENNIALS: CONFIDENT, CONNECTED, OPEN TO CHANGE* (2010)

Confident

According to a Bayer-Gallup *Facts of Science Education* survey, 84 percent of today's young people believe someone in their generation will become the next Bill Gates, 66 percent believe they personally know such a person, and 25 percent believe they actually *are* that person. When today's older generations came of age, it was common to wonder if you had what it takes to succeed. Millennials spend less time wondering. They are more inclined to assume that they can meet any standard and beat any challenge. As one 16-year old boy quipped in a recent survey, "even the most average students can shoot for the moon if the opportunity is presented."

To be sure, many Boomer and (especially) Gen-X youths boasted about how they could defy the odds and end up a millionaire. Yet even this swagger implied that they would be an exception because most of their generations was not expected to succeed. What's remarkable about Millennials is their collective optimism: how confident they are, as a group, that nearly all of them will attain their life goals. They understand, in theory at least, that attaining these goals will require substantial planning, work, and sacrifice. Some, receiving appropriate guidance from older generations, are able to channel their energy effectively toward their goals. Others just spin their wheels while confidently waiting for their moment to arrive.

Behind this generational confidence lies the high hopes of their parents, along with all of the hopeful messages Millennials have heard throughout their childhood about believing in yourself, aiming high, and not settling for less than your dreams—messages that have been roundly criticized in some quarters for failing to prepare this generation for the grim reality that awaits. This does point to a real concern: Millennials are more likely than prior generations to feel derailed when everything doesn't go as planned, from not getting into the college of their choice to having a disappointing first job. And with the recent recession, there is plenty of derailing going on.

Yet there is an important positive side to this confidence. It energizes Millennials to set high standards and try to meet the very highest educational and professional expectations. If (as much psychology research suggests) optimists learn faster than pessimists, then today's youth ought to have plenty of momentum behind them.

The new youth confidence is widespread, but it is especially prominent among young women, who are more likely than their male counterparts to do well in school and to attend and graduate college. Educators will need to respond to this gender disparity as they prepare for the next generation of young workers.

Implications for Educators

Millennial students have lofty career expectations. Unlike young Gen Xers, who started out with a "reality-bites" outlook on their job prospects, today's students don't believe that personal fulfillment and good pay is a necessary tradeoff. Many believe that they can have it all. They think they should be able to start right off doing interesting work that will have a real impact on the company, rather than "serving time" with busywork or rote tasks. The share of youth age 18 to 25 who predict they will be "financially more successful than their parents" has been rising over the last decade, reaching 65 percent overall in 2005, and 75 percent for young blacks and Latinos.

While the economic dip of 2003 and (even more) the severe recession beginning in 2008 have triggered steep hikes in the youth unemployment rate, youth confidence remains high. In the spring of 2008, 61 percent of teens remained "very confident" (and another 31 percent "fairly confident") that they would achieve their career goals. By the spring of 2009, as entry-level job offers hit record lows, most Millennials patiently stuck to their long-term career goals— interning or going back to school (even if it meant living at home) rather than accepting a second- or third-choice occupation.

Many educators worry that excessive optimism may be setting this generation up for a hard fall. They are right to be concerned. The hardscrabble pragmatism of young Gen Xers, who didn't mind "trying out" whatever was available, often helped them bounce back from career disappointments. With their aversion to risk and unplanned detours, Millennials don't show the same resilience. Whether they have trouble getting hired, difficulty getting along with a boss, disappointment over their assigned tasks, or (especially) distress upon getting laid off, today's young workers have a harder time bouncing back from career setbacks.

Yes, educators need to temper the Millennial optimism with realism. But they should avoid the temptation to go negative and deliver "tough love" lectures about how hard the world really is. Shock therapy won't work. Few Millennials will believe the grim message, and many will simply resent the grim deliverer. By attacking optimism directly, moreover, educators may end up shattering the dreams that incentivize Millennials to work, plan, achieve, and stay true to their long-term goals. Even if the attack succeeds, it fails.

A better approach is to deepen and broaden the Millennials' understanding of their career dreams. Deepening, for example, means explaining to students who want to be MDs the full facts about their intended profession: the courses they must take, the grades they must earn, the colleges they must enter, the competition they will encounter, the age at which they will first earn a full salary, the tradeoffs among specialties, the median (not average) salary of that specialty, the political forces likely to shape the future of the medical profession, and so on. Broadening means expanding the range of careers that lead to their dreams: You don't have to be a veterinarian to work with animals, nor a lawyer to work in a courtroom, nor a star athlete to work in pro sports, nor a professor to teach. And yes, like it or not, entry-level jobs involving busywork or manual labor can indeed be gateways to perfect careers.

More generally, educators should prepare Millennials by integrating contextual ("real-world") applications into their academic curriculum and by informing students about the full range of professional opportunities available to them. One promising strategy is to replace traditional classrooms with career academies. Studies show that career academies often boost the engagement, retention, and test scores of high school students (boys especially) by showing them how their classroom learning will help them on the job. Not surprisingly,

The Argument for Career Academies

Career academies represent a shift away from the traditional separation of "academic" and "vocational" tracks to an educational model that combines academic rigor and career application for all students. What is a career academy? First, career academies are *small learning communities* of high school students who take classes together for at least two years. Second, they use a *college preparatory curriculum with a career theme* that highlights the connections between academic disciplines and their various career applications. And third, they rely on *partnerships* with employers, the community, and local colleges.

The career academy model was developed in Philadelphia in 1969 by Charles Bowser, the executive director of the Philadelphia Urban Coalition. Bowser partnered with the Philadelphia Electric Company and Bell of Pennsylvania to create a program that would help disadvantaged students develop better employment skills and provide local employers with a qualified entry-level workforce. In the early 1980s, the model spread to California, beginning with two programs in Bay Area high schools. The success of these schools prompted the state legislature to establish and fund other "partnership academies." Over the past twenty years, career academies have expanded rapidly across the country, supported by both state and business funding. Today, there are programs in more than two thousand high schools nationwide.

The rising popularity of the career academy model coincides with the arrival of Millennials into America's high schools. Why do academies appeal to Millennials?

■ The small-school environment provides the individual attention and sheltering that Millennials crave. The continuity of teachers and students across multiple classes and years creates strong, supportive communities in which Millennials thrive. The numbers clearly bear this out. In 2003, the Sacramento City Unified School District changed to a district-wide small learning community and career academy system. Over the next three years, the district's graduation rate rose from 76 to 87 percent, and the dropout rate fell from 13 to 7 percent. Suspensions and expulsions also declined dramatically.

■ Contextual, project-based learning is especially effective with Millennial boys, who are less likely than their female peers to follow a prescribed academic path without understanding its relevance for "real life." Internships, job shadowing, and mentors allow both boys and girls to think of themselves in professional roles, achieving according to professional standards. Gen-X parents are also drawn to career academies' practical payoff in future earnings. A 2004 study found that, four years after completing high school, males who had enrolled in career academies earned $2,500 more than their peers annually. A 2006 survey of a Florida district estimated that career academy graduates earn an additional lifetime income of $298,915 relative to typical high school graduates.

■ Numerous studies have shown that career-focused learning doesn't detract from, but rather improves, academic achievement. Millennials don't rebel against non-relevant curricula—they just tune out and sit through it. But a practical problem-solving and career orientation can wake them up again. High school math and reading test scores in Sacramento City Unified District rose for all grades in the first three years after the district converted to the career academy system, and the number of Advanced Placement classes rose by nearly a third. A study of career academies in the California Bay Area showed that students enrolled in academies had GPAs nearly 0.5 of a grade higher than non-academy students in the same schools, and test scores 30 to 40 percent higher.

■ Many programs have "multiple-pathway" systems that require students to try out different career tracks before choosing a concentration. This allows Millennials to test a variety of careers in a structured, guided environment so they can choose the right career with no mistakes or doubling back. Some states—including Florida, Ohio, and California—shape their career pathways to help create a future workforce whose skills match the needs of local industry.

■ Career academies create a Millennial-friendly pipeline from high school to postsecondary education and into the workplace. Joint high school and college course credits, organized visits to local colleges, and long-term connections with future employers create a smooth transition for students. When Sacramento switched to a district-wide career academy model, they experienced a ten percent rise in the share of students completing University of California qualified coursework. In the California Bay Area, 8 percent more of the career academy students continue on to two-year colleges compared to non-academy students in the same schools, and 16 percent more continue on to four-year colleges.

many states are now implementing or studying the career academy model. Another strategy is to give high school students better guidance about career options that do not require a four-year college degree. Apprenticeships, trade schools, technical institutes, and colleges offering two-year degrees are quicker and cheaper than a four-year college and pose less risk of a very bad outcome, like dropping out with large debts and no degree. They also offer excellent preparation for many of the understaffed, high-growth industries of tomorrow, from information technology to health care.

If the Millennials' confidence often seems unrealistic, educators themselves must be held accountable. Because counselors so often give the impression that "success" requires a four-year degree, most Millennials figure no other option will help them achieve their goals. According to a recent survey, 68 percent of today's high school students say they will go to a four-year college or university, while only 26 percent plan to attend a community college or technical trade school. These plans do not pan out: A much smaller share actually gets a four-year degree, and a much higher share gets a two-year degree or certificate. Thus far, most Millennials do appear to be moving into their desired careers when they enter the workplace—yet many are doing so after wasting a great deal of time and money on the wrong postsecondary programs. And they are choosing these programs after trusting the advice of adults who indiscriminately pushed them towards the abstract goal of a four-year degree.

All this is needless. Millennials would love to focus their confidence on a more targeted, tangible, and realistic vision of their future, if only educators would help them. Educators need to acquaint them earlier and more intensively with a wide range of real-life careers and the skills and preparations necessary to succeed in these careers. This is something today's young people cannot do on their own. Keep in mind that a declining share of young people have any paid work experience as teens and that a rising share assume (often rightly) that in today's globalizing economy they will be unable to follow in the career footsteps of their parents.

Growing confidence does not characterize all parts of the Millennial Generation to an equal degree. Compared to Boomers and Gen Xers at the same age, surveys show a bigger confidence boost (see our discussion in Chapter

4) in lower-income over higher-income families, in urban over rural families— and in girls over boys. By the time they graduate from high school, Millennial girls are more likely than Millennial boys to say they "like" school, to take challenging courses, to get good grades, to engage in extracurricular activities, and to have concrete career plans. Girls are more likely to enter four-year colleges and more likely to complete four-year, graduate, and professional degrees. The energy and optimism of Millennial "girl power" are becoming proverbial.

Many educators wonder how they can get the boys as fired up as the girls. The key is to appreciate gender differences in motivation: Whereas today's girls (according to teacher surveys) are more likely to work hard simply to please the teacher or to earn the credential, today's boys require incentives that are both more practical and more intrinsic. They need to know how the school work will lead to a career, earn them a living in the real work, and make them a better or more effective person.

To motivate boys, educators must help them grasp all of the step-by-step connections between the courses they attend today and the personal, social, and professional success they hope to gain tomorrow. High schools should emphasize contextual and project-based programs and make sure boys have plenty of access to workplaces and postsecondary institutions where they can witness how academic learning gets applied on the job. (Not unexpectedly, research shows that career academies have a bigger positive impact on the retention and future outcomes of boys than of girls.) Traditional four-year colleges, which are often less explicitly geared towards the real-world job market, struggle most to attract and retain men. An effective strategy for these colleges will be to track the local economy, develop data that can prove that student learning is relevant for practical employment, and offer counseling, placement, and alumni-networking programs to reinforce those outcomes.

On the flip side, today's girls often need to be cautioned in the opposite direction. So busy are they to get good grades, fulfill requirements, and move on the next level that many young women in high school and college forget to ask themselves whether it's all leading to the career they want—or even whether it leads, realistically, to any career at all. Among the Millennials who are now beginning to earn postgraduate degrees in academic specialties such

How Millennials Learn, by Gender

Millennial women are more engaged in the formal academic system, while men are more likely to engage on their own outside the system.

Frequent Academic Activities in the Past Year	Men	Women
Took notes in class	52%	**79%**
Asked questions in class	50%	**57%**
Sought feedback on academic work	40%	**53%**
Discussed grades or assignments with instructor	54%	**60%**
Improved at memorizing facts, ideas, or methods	66%	**74%**
Improved in writing clearly and effectively	66%	**71%**
Explored topics on my own, even if not required in class	**35%**	28%
Worked with classmates outside class	**50%**	44%
Reported improvement in solving complex, real-world problems	**65%**	60%

SOURCES: *Annual Report 2007*, National Survey of Student Engagement (2007); and *The American Freshman*, Higher Education Research Institute, UCLA (2009)

as the humanities and social sciences, women comprise a rapidly growing share who do not intend to seek academic appointments. Many will be disappointed to learn that the degrees earned at such a large sacrifice of time and money may have few other applications.

While many young Millennial men need to be reminded that formal schooling helps you obtain what you want in life, many young Millennial women need to be reminded that they may want more in life than formal schooling can offer.

Implications for Employers

When recruiting new employees, employers quickly find out that most Millennials are supremely confident about the value of what they can offer. Almost from day one, they expect to do interesting work that will have a real impact on the company and to be amply rewarded in both pay and recognition. According to a 2007 CareerBuilder survey, 87 percent of hiring managers and HR professionals say Millennial workers feel more "entitled" than older generations in terms of compensation, benefits, and career advancement. According to a 2007 MonsterTRAK survey, young employees are more likely than older employees to agree with statements such as "I know that I have more natural talents than most."

This confidence—some would say cockiness—has triggered predictable howls of complaint from Gen-X supervisors and Boomer executives. Gen Xers figure there must be something soft about a generation that expects so much from a mere "job," or something idiotic about new employees who want to contribute so much. Boomers figure every generation should have to "pay its dues" and work its way up the tedium ladder the way they once did. Many Boomers believe that entitlement corrupts, adversity purifies, and a hardy work ethic must be honed against the fire of a hateful establishment (the way theirs once was).

Millennials, meanwhile, wonder why older managers insist on a system of "generational hazing" (whereby the old mistreat the young simply because the old were themselves once mistreated), which diminishes productivity, undermines morale, and makes the jobs less appealing. "Just because older generations of working Americans disliked their jobs but stuck with it and did it anyway, why does that mean we have to?" reasons Ryan Healy, 25-year old cofounder of the blog "Employee Evolution: The Voice of Millennials at Work."

So how should older managers respond to the high expectations of young hires? Don't roll your eyes—and don't bother lecturing them about "impatience," how hard it "used to be," or other irrelevancies. Instead, leverage this confidence to your advantage just as you learned to leverage their specialness. Let young workers know that you respect their lofty goals and will do your best to help them achieve their ambitions—by giving them a whole lot of serious work to do. Make it clear that if they apply themselves and excel than you will give them challenges worthy of their talents. Companies like Chesapeake Energy make *Human Resource Executive* magazine's short list of "Millennial Magnets" (favorite Millennial employers) by earning a reputation as a workplace where young employees are allowed to take on high-level tasks early and be promoted for excellence regardless of their age.

Employers who use Millennials' high expectations to motivate them in the workplace may be surprised by how often today's youth will rise to the occasion. High maintenance and high performance often go together, not just in car engines but in people as well. Boomers who worry about undermining the perks of seniority (like higher pay) should relax. According to a 2006 survey by the global staffing firm Randstad, workers born after 1980 were the most likely to be interested in learning new skills (31 percent) and to value a good career path (19 percent) than any age group, yet they were the least likely to be interested in pay increases. In practice, Millennials who are pushing themselves to the limits of their ability are *less* likely to complain about Boomer obstructionism and *more* likely to inspire Boomers to provide the visionary leadership organizations need.

As they scale the corporate or professional ladder, Millennials will want their voices to be heard. Unlike today's older generations, they have grown up on close and familiar terms with nearly all of the adults in their lives, starting with their parents. They are accustomed to having their opinions taken seriously by older people—and are baffled by the brusque you're-too-young-to-count attitude that prevails in many corporate suites. Fully 81 percent of Millennial employees say it's important to have direct access to senior management, a far larger share than older generations. A growing number of companies are figuring out that Millennials will perform better and stay longer if they feel they can speak up in office meetings, go to a manager with a new idea, and have their opinions valued by coworkers. At Deloitte, young hires are encouraged to contribute in meetings that routinely include senior-level executives. Google bypasses corporate hierarchy by granting high-achieving Millennial managers direct access to the company's co-founders.

Many employers view questions or suggestions from Millennials as annoying (they're wasting my time) or even threatening (they want to show me up and take my job). Some Boomers in particular, recalling their own raucous youth experience, may misinterpret brimming confidence as willful antagonism. Yet other employers will make time to listen to their new Millennial hires and either learn from them or, if their suggestion is a bad one, use the occasion as a teaching moment, an opportunity to mentor the young and explain to

A Generation of Multitaskers?

Millennials are the first generation in history to grow up, from their earliest childhood, immersed in interactive digital media—from the networked PC and PDA to the MP3 player and mobile phone. This has led some commentators to make extravagant claims about how the digital age has fundamentally altered the way this rising generation reads, learns, processes information, and solves problems. They say that Millennials, as a "Net Generation" of "digital natives," possesses "altered cognitive wiring" that processes information in parallel, that is, everything at once. Meanwhile, older "Gutenberg" generations, as "digital immigrants," continue to think the old-fashioned serial way, one thing after another.

Proof positive, they say, is the obvious talent Millennials have for multitasking. Whether in their bedrooms, their dorm rooms, or their offices, today's young people can do everything at the same time—text, game, read an assignment, watch a sitcom, do research on Google, and keep the TV on—without (apparently) missing a beat. According to the Kaiser Family Foundation's *Generation M2* survey, this is how 8- to 18-year olds cram 10:45 hours of video, music, and reading into 7:38 hours of actual time each day.

Question: Are Millennials wired differently by their upbringing, endowed with an ability for multitasking that older generations don't share?

Answer: No, not really. Or rather, no in all but the most qualified sense that Millennials do better at something that every generation does poorly. The best defense Millennials have for multitasking is that it can often save them time when no more than one of their activities requires any real focus or thought.

Let's start with the basics. According to the vast majority of neurologists and psychologists, there is no such thing as multitasking, in the sense of lending conscious attention to more than one "task" at the same time. The seat of consciousness and recallable memory, the brain's cerebral cortex and hippocampus, can only focus on one thing at a time. When people "multitask," what they are actually doing is moving their attention rapidly back and forth between tasks—and this juggling results in a sharp deterioration in the ability of any person, no matter what their age, to carry out any task. Countless clinical experiments (often involving computer screens) confirm this finding among all age groups: Tasks done one after the other, in a serial and focused fashion, are completed faster and with fewer errors than tasks that are "juggled" simultaneously.

Now for the qualifications. Experiments confirm that young adults are relatively better at multitasking than older adults. Surveys also show that young adults do multitasking and enjoy multitasking more than other age groups. The "digital natives" crowd says, well, they do it more because they're better at it. But clearly this doesn't make sense, because—despite their relative advantage—they would get even more done if they didn't multitask at all.

An alternative explanation is that young people multitask more simply because they enjoy it more—even if their overall performance suffers. Why do they enjoy it more? Because they're young. Over two millennia ago, Plato and Aristotle commented on the impulsiveness and volatility of youth. Over a century ago, the psychologist William James wrote eloquently of the "extreme mobility of attention" and "distractibility" of the young mind. Most contemporary psychologists agree that the brain itself does

them how the business really works. These employers understand that most outspoken Millennials are just trying to be helpful and contribute—an urge that should not be thwarted but encouraged. These are the employers who end up earning young workers' loyalty.

Employers adjusting to this new generation's workstyle will have to tool up an old (and often underused) skill: positive feedback. Throughout their schooling, Millennials have received a widening torrent of grades, gold stars, not become fully mature in its executive function until the mid-twenties. In other words, it's not digital IT that makes youth flighty. It's the flightiness of youth that makes them use digital IT the way they do.

A Stanford University study, published in 2009, reinforces this interpretation. The researchers separated out those college students who do the most multitasking and who evaluate themselves as especially good at it. Remarkably, the study found that these students performed worse in every type of multitasking exercise than other students. According to the authors, these "expert" multitaskers were hobbled by their inability to shut out one task while focusing on another. They were too distracted by every new stimulus to stay focused. The study's findings are suggestive: Those who multitask a lot do it not so much because it helps them, but because they cannot help themselves.

Now for a further qualification. Our brains do allow us to multitask very well if only one of the tasks requires conscious focus and the rest are all learned or passive tasks requiring little focus. (This has been called passive background tasking—as opposed to active switch tasking). That's how people talk and eat or listen and drive at the same time. And that's how teens can IM while watching a video. Either the IM or the video is not requiring much attention. By doing such tasks at the same time, busy Millennials

with a lot going on in their lives will be able to squeeze more hours out of each day.

Few employers can afford to overlook the cost of multitasking in lost productivity (and employee stress). The Institute for the Future reports that the typical "Fortune 1000" employee sends and receives 178 message per day and is interrupted three times per hour. Some tips:

■ Inform your employees about how and why multitasking can undermine their effectiveness, especially when they are working on challenging and high-performance tasks. Many young people have never been told this—even by their own parents. Millennials are used to lessons on time management, but often need help in drawing boundaries between themselves and the group. Many think (wrongly) that being a good team player means leaving your front door open at all hours.

■ Give employees tasks that are creative enough to give them an incentive to focus. Make sure they grasp the point of what they're doing. Many switch-taskers say they don't care how productive they are because their work is "just dumb." And background-taskers often learn to carry out their job repetitively with little thought (in which case, multitasking may or may not be a problem).

■ Avoid blanket restrictions on Internet, PDAs, or mobile phones, except at meetings or in the classroom (Millennials will want specific rules here). But there is still plenty you can do to help your employees avoid distractions. Make it easy for them to hold all office calls, to take their email off ping, to press one key to block all incoming online communication, or (with software like WriteRoom) to black out everything on their computer screen except for the text window they're working on.

■ Frequent meetings and ad-hoc coworker interruptions (virtual or face-to-face) are the single biggest cause of involuntary multitasking. Consider formalizing the process of setting up a meeting to ensure that every meeting has a clear purpose. Reduce interruptions by encouraging recurrent weekly meetings between team members in which a week's worth of issues can be discussed. Institute meeting-free Fridays (a growing favorite) or even email-free Tuesdays or Thursdays. Most Millennials will appreciate such efforts to structure the workweek.

■ Make sure that the desirable norm in your workplace is calm focus, not multimodal madness. Leadership by example is indispensible.

and weekly online interim reports. In the workplace, they will continue to expect positive recognition for work well done. A number of employers are already boosting employee recognition by offering little awards for a wide variety of employee achievements, regular thank-you emails, and weekly meetings to acknowledge good work. As NPR recently reported, some firms go so far as to have an "employee of the day" ceremony each morning. Clifton Gunderson dramatically reduced turnover by implementing a three-tiered system of recognition and rewards, where managers can give bonuses and time off to top achievers, and present small rewards like gift cards on the spot for just about anything they deem praiseworthy.

To be sure, the Millennial hunger for praise-heaped-on-praise—six in ten twenty-something workers say their boss does not give them enough—has attracted much roasting from the business media and older employers, who sometimes ridicule Millennials with names like "Generation Me." "Do I have to give them a gold star just for showing up for work on time?" intoned a recent sarcastic email that made the rounds of HR Web sites. Yet Millennials see it very differently, observing that most Boomers and Gen Xers rarely praise anyone for anything. In their eyes, Boomers and Gen Xers have created unfriendly office environments in which positive work attitudes are thwarted by regulatory prohibitions, dark rumors, cynicism about work, outright threats, and distrust about the company's basic purpose. By contrast, today's young workers will be drawn to—and will gladly help foster—upbeat workplace environments where people articulate positive messages about one another's accomplishments and about the institution's mission.

The Praise Industry

- Bank of America created the management-level title, "senior vice president of recognition and rewards."
- Managers at Universal Studios recognize good work with "Applause Notes" that are redeemable for free movie tickets.
- Bronson Healthcare Group requires managers to write at least forty-eight praise notes a year.
- Bob Nelson, consultant and author of bestselling 1001 Ways to Reward Employees, is the self-titled "Guru of Thank You."

Millennials aren't just whining when they talk about recognition. Among all the survey results tabulated by the Leadership IQ survey, a positive response to the question "my boss recognizes and praises my accomplishments" is the single best predictor of Millennial workplace satisfaction. Ignore it at your peril. Indeed, workplace surveys in several industries show that the number one professional complaint of employees of all ages is the lack of recognition for good work.

Motivating a generation that has lofty workplace expectations requires some strategizing when the work is menial, low skill, or traditionally low prestige. One good approach is to frame the job as an important contribution to the organization and even to society as a whole—and to formalize recognition (for example, through weekly team ceremonies). Another is to pose the job as a personal challenge and to use its very difficulty to appeal to youth's sense of honor or idealism. Military, security, and emergency organizations often find success here, as do nonprofits recruiting young people as missionaries, public health aides, or expeditionary teachers (like the Peace Corps or Teach for America). Finally, employers can package menial work as a perfect stepping stone to future success by providing money, experience, references, or other benefits. Both the U.S. Army and McDonald's now brand themselves as skill-building employers who put recruits on a secure path to salaried corporate careers. To make the path credible, employers should offer a college tuition bonus or negotiate a secure pipeline with local postsecondary schools.

Effective motivation differs by gender as well. According to the 2007 MonsterTRAK survey, young men are more likely than young women to consider themselves exceptionally talented. They also rank "chance for promotion" and "high income" higher in their criteria for job decisions, while young women lean toward "job security" and "geographic location." This young male bluster may seem standard issue for all generations—but keep in mind that Millennial women now have a sizable advantage over Millennial men in educational attainment, career planning, and sense of life direction. Employers take note: When recruiting young men, it usually helps to emphasize how their jobs will push both them and the organization to a new level—and when recruiting young women, it helps to emphasize how their jobs will fit perfectly into their life plans and be greatly valued by the organization.

In the years ahead, these two flavors of Millennial confidence will make a profound impression on the economy if, as we are beginning to see, young women and young men are attracted to different sectors. Millennials are almost certain to feminize the credentialed professions (medicine, law, academia) and the personnel of large, structured corporations and public agencies. Meanwhile, this generation is likely to masculinize the more fluid, market-oriented sectors (technology, marketing, startups). Most Millennials will view these gender differences, not as antagonistic, but as complementary—all part of their larger effort to lift the optimism of American workers and the mood of the American workplace.

Implications for the Public Sector

Unlike Gen Xers, Millennials are drawn to the structure and stability of public-service career ladders. Many prefer them to the high risk and high turnover of "flat" organizations. But with their big career expectations, today's youth are often repelled by government's reactionary and categorical attachment to seniority over performance. This generation expects to take on high-level tasks and be promoted for excellence regardless of their age. They are not thrilled by the prospect that a petrified bureaucracy might stand in their way.

To recruit and retain Millennials, public-sector employers must therefore strike a new balance between structured hierarchy and performance-based rewards. This should include a regular promotion schedule that operates in tandem with a more flexible reward system for excellent work (and safeguards for anyone falling behind). Over the past decade, pay-for-performance measures have been on the rise in government agencies. But most of these have been structured as ad-hoc bonuses and add-ons that appeal to Xers. Millennials, who care more about institutional structure, will expect performance-based rewards to be integrated into a reliable, agency-wide system.

The highest-achieving Millennials value access to senior management and the ability to take on important tasks—even more than they value monetary incentives, according to a 2009 Deloitte study of young government employees. Yet most public-sector employers fall woefully short in this area, effectively screening out the most capable candidates. According to OPM, federal employees are much less likely than private-sector employees to feel that they are encouraged to innovate or that they can communicate with senior management. Government agencies should find creative ways to change this image. The General Services Administration holds a quarterly new-employee celebration where senior leaders mingle with young hires. The Nuclear Regulatory Commission snagged the top ranking in Partnership for Public Service's 2009 *Best Places to Work* in the federal government in part because management holds regular meetings to listen to staff.

Confident Millennials are motivated by a positive workplace tone, from upbeat team-building exercises to a steady stream of praise from managers. Some veteran Boomer and Xer civil servants create an opposite tone: burned out, past caring, and cynical about the agency and their own role there. Managers should be attentive to these negative attitudes, recognize that they are toxic to Millennials, and (if they cannot eliminate them) take these veterans out of the chain of command. Like their private-sector counterparts, agencies can improve the workplace tone by bolstering positive recognition. Fewer than half of all federal employees are satisfied with the recognition they get for doing a good job, according to OPM. In North Carolina's study, young state employees agree that improving recognition programs would help retention.

Public employers are better positioned than their private competitors to frame traditionally low-prestige jobs as an important societal contribution. The USDA Forest Service ramped up recruiting for trail clean up by offering course credit while *reducing* the pay rate. They took a menial paid job and successfully transformed it into a world-saving, résumé-enhancing experience. Another Millennial-friendly strategy is to present jobs as a worthy challenge for a special few with the right skills and dedication. The Marines and Teach for America have used this message successfully to recruit high-achieving students for the most challenging of callings.

Millennials' confidence will also have important implications for public policy.

Just as today's youth want to create a more upbeat workplace environment, they will also seek a more positive tone in politics. Surveys indicate that they are more distressed than older generations by the negative tone in Washington (including the pessimistic Boomer talking heads whose opinions now dominate the media). Policy makers can learn from President Barack Obama, whose "yes we can" message resonated especially well with this confident generation.

Nowhere is a positive tone more important than in policies relating to youth themselves. For decades, legislators have increasingly discussed youth in gloomy tones, with downbeat predictions about "failing" and "at-risk" youth populations. Now, with Millennials coming of age, they should shift to a more positive, solutions-oriented tone about how to help young adults reach their full potential. Rather than harping on crime and drugs—which in any case are trending down in the Millennial youth era—policy makers should focus on helping young people excel in college, volunteer in their communities, launch businesses, and jump-start eco-friendly industries.

With their positive outlook on the nation's future, Millennials will enthusiastically support sweeping, ambitious policies designed to make America's core institutions, and their own lives, work better. This will feel very different from the incremental policies targeted to older generations. Surveys show today's youth favor large-scale, national solutions for everything from poverty to global warming to the national deficit.

09

Team Oriented

"I would give today's young employees very high marks for teamwork. When they were growing up they were structured and their class work was all team based. Now our teams work very well."

— **MARK FINGER**, VP OF WORLDWIDE HUMAN RESOURCES, NATIONAL INSTRUMENTS (2008)

"Community service is part of their DNA. It's part of this generation to care about something larger than themselves. It's no longer about keeping up with the Joneses. It's about helping the Joneses."

— **MICHAEL BROWN**, COFOUNDER AND CEO OF CITY YEAR (2009)

Team Oriented

Workplace veterans have been noticing something unusual about today's entry-level employees. When managers assign them group projects, they look relieved rather than irritated. Staff meetings find them striving for consensus while minimizing argument. Offices ping with the sound of instant messages as young workers exchange constant advice and support. Surveys confirm this impression of rising teamwork. According to a 2007 SelectMinds survey, 77 percent of Millennial workers say the social aspects of work are very important to their overall workplace satisfaction, ten points higher than older generations.

Boomer and Gen-X managers are often baffled by this team attitude. But to anyone who has been tracking the attitudes of Millennials from K–12 schools to college and beyond, the trend is no surprise. From team grading and career academies to community service and Facebook, Millennials have been developing strong team instincts and tight peer bonds. Today's youth have adapted instant messaging and digital-mobile technology to increase their level of interconnection to an unprecedented level. From one generation to the next, the catch phrase has changed from "just do it" to "let's do it."

As Millennials enter the workplace, they are bringing their inclusive style with them. They expect constant communication and collaboration with their bosses and colleagues, both virtually and face-to-face. They get excited at the prospect of bonding retreats, group projects, and team compensation plans. Employers in traditionally competitive, individualized professions, such as law and finance, need to contemplate dramatic changes in their workplace structure and company brand if they want to remain a cool place to work to the new youth elite.

Millennials' increased ethic of teamwork goes beyond their own social circles. This generation feels a strengthened connection—and civic obligation—to their communities, their nation, and their world. A record share say they want to help "others in need" and are signing up for community service. Youth voting rates have surged ever since the oldest Millennials reached age 18, and reached the highest level in decades in the 2008 presidential election. Surveys show that today's youth are strongly attracted to "helping" professions like government, teaching, and nonprofits. Fully 79 percent of 13- to 25-year olds say they want to work for a company that cares about how it affects or contributes to society.

To attract the best and brightest, companies of all stripes, even those not generally associated with public service, will need to emphasize their positive impact on the community and offer greater service opportunities.

Implications for Educators

Through their K–12 years, Millennials have come to expect that working and learning as members of a team will be a central part of their future careers. Today's teens list "working well in teams" as one of the four top work skills. NACE reports that the share of college grads who believe that their community is more important than their job has doubled since 1982. (According to NACE, this is the single largest difference in *any* basic value shift between graduates surveyed in 2008 versus those surveyed in 1982.)

Educators should tap into this generation's team instincts to deepen commitment, raise retention, and achieve better overall results. Expand on group learning opportunities, including peer-to-peer counseling, tutoring, and group projects with team grading. Many colleges are encouraging students (or, with freshmen, requiring them) to enroll in learning communities where two or more courses are team-taught with coordinated curricula and student collaboration. Millennials are especially attracted to living-learning communities, in which both the enrolled students and the faculty live in the same dorm and can conveniently schedule intensive group study and discussion.

Peer grading and team grading are touchy issues, even among Millennials, who will care deeply whether group evaluations systems are fair. When students grade students, the graders should be required to give multiple scores covering multiple aspect of the gradees' work so that the teacher will be able to distinguish the strengths and weaknesses of both the graders and the gradees. Educators can avoid the most common complaint about team grading—that it allows freeloaders to coast on the efforts of achievers—by being sure to assess each member's relative contribution. The simplest assessment method is simply to ask team members to evaluate each other's effort.

Increasingly, colleges are changing the classroom experience itself to better suit the collaborative and interactive Millennial learning style. A growing number of teachers are launching class Facebook pages so that students can plug into group discussions or check due dates (via laptops or cell phones) anytime and anywhere. Some administrators claim course-specific social networking is actually raising their retention rates—especially at urban community colleges where students rarely see each other outside the classroom. A growing number of colleges are adopting electronic hand-held student response systems in the classroom, which allow real-time interaction between teachers and students (for example, a teacher can poll students in seconds to find out if they know the material) or between students (when they break up into teams). Where these fancy electronic systems are unavailable, Twitter is often a cheap alternative. The traditional single-lecturer mode is no longer the only classroom experience, but just one among many options, most of them more group oriented.

With Millennials on board, even traditionally cutthroat careers will take on a more team-oriented flavor, pushing some professional schools to shift their focus towards team skills and group learning. Business schools such as Rutgers Center of Management Development report that today's students are showing increasing interest in courses that teach partnership skills, like management and labor relations, over the individual-skills courses Gen Xers valued, like finance and marketing. New collaborative trends in fields like law and medicine will soon influence training curricula and put greater emphasis on effective group decision making and the ability to assume both support and leadership roles.

Colleges are even beginning to develop formal, group-oriented curricula for careers that have traditionally been regarded as purely do-it-yourself territory—

like starting a new business or nonprofit. To Boomers and Gen Xers, the "entrepreneur" is a mythic risk-taker who sets out on his or her own, breaks rules, and defies the world. By contrast, Millennials who want to launch their own software company or their own line of clothing are eager to learn about how to minimize risk, unify a team of employees, and create a strong network of investors and customers. They then go forth with an entrepreneurship credential.

Writ larger, the Millennial team ethic translates into stronger attachments to the local community. After graduating high school, a growing share want to learn and train in nearby neighborhoods and towns—a trend also pushed by the Millennials' aversion to risk, their growing desire to live near their parents, their parents' own worries about their children's safety, and (recently) the recession squeeze on family budgets. The bottom line for every kind of higher education: You need to focus more of your recruiting dollars on local schools. Many colleges that once tried to market special programs or online degrees nationally are now finding they have better luck in their own backyard. Since the new localism influences where Millennials want to work as well, major corporations are also sensing the need to "grow their own" talent in their own neighborhoods. Companies in aerospace (Seattle), in design (Los Angeles), or in health technology (Boston) are turning away from anonymous national recruiting drives—and starting to favor building or funding local institutes and colleges where they can gradually develop their own home-grown talent.

Whether near or far from home, many Millennials are driven by a desire to serve other people or some cause larger than themselves. When high school teens were asked in 2002 why they chose their preferred career, three times as many said because I "want to help people" than because it "pays good money." By 2009, the share of incoming college freshmen who reported doing community service during their senior year of high school rose to an

---

The Public-Service Elite

In 2009, 11 percent of all Ivy League seniors applied to serve in Teach for America.

Average SAT score of all applicants to Teach for America:	1344
Average SAT score of all applicants to Ivy League Colleges:	1323

SOURCE: Teach for America (2009); average SAT estimated as the midpoint of 25th and 75th percentile, published online for all Ivy League colleges (2010)

all-time high of 85 percent. The proportion who said it is "very likely" they will volunteer in college is also at an all-time high. For Boomers, community service was often regarded as a way to escape the draft or to defy the "system" as an activist. For Gen Xers, it was frequently imposed as punishment for misbehavior. For Millennials, it's simply the norm—an expected part of anyone's educational experience.

Schools can harness this desire to serve the community by increasing the variety and depth of their service-learning offerings—in effect, expanding the ways in which Millennials can serve in return for course credit. Job shadowing, skill development, and apprenticeships in fields such as health care, accounting, law, engineering, and construction can all be carried out in the context of community service. Or counselors can help students choose a concentration of study by discussing with them the volunteering roles they most enjoy. Most schools and colleges are bus-

College Senior List of "Ideal Employers": Top Ten Selections, 2001 and 2009*

Rank	2001	2009
1	3M	Google
2	Amazon	Walt Disney
3	Accenture	Apple
4	IBM	U.S. Department of State
5	Walt Disney	FBI
6	Microsoft	Ernst & Young
7	Cisco	Peace Corps
8	BMW	NASA
9	Abbott Labs	Pricewaterhouse Coopers
10	DreamWorks	Teach for America

* Public and nonprofit employers shaded
SOURCE: Universum Communications (2009)

ily pushing their curricula in the direction of service. At the cutting edge is the enormous California State University system, which now maintains 2,500 service-learning courses for more than 65,000 students; over the past decade, CSU students have contributed roughly thirty million service hours.

Career counselors take note: The Millennial urge to contribute to the community is making the "helping" aspect of careers more important than it was to prior generations at the same age. Service-oriented fields such as criminal justice, forensics, public health, and civil engineering have surged over the past decade. The quality of applicants to nursing schools and military academies has never been higher. Meanwhile, the allure of teaching is white hot. In the 2003 and 2005 Gallup surveys, teaching became a top-ten career choice among teens (and for both boys and girls) for the first time since 1977. In 2008, 11 percent of Yale's senior class, 9 percent of Harvard's, and 10 percent of Georgetown's applied to Teach for America.

On a 2009 Universum survey, college seniors ranked public-sector careers (the U.S. Department of State, the FBI, and NASA) along with major service callings (Peace Corps and Teach for America) at the very top of their list of ideal employers. Even fields like business, which have not been traditionally service oriented, are feeling the change. In 2007, 26 percent of MBA students said that an important factor in their job selections will be "the potential of making a contribution to society," up from 15 percent in 2002. More MBA students now rank "creating value for the communities in which they operate" as a primary business responsibility. Millennials want careers whose value will benefit—not come at the expense of—their friends and neighbors.

Implications for Employers

"The Apprentice," NBC's bare-knuckle reality show about young competitors in the boardroom, began losing popularity just when Millennials started to be noticed in the workplace. Coincidence? Probably not. About the same time, "friending" on Facebook was becoming the hot new fad among employed twenty-somethings. And the U.S. Army finally jettisoned its "Army of One" slogan, whose loner theme was clearly failing to attract recruits.

Today's new employees are moving away from a winner-take-all workplace culture and towards a culture of group recognition. And that's having an impact. By all accounts, employees are doing more work in groups and less work on their own. In offices, individual (cubicle) workspace is shrinking while multipurpose common rooms are expanding, according to a study by the International Facility Management Association. A 2007 MonsterTRAK and Michigan State University survey reports that Millennial employees rank "being able to work independently" 11th out of 15 characteristics important to their job search, significantly lower than the ranking given by older employees.

From their very first contact with potential young recruits, employers should leverage the new team ethic. Many Millennials don't want to get hired alone. They want to get hired with and through their friends. So let them. Avon now has young salespeople invite their friends to "beauty bashes" (reminiscent of the "Tupperware" parties of the 1950s) where many of the friends agree to sign on and join Avon. In 2006, the U.S. Army, Army Reserve, and Army National Guard instituted a novel Referral Bonus Program that paid soldiers a bonus (eventually, $2,000) to recruit their friends. The program was hugely successful and is credited with turning around a slide in enlistments. Another popular new offering is the Army's Buddy Team Enlistment Option, which allows friends to enlist at the same time and go through basic and advanced training together.

Many businesses that recruit online report that harvesting social networks generates faster, more targeted, and higher-quality results than using anonymous job search sites. The social networking software Jobster, recently adopted by the U.S. State Department, lets employers reach out through viral emails forwarded by employees to their acquaintances. Ernst and Young gives interns video cameras to create "vlogs" for the firm's Web site. A rising number of employers are using Facebook as a recruiting tool. A Facebook widget called "Work With Me" enables employees to post a link about their workplace on their own webpage. If the widget results in a new hire, the employee who posted it can be rewarded—for example, paid a bonus. In an emerging tech-sector trend called "team hiring," many employers are hiring groups of classmates or workmates and, after one or two stints, these teams are openly selling their services as a group package. Like the Army, tech employers are finding that they can lure desirable young candidates to the company by hiring their friends and siblings—a tactic rarely tried or even imagined when free-agent Gen Xers were their age.

As soon as the new hires arrive, employers should work hard to forge a close-knit, team-oriented environment. Nearly half of Millennial workers rate the availability of networking and support programs for employees with common interests as a very important factor in their decision to join or remain with an employer. The engineering firm Kimley Horn, recognized as a "Millennial Magnet" employer, offers lunchtime forums where employees socialize and share their knowledge and perspectives. Anyone visiting Deloitte's internal

Web page might mistake it for a social networking site: Employees can create joint blogs, network with coworkers interested in similar hobbies, and sign up to make a movie about their experience at the company. Elite consulting and tech companies like Accenture and Qualcomm offer immersive orientations—basically multiweek boot-camp retreats only more fun—in order to bring young employees together into communities of trust.

Once on the job, make sure Millennials know that they are expected to help their peers and that their peers will be expected to help them. Many of the most effective recognition and reward programs for young employees, for example those at Best Buy or Scottrade, focus on the group. These programs either reward teams for their collective performance or have everyone on the team award members who contribute the most. A rising number of companies—today 12 percent of all privately owned firms, mostly in manufacturing—are implementing team-based compensation plans, in which a significant share of salary depends upon the performance of the group. Millennials will find these plans attractive. As with team grading in high school or college, of course, these plans will only work well if they are carefully designed and supervised: Rewards must be exactly aligned with desired performance, and safeguards against free-riding or gaming the plan must be enforced. As a rule, groups who work the best together are groups who socialize the best together. The most successful Gen-X supervisors are likely to feel, from time to time, like summer camp counselors.

In many expert fields like law and medicine, which have traditionally been structured around competitive and independent professionals, the coming shift to team-based models may come as something of a shock. No longer will all the decisions be made by a few workaholic superstars surrounded by minions. Instead, professionals will work together and fill in for each other. This is already beginning to happen as law firms and health-care facilities cut costs by hiring teams of paralegals and physician assistants to complete tasks that were formerly done by a single physician or lawyer. Many employers are noting the advantages of the new team-based model, including more scheduling flexibility, greater depth of expertise, and (due to mutual oversight) fewer errors.

With Millennials on board, employers may have to rethink their training and evaluation priorities. If Millennials are strong when it comes to team skills, they can often be weak when it comes to individual initiative. College professors report that fewer students now think outside the box on assignments or disagree with the peer consensus. Managers accustomed to self-starting Gen Xers are sometimes disappointed by Millennials' growing attention to rules and to fitting in with coworkers. Managers should respond by making sure that youthful teams listen carefully to dissenting opinions, rather than assuming there is safety in numbers. Millennials who like to take charge need to be reminded that an effective leader must possess the ability to take a calculated risk, go against the grain, or stick up for an unpopular opinion (their own or someone else's). Teach these lessons as workplace "skills" Millennials can put on their résumé. Better yet, hook them up with Gen-X mentors who can show them what a little top-gun moxie feels like day to day.

Employers will also have to adjust to a range of new communication styles. Today's young people are legendary for being glued to cell phones, buddy lists, and social networking sites, all in an effort to keep in touch with large circles of colleagues, bosses, friends, and family. The *LexisNexis Technology Gap Survey* reports that Millennial workers spend an average of 10.6 hours a day using online tools, twice the daily hours spent by Boomers.

So how should managers feel about this nonstop traffic in IMs, texts, tweets, and news feeds? Some try very hard to suppress it as a useless distraction. This is a mistake. Smart managers understand that lots of digital traffic is crucial to the Millennials' collaborative workstyle and empowers their greatest workplace strength: a willingness to share information, advice, and instruction. Even communication with outside friends and family is often about solving workplace problems or resolving personal logistical headaches and freeing up time for more play—or more work. If today's young workers seem to be spending too much time photo-shopping images on their Facebook wall, the usual problem is that they don't have enough serious work to do. Come up with new ways to challenge them.

Yes, there are potential downsides to Millennials' digital multitasking acumen. It works better in fast-paced, high-pressure environments than with tasks that require extended deep concentration. But rather than instituting a blanket ban, managers should help Millennials understand when it's better to power-down digital stimuli, and why. Don't imagine that by putting them under a bell jar you're improving productivity or morale.

Many employers justify tight restrictions on public digital networks in the name of privacy and security. This is a legitimate concern for many institutions—for example, in defense, intelligence, and law enforcement, or in finance, law, and health care. Yet here the restriction should only apply to departments handling secure information. And even these departments should have access to secure in-house networks, which can range from custom-built and super-encrypted intranets (for the highest security needs) to much cheaper off-the-shelf options like LinkedIn Company Group, Yammer, and PBWiki (where the security needs are not so extreme). However employers can make it happen, they must keep pace with the voracious communication needs of this "net" generation.

Figure 24 ▶

How People Communicate with Friends While at Work, by Age

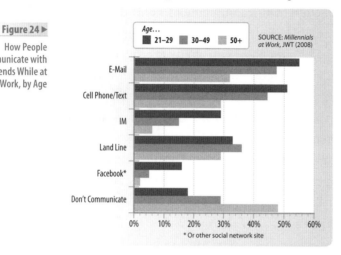

With Millennials gradually filling the workplace, racial and ethnic diversity will take on a new tone and meaning. Most of this generation welcomes diversity and, if given the choice, prefers a "more diverse" over a "less diverse" workplace environment. Numerous surveys show that, of all generations, Millennials are the most welcoming of diversity, that they believe they handle diversity better than older people, and that older people agree that they handle it better (according to a 2009 Pew Research Center survey, this is the only positive youth trait decisively acknowledged by older people).

The implications for employers are clear. Showcase diversity, but showcase it in the Millennial style—which sees diversity as positive and necessary, something that adds but never subtracts from the team's ability to achieve common goals. Millennials favor a "trans" racial more than a "multi" racial

The Wiki-Workplace

One of the most surprising and significant trends in networked IT over the last ten years has been the rapid development of "free" information services that generate tremendous value to users simply through voluntary collaboration. People make use of these free Web services every time they check a fact (*Wikipedia*), evesdrop on a celebrity (*CelebrityTweet*), monitor a political opinion (*Daily Kos* or *Free Republic*), locate an instructional video (*YouTube*), query an expert (*Aardvark*), or shop around for virtually any good or service (*Amazon, Hotels, Cars, Fandango, Yelp, Urbanspoon, Zagat*). With Web giants like Google and Microsoft designing ever-more flexible "platforms for participation," the variety of networked information services continues to grow every year.

This trend—which business-practices guru Dan Tapscott calls "wikinomics"—coincides with the maturing of Web technology and the expansion of bandwidth. It also coincides with the coming of age of a new generation, whose ability to team up, trust each other, heed peer opinion, and build communities is ideally suited to these participatory tasks. Millennials define the cutting-edge of wikinomics. For this generation, it isn't just about collaboration among consumers. It's about collaboration among friends, students, parents, businesses, voters—and, of course, coworkers.

Employers, take note: Millennials on the job regard networked IT as an invaluable force multiplier—something that replaces the power of one with the power of many. In the "wiki-workplace," with just a few keystrokes, Millennials are able...

■ to **query**: An employee is working on a project and doesn't recall a particular term, step, or code. He could rummage through manuals for an hour, or he can query the collective mind of several dozen coworkers—and get the answer back in seconds.

■ to **teach**: Now reverse the situation. An employee is the expert on something that everyone keeps bugging her about. To instruct them all, she can text everyone an e-lesson. Or, for a more personal touch, she can broadcast an e-video. Or, if she has a flair for the dramatic, she can invite them all for a half hour into her *Second Life* classroom.

■ to **understand**: A lengthy and complex project involving many collaborators can almost always benefit from a dedicated wiki, where the group's understanding of every moving part can be steadily broadened, enhanced, or updated in real time. The wiki is around 24/7 to impart or receive wisdom, and will faithfully bring any differences of opinion to the group's attention.

■ to **team up**: Why do high-pressure professions like law or medicine depend so heavily on the never-sleep workaholic? One main reason is that it's just too difficult to synchronize group hours or to "hand off" client or patient data from one colleague to another. Sophisticated project software is starting to change this. In the wiki-workplace, the whole team "owns" the

data and any team member, present or not, can backstop a critical decision.

■ to **estimate** or **forecast**: When it's important to know something about an organization's future (whether a deadline will be met, whether costs will be within budget), team leaders could consult a few experts. Or, for a better estimate, they can consult their own fellow workers—either by getting every employee to vote or by inviting them to "bet" in an internal futures market. (Research shows that these internal markets consistently outperform official company forecasts.)

■ to **deliberate**: To lead is to choose. To lead well is to make choices that are informed by your organization's collective wisdom. Before making important decisions, cutting-edge managers are using networked IT to sound out the rank and file, sift through suggestions, and invite the dissenters to make their case. Today, among Boomer (or even Xer) managers, not many are at this cutting edge. But tomorrow, when Millennials become the managers, collaborative leadership using tools of virtual deliberation will become the norm.

society, an image better conveyed by blended pigments than white next to black, by dozens of races cooperating rather than two or three races pulling in different directions. Older diversity trainers and counselors must adjust their workshops accordingly. The edgy and moralizing shock-therapy mode that young Gen-X workers enjoyed (or shrugged off) back in the 1990s may trigger serious pushback from Millennial workers. Why so negative, many will ask? And when it comes to tolerance, why are *you* lecturing *us*?

While on a micro level the Millennial team ethnic means close bonds with coworkers, on a macro level it is pushing a growing determination to contribute to the community as a whole—from the neighborhood and town to the state, the nation, and the world. The hands-on "helping" aspect of careers is thus becoming a more important attractor for young recruits than it was ten or twenty years ago. Quite simply, they want to work for companies that reach out to the community and make it possible for employees to lend a helping hand. A 2007 Deloitte *Volunteer IMPACT* survey found that nearly two-thirds of 18- to 26-year olds polled would prefer working for employers that allow them to contribute their talent to nonprofit organizations. Laysha Ward, president of community relations for Target, says recruiters from all regions are hearing young job candidates bring up the company's "commitment to the community as one of the number one reasons they want to work for us."

Some businesses now go to great lengths to pursue the community service angle in their employer brand. Goldman Sachs, JPMorgan, and Amgen, for example, have formally teamed up with service programs like Teach for America to improve their image on today's campuses and compete for top graduates. Pfizer and Ernst and Young have even developed oversees initiatives where new employees spend a few months volunteering with small businesses and nonprofits abroad.

Less exotic—and a lot more typical—are employers that go out of their way to coordinate office-wide community service activities or give employees time off to do community service independently. Accenture recently launched a Web page where employees can search and sign up for volunteer activities. Many law and accountings firms now provide several paid days annually for volunteering with local schools and nonprofit organizations. PNC sends employees to volunteer their professional skills at about 200 nonprofits nationwide. Common Impact, a nonprofit founded in 2000, now serves as a bustling switchboard connecting young professionals at for-profit companies with local nonprofits that need their services. Employers are finding that sponsoring community service is a win-win deal: Not only does service boost recruitment and reduce turnover, but it also teaches valuable leadership skills that young workers can bring back to their regular jobs.

Implications for the Public Sector

Public-sector workplaces can be a good home for team-oriented Millennials. According to OPM, 84 percent of federal employees agree that "the people I work with cooperate to get the job done," four points higher than the private sector. It suits Millennials that public employers are less likely than private employers to foster competition among colleagues and more likely to stress standardization and group projects.

Unfortunately, government agencies often fall short in providing the networking and communications technology that actually enables Millennials to work in groups. Social media sites, streaming video, wikis, and blogs are often discouraged or even prohibited by public agencies, which cite the need to protect secure information—and in any case are plagued by slow technological procurement and a rule-bound culture. Many government middle managers also resist attempts to implement networking technologies in the belief that, in hierarchical agencies, controlling access to information enhances their authority. There are some encouraging signs. In 2006, the CIA launched "Intellipedia," a Wikipedia-inspired forum for intelligence analysts to share information. Soon after, the State Department launched "Diplopedia." Public employers are beginning to understand how such tools can help unleash the potential of today's rising workforce. Yet the shift towards collaborative technologies in the public workplace still has a long way to go.

To energize Millennial teamwork, agencies should consider using Gen Xers as in-person leaders and organizers. Compared to Boomers, Xers are more tech savvy and, of course, they are closer in age to Millennials. The predominance of Boomers and the shortage of Xers in many public agencies can make these workplaces seem staid and unsocial to today's young hires. Bringing in or reassigning charismatic Xers to manage Millennial hires will help galvanize their team ethic and project a youthful and purposeful image to new applicants.

On a broader level, Millennials' unprecedented attraction to public-sector careers is driven in large part by their desire to help the community. On Universum's *Ideal Employer Survey*, students ranked "Government/Public Service" first out of 46 industry options. And when asked why they might be interested in a government career, nearly 75 percent cited "opportunity to make a difference" and "ability to help people."

Public employers should leverage Millennials' new community focus by playing up the "helping" aspect of government careers. During the Gen-X youth era, many agencies stressed the marketplace competitiveness of their employment packages (such as individual pay and advancement) more than their public mission. In the Millennial youth era, this trend is reversing. Public employers at all levels are attracting new recruits with a message of community service. For example, in 2004 the Social Security Administration launched a new recruitment slogan: "Make a difference in people's lives and in your own." Vermont's state government also recently launched the Millennial-friendly slogan, "Great jobs. An even greater purpose."

With their strong attachment to parents and tight circles of school friends, Millennials are particularly drawn to helping their local communities—something state and local government employers can use to their advantage. When asked what factors influenced their choice of employer, 41 percent of Millennials in state governments said " location" was a key factor, versus 35 percent in the private sector. State and local public employers in particular should reach out to local students and emphasize the opportunity to impact their home community.

Millennials' team orientation will also have important implications for public policy.

For decades, policy makers have assumed that young people naturally resist any sense of obligation to government—but in the years ahead, it will be older Gen Xers and Boomers tuning out the call to serve, while younger citizens line up behind community initiatives. As more Millennials come of age, policy

Millennials and
National Public Service

Responses from a nationwide poll of 18- to 29-year olds:

Government isn't doing enough to encourage young people to enter public service	
Agree	33%
Disagree	7%
Strongly support the creation of a national Public Service Academy	
All	88%
Democrat	86%
Republican	92%
Independent	89%

SOURCE: United States Public Service Academy (2008)

makers can expect them to become a political powerhouse. Whether looking for voters, organizers, or volunteers, forget older adults and start targeting the young. In labor relations, expect a wave of self-organizing young people that may be entirely independent of the older union leadership.

Policy makers should give this generation opportunities to become fully involved in public service, perhaps by broadening in-school service learning, creating a summer-service "rite of passage," and using large-scale service programs like AmeriCorps and Teach for America to help fill positions in shortage professions. Particularly if the economy remains weak, a large young-adult volunteer corps can help local organizations fill gaps caused by budget cuts and layoffs.

Government agencies should tap into Millennials' large social networks to coordinate support and group action on a wide range of initiatives. Community agencies can publish online a list of public agendas (painting schools, cleaning playgrounds, reducing graffiti) and ask citizens to organize plans to accomplish those goals. Agencies can even offer certificates for completing such projects and promote them as professional, skill-building opportunities. Public leaders may be surprised at how quickly Millennials will respond, organize themselves into teams, and get things done.

10
Conventional

"While media portrayals often depict youth as irresponsible, lazy, and morally corrupt, our study offers a different perspective, in which youth… make responsible choices and refrain from risky behaviors, demonstrate a strong sense of civic commitment and engagement, and are strongly influenced by parents, families, and religion when confronting moral dilemmas."

— *GOOD INTENTIONS SURVEY OF MILLENNIAL ATTITUDES,*
GIRL SCOUT RESEARCH INSTITUTE (2009)

"Older generations that couldn't wait to proclaim their independence can't comprehend this generation's need for parental guidance and influence."

— *HR MAGAZINE* (2007)

Conventional

When today's young employees were in elementary school, the best-selling children's book of all time, *Harry Potter and the Sorcerer's Stone,* gave the world a glimpse at the more ordered side of the Millennial Generation. Everyone recalls the image of Harry in movie ads: a bright-eyed boy in glasses looking very proper in a uniform dress shirt and tie. This primness resonated with Millennial children, who were themselves struggling to excel and have fun in an increasingly structured institutional environment. Like his Millennial readers, Harry and his friends are always working towards grades, exams, deadlines and contests. Yet few of them feel alienated or oppressed. They accept their mission—to defend their teachers and parents against the forces of chaos—without complaint. It is enough to save the system, excel within it, and happily fit in.

When Millennials are asked about their ultimate life goals, the very *ordinariness* of their answers often surprises Gen Xers and (especially) Boomers. When surveyed, they say that "balance" is important and that they want to become friendly neighbors, good citizens, and reliable friends. In recent years, a record share of collegians (according to UCLA's *The American Freshman* survey) have been saying they want to get married and have kids. They trust big institutions like government more than older people do. Roughly half are sometimes bothered by too much sex and violence on TV. Ask them about how they would rather spend their time, and they'll say with their family. They think joining the middle class is a desirable—if today sometimes elusive—aspiration.

Millennials cannot be described as "conservative" according to the usual political or ideological definitions of that word. The Millennial commitment to "the family," for example, includes actual families of every variety, from gay couples to single-parents. The term "conventional" fits this generation better.

They're not seeking to return to some bygone decade. Instead, they want to re-craft and update time-tested values and use them to make everything work better in twenty-first century America.

As this new crop of youth acquires "skills" and makes the round of internships, carefully cultivating qualifications that will fulfill recruiters' expectations, employers seldom reflect on how different this approach to the future is from what they and their peers were doing in their own youth. Today's young workers are not like the free-spirited young Boomers who defied the system and burned to define their own paths, nor like the free-agent young Gen Xers who ignored the system and kept a sharp eye out to seize opportunities.

Millennials would rather do without the defiance and the risk. They want to plan and build their careers step by step. They put an increasing premium on stable work-life balance—which, as we will explain, is more accurately described as a work-life blend. They are attracted to workplaces with clear structure and big-brand clout—though their need to make a personal connection makes them also look for informal, casual settings. They are moving away from the first-break-all-the-rules workstyle in favor of carefully regulated environments where everyone is accountable to the organization and feels close to the group.

Implications for Educators

Before they even begin to advise Millennials about their career choices, Gen-X and Boomer educators need to step back, reexamine the lessons they have drawn from their own lifecycle experiences, and make sure they are not blindly projecting those lessons on their students. When today's educators were themselves in school, G.I. and Silent career counselors told them to get their degrees, follow the rules, and march down the path to a stable job and a house in the suburbs. Many of these students responded by doing just the opposite. They traveled to far-flung places, "found themselves" through unusual vocations, started their own businesses, and took entrepreneurial risks. Many years later, they assume the same impulses motivate today students—and can't imagine most young people wanting to plan how they will scale the rungs of a big institution's career ladder.

But they're mistaken. They were never like today's youth and today's youth will never be like them: That's what happens from one generation to another. When Millennials look up at their elders today, in fact, they often draw very different lifecycle lessons—such as how *not* to end up in midlife, after decades of impulsive choices, with poor pay, few benefits, no retirement plan, little job security, and weak ties to their neighbors. Gen-X and Boomer job counselors often tell today's students reassuringly that it's OK to chart your own path and that a couple of career failures and dead ends can be a growth experience. But hearing that, the students don't feel reassured. They feel dread, and many tune out. What the counselors are saying is not exactly wrong. It's just not the approach these students find helpful.

To connect better with Millennials, educators should think more conventionally. They need to respect the aspirations of today's youth for a career (and matching lifestyle) offering regularity, steady advancement, security, safety nets, an affordable home, and a close community. Millennials want to join, identify with, and take pride in the organizations associated with their careers: their company, agency, foundation, union, profession, or trade. They speak the vocabulary of service—words like commitment, duty, honor, responsibility, and mission—without irony.

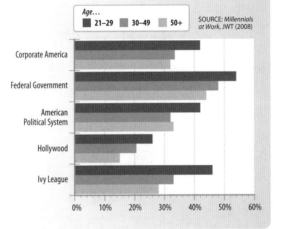

◄ **Figure 25**

'How much respect would you say you have for... ?' Share Saying They Have Respect, by Age

Educators should understand that most Millennials don't want to pursue extreme life goals. According to the *LifeCourse-Chartwells College Student Survey*, today's college students overwhelmingly agree (68 to 8 percent) that a "very" or "extremely" important reason to go to college is "to become a more well-rounded person." Millennials want to demonstrate that they are worthy of their work credential or title. And in a very conventional fashion, they want to celebrate the attainment of such credentials with ceremonies in front of their peers (a habit, beginning in grade school, which explains all the ribbons, stars, trophies, and certificates stored away in their bedrooms).

Most of all, educators need to accept the Millennials' insistence on having an explicit strategy to get them to where they want to go. They want step-by-step guidance on how to prepare and plan. They want to know all the timetables and costs and deadlines and options. And once they get the information, they won't want to evaluate it alone. In conventional Millennial fashion, they will want to evaluate it together with all of the trusted people in their lives—most of all, their parents, but also their close relatives, teachers, counselors, and friends.

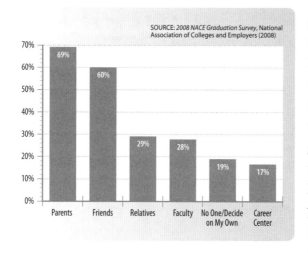

Figure 26 ▶

Asked of College Seniors Looking for Employment: *Who do you review a job offer with?*

SOURCE: *2008 NACE Graduation Survey*, National Association of Colleges and Employers (2008)

To appreciate the generational shift over time, recall how young Boomer actors and musicians once started their careers: They told their parents to go to hell, and they set up shop on their own. Now look at today's young Millennial stars (from Hilary Duff and Amanda Bynes to the Olsen twins and Miley Cyrus) who launched their careers surrounded, trained, prepped, and groomed by their families every step of the way. The same youth music that once signified the desire to rebel against adults now signifies the quest for their approval.

Because many Boomer and Gen-X parents are anything but traditional, Millennials can be torn between competing conventional ideals—following in their parents' footsteps, or pursuing a path in the mainstream of their own generation. This raises dilemmas that Boomer and Gen-X educators may have trouble recognizing. Imagine for instance a student with an entrepreneur mom ditching a business major in favor of public health or officer candidate school.

Or imagine a young student whose dad works in construction enrolling in a full-time community college program but feeling guilty that he's not helping with his family's business. In both cases, the Millennial wants to make the approved choice, yet still feels torn.

Everyone agrees that a close bond between parent and child is usually a good thing. Yet most people also agree that sometimes this close bond is a problem. Educators are noticing a rising share of students who lack initiative and enthusiasm because they are preparing for a career only to please their parents. What can counselors do when there is just *too much* parenting going on?

Rule one: Do not confront the parent. The closer the parent is to his or her child, the more that strategy is likely to backfire. Rule two: Use indirection. Explain to the parent that a change of pace and a different type of educational experience—a summer program abroad, a service-learning semester, or a gap year—might actually rekindle the student's enthusiasm toward the intended goal. Then urge the student to branch out and try a broader spectrum of electives, extracurriculars, or internships. The ultimate goal is to push the student into an activity that will "click." Off-campus temp work (not the usual résumé-stuffing internships) can be an excellent way to push unmotivated college students through a wide variety of roles and settings and teach them what real paid work feels like, day to day. Colleges and training institutes would benefit greatly by partnering with local contract labor firms and packaging a structured program.

"Conventional," it must be stressed, is an adjective that better describes this generation's life aspirations than its as-yet acquired social habits. Indeed, if head-shaking older generations know anything for sure about Millennials, it is their ignorance of so many ordinary conventions of proper workplace behavior. Fifty-somethings talk about it all the time: Today's young people don't know how to dress properly, how to eat properly, how to shake hands and talk on the phone, or how to speak concisely, politely, and without serial repetition of the word "like." Many Millennials are guilty as charged, and for a simple reason—Boomer and Gen-X parents never taught their Millennial children these so-called "soft skills," whether because the parents rejected them, forgot them, or never cared much about them.

Dressing Down Millennials

It's no secret that Boomers, and yes, even Xers, criticize Millennials for how they dress in the workplace. Managers complain about young employees who clomp down office hallways in flip-flops, glue iPods to their ears, and sport inappropriate tattoos and piercings. Such behaviors, they claim, show a lack of respect for authority and for office norms.

Not true. What such behaviors actually show is not a lack of respect, but rather a lack of knowledge. Today's youth typically dress inappropriately on the job because their Boomer parents never taught them about corporate norms—and employers, for all their complaints, are rarely specific about what they require.

Millennials who dress casually in the workplace believe they are following the norms of their elders, not flouting them. After all, Millennials have been seeing older generations dress down for as long as they can remember. Many saw Boomers pioneer the casual dress movement in the 1980s, wearing their famous Levi's to the office. Nearly all of them saw Xers take casual to a whole new level in the 1990s, with Silicon-Valley executives running strategy meetings in sandals and t-shirts. Interviews with grungy tech superstars now stream on wsj.com, and images of tattered CEOs monopolize the covers of *Wired* and *Fortune*.

In fact, the social rules governing proper dress and behavior have now become very complicated—with a lot more edginess allowable in some settings than in others. (Is your office in San Francisco or Columbus? Is your industry media or banking? Are you meeting with creatives or with stockholders?) Boomers and Xers may assume that Millennials understand these rules, but often they do not. Most simply do what older generations did when they were young (and the rules were much simpler): They look at older images of success and say, OK, that must be the norm.

Boomers and Xers also assume that every youth generation pushes the envelope on dress, as they once did. But most Millennials aren't pushing, and many are self-consciously adjusting Xer-pioneered fashion trends to fit their own more mainstream style. Clothing colors have shifted from black to bright. Prep, once out, is now in. The signature urban look is less about open-collared attitude and more about buttoned-down success. Compared to Xers at the same age, a slightly larger share of Millennials are getting tattoos—but the new Millennial trend is to opt for smaller tattoos and to hide them beneath clothing, with 70 percent saying their tattoos are not usually visible.

Even before they entered the workplace, Millennials easily adjusted their personal style to fit institutional norms. Starting in the 1990s, large numbers of public K-12 schools began instituting formal dress codes—or even school uniforms—in an effort to improve behavior and achievement. Few Millennials ever objected. Most came to expect dress codes or uniforms as a standard feature of any well-ordered institutional environment.

Today, this uniformed generation actually expresses more support than older generations for conventional workplace attire.

According to a recent JWT survey, 67 percent of Millennial respondents agree that "a formal appearance at the workplace is important for career success," compared to 54 percent of forty-somethings and 56 percent of fifty-plus respondents. Millennials are even willing to train in advance on how to dress for success in the workplace: The College of Business at Illinois State University recently implemented a dress code for classes, to no complaints from the student body.

Boomer and Xer managers, pay attention:

- If you believe that the dress and behavior of young workers is sometimes inappropriate, treat it as a knowledge and training issue, not an attitude issue.

- Announce to everyone exactly what the problem is and why. Draft a specific code on dress or a specific do-and-don't list on behavior.

- Set up workshops (with a mastery "star" or "certificate") if concrete instruction is required.

- Be fair and use common sense in tracking compliance, and make sure that you and other older workers are meeting the same standards.

The improved conduct will soon become second nature, and it is unlikely you will encounter any significant pushback from Millennials along the way. Some may even thank you.

Millennials' genuine unfamiliarity with politeness norms points to a key difference between them and their parents. When Boomers dressed down on campus in the 1970s, they typically knew the difference between dressing up or down—G.I. and Silent parents lectured them about it all the time. Their casualness was therefore an intentional statement about their disrespect for authority. Today's Millennials have no such intention. When (to cite a typical incident) members of Northwestern University's women's lacrosse team showed up at the White House in 2005 wearing flip-flops, the media decried their disrespect of the Presidential office—much to the astonishment of the young women, who had no idea they were being rude. They had grown up wearing flip-flops nearly everywhere.

Millennials, unlike their parents when young, appreciate the importance of politeness norms and sincerely wish that they could better learn what these are. In a 2008 NACE survey, 67 percent of Millennials agreed that "formal appearance on the job is important for workplace success"—versus only 55 percent of workers over 40. The problem is that today's youth don't understand what phrases like "formal appearance" really mean. Where are they supposed to find out? Watching the MTV Video Awards? Every time a college offers a credible curriculum on learning social skills in the workplace, the course is mobbed and long waiting lists appear.

To a modest extent, educators are catching on. Some high schools, community colleges, and universities are beginning to offer courses that teach students everything from how to address a formal letter to which fork to use at a formal business meal. George Mason University now offers a "Professionalism at Work" course that covers what clothing is too casual, how to write appropriate business emails, and when it's acceptable to listen to an iPod while working. Towson University fields seminars where local recruiters give students pointers on proper ways to shake hands, make eye contact, and follow up with email or phone calls. At High Point University, first-year students are actually required to take a "Life Skills" course that includes lessons in business etiquette, time management, financial literacy, and communication conventions.

Boomers often resist teaching rote behavior, preferring to "dig deeper" and transform feelings and attitudes (pragmatic Gen Xers have far less trouble).

Boomer educators will have to shift this mindset. They need to become less moralistic and more practical. Millennials have no problem respecting the authority of the White House or their employer—they just need to be taught how exactly to show that respect.

Implications for Employers

Every generation finds a new and different way to reconcile work life with personal life, and the Millennial Generation is no exception. Employers are still trying to figure this one out.

Consider the progression of "work-life balance" over three generations. With their zealous youth crusades and obsessive quest for meaningful careers, Boomers have been famously *unbalanced* about the vocations they have they pursued. They are more likely than other generations to describe their work as a "calling" or themselves as "workaholic." They are attracted to solo challenges and willingly bring their work lives into their "home" or private life. For Boomers, to paraphrase an old '60s slogan, "the professional is personal." Gen Xers entered the workplace with a new bottom-line outlook: Extract the maximum advantages from work (pay, bonuses, free time) with the minimum cost to your personal life. Gen Xers popularized the concept of work-life balance, seeking flexible hours and telecommuting to get the most out of their personal lives. The professional isn't personal—it's just neutral. The winners are those who, through luck or skill, make it all pay off to their best advantage.

Millennials are coming on board with yet a new set of priorities. Unlike Boomers, few Millennials see the individual pursuit of career success as their primary path to life satisfaction. Surveys show that they are far less likely than Boomers were at the same age to agree with statements like "the most important things that happen in my life involve work," and "life is worth living only when people get absorbed in work." They are even less likely to agree with Boomers who use income as a proxy for career success. Three out of four Millennials say that how they spend their time is more important than how much money they make, according to a recent Harris Interactive poll.

Yet unlike Gen Xers, Millennials refuse to regard "work" and "life" as separate and mutually hostile priorities, allowing no really happy outcome. As

Ryan Healy, a Millennial founder of the blog "Employee Evolution: The Voice of Millennials at Work" explains, "'work/life balance' implies a dichotomy that Millennials find distasteful.... This whole notion of needing to separate work and life implies that your career, which takes up 75 percent of your day, is something you simply try to get through so you can go home and do what you really enjoy for the other 25 percent. What a terrible way to live."

Millennials are pioneering a more optimistic and integrative solution: a work-life *blend*, in which work and life intermingle throughout the day. Their approach reverses the original Boomer solution in a conventional new direction. Because Millennials expect to have a comfortable, committed, and mutually trusting relationship with the institutions that employ them, they willingly bring their "home" or private lives back into their work lives. For today's rising generation, the personal is becoming professional.

Already, employers are noticing this shift. Young employees are using cell phones, instant messenger, and social networking sites to keep in touch with peers and parents during the workday. They fill their cubicles with personal paraphernalia, lounge after hours with coworkers in workplace common spaces, and generally make themselves at home in the workplace. Some employers criticize all this personal chatter and casualness as an unproductive distraction—but Millennials see it differently. They view friends and family as constructive supporters of their work who should not be walled off during the day. They want to trust their employers and commit to them as whole people, in a comfortable environment that lets them bring together their personal and professional strengths. And, in return, they want employers to trust them to balance (or blend) their personal lives with effective work habits.

Some of America's most successful corporations are willing to accept this new Millennial deal. Consider the headquarters (nicknamed "campuses") of Google, Starbucks, Apple, Nike, eBay, or Disney. These employers encourage young employees to think of the company workspace as their own personal living space, complete with informal coffee bars, video-game corners, and living-room-like offices. Google even encourages young workers to set aside a certain percentage of their work time for personal pursuits. In so doing, these corporations persuade the best and the brightest of today's rising generation to dedicate most of their waking hours on behalf of stockholders. Not a bad deal. What's more, most of these Millennials aren't putting in heavy schedules just so they can cash in and quit after a few years (which has been the Gen-X norm), and they are less likely to burn out since there is room for personal time. Many Millennials will gladly keep up this level of commitment to the same company for their entire career.

To be sure, not all companies can build extravagant surroundings to facilitate the Google-campus version of work-life blending. But most employers can easily find effective ways to make young hires to feel "at home" while at work—like providing comfy places for coworkers to gather at lunch and allowing personal communications with friends and family during the workday. Employers can also make them feel literally at home by offering the kind of flexible hours and telecommuting options that have been so attractive to Generation X. But there is one big difference. For Gen Xers, the whole point of flextime—so common now in consulting and professional services—is to minimize plugged-in "face time" and maximize unplugged personal time. That's not the point for feedback-craving Millennials. For them, employers need to find new ways to make young workers feel like part of a structured community even when at home, from scheduled phone check-ins to *Second-Life*-style virtual meetings where employees and managers gather at a virtual location. Wherever Millennials work, they want to integrate their lives into a community that knows them, needs them, and looks after them.

The quest for structure is a key Millennial trait. On a day-to-day level they prefer a scheduled work culture with clear expectations, mirroring the rule-bound world they have lived in from kindergarten on up. Employers should provide detailed job descriptions where everything is clearly defined, including the boundaries between superiors and subordinates, department responsibilities, and individual, department, and corporate goals. Formal job titles, which went out of fashion in Gen-X-style "flat" organizations, may make a comeback. Performance reviews, scheduled promotions, detailed project timelines, and other formalized procedures are almost certain to grow in popularity.

Millennials not only want to adopt a conventional workstyle, they want to join a company that openly embodies conventional values. In the Gen-X youth era, businesses went out of their way to project an edgy, individualistic employer brand. Recall the slogan, "At Southwest, freedom begins with me," or the famous U.S. Army tagline, "Be all you can be." In the Millennial era, successful employers are targeting the mainstream and emphasizing what is honest, upright, and time-tested. Recruiting ads are beginning to use phrases like "timeless commitment," "tradition of excellence," and "cornerstone of the industry"— phrases that would have fallen flat with young Gen Xers. Consider what Target now announces about its workplace: "Our goals are clear, challenging, and met through teamwork." Or Campbell's: "Character. Competence. Teamwork." Or Whole Foods: "We also look for well-rounded human beings who will help build our locations into profitable and beneficial members of their communities." When targeting Millennials, lose the edge. Instead, emphasize deeply held traditions, unchanging values, and a community (or national) reputation.

The employer message is not credible, of course, unless it is backed by employer behavior. Millennials want to believe in big institutions and are much impressed by managers who, in their character and judgment, conduct themselves as exemplars. According to a 2006 NACE survey, two of the top three criteria Millennial college students use to evaluate employers are the integrity of the organization and ethical business practices. In another recent survey, Millennial workers rated working with a boss they can respect and learn from as the most important aspect of their work environment. With supervisors they trust, Millennials want to be friendly and relaxed—but not intimate. They're fine about dressing down off-duty or using first names—but don't try to "friend" them on Facebook or share personal-life secrets (which are far more likely to traumatize them rather than you).

Like educators, employers will have to cope with new hires who are unfamiliar with many "soft" workplace skills, from formal communication to acceptable attire. Don't waste energy blaming them for the social rituals their Boomer and Gen-X parents never taught them or for the employment experience they never had. Instead, take advantage of their eagerness to learn what's expected of them and their desire to emulate older adults they trust.

Some employers address the soft-skill gap with a creative flair. Merrill Lynch brought Prada stylists to a women's dress-for-success night at the University

"Appropriate" Technology

Share agreeing that...	Workers' Age	
	Under 28	44 to 60
Personal digital assistants (PDAs) and mobile phones contribute to a decline in proper workplace etiquette.	46%	**68%**
Using laptops or PDAs during meetings is distracting	49%	**68%**
Using laptops or PDAs during meetings is efficient	**35%**	17%
It is acceptable to blog about work-related issues	**41%**	28%
It is appropriate to "friend" a client on a social networking site	**47%**	24%
It is appropriate to "friend" a colleague on a social networking site	**76%**	38%

SOURCE: *LexisNexis Technology Gap Survey* (2008)

of Pennsylvania. (Tips: avoid bright red nail polish and wear closed-toed shoes). Goldman Sachs sponsors workshops at more than fifty schools, covering résumé-writing and workplace comportment. (Tips: always have a short pitch on your current project prepared in case you land in the elevator with the CEO). Other employers take this a step further with training seminars covering everything from phone etiquette and memo-writing style to appropriate ways to approach a supervisor or interact with a client. Major Wall Street firms are enrolling their new employees in formal business communications courses. PRC, a customer relationship company based in Fort Lauderdale, Florida, offers employees a course titled Business Communications and Writing to wean young workers off of text messaging shorthands like "btw" and "imo."

As educators have already discovered, this generation responds well to hands-on, interactive learning in a formal setting (especially if they're given "credit"). Employers can even offer young hires certificates or some other mark of completion, which this generation always appreciates. Like their hero Harry Potter, Millennials are used to being officially recognized for the good deeds they accomplish.

Implications for the Public Sector

In some ways, public-sector jobs are the perfect fit for conventional Millennials: stable, structured, and big-brand, with long traditions and an enduring purpose in the community. Yet most government employers aren't leveraging these strengths—or even regard them as weaknesses. A Booze Allen Hamilton report found that few government agencies discuss the mission, vision, or culture of the agency when orienting new workers.

To target today's youth, public employers need to begin playing up their conventional strengths. The armed services alone have figured it out, perhaps because they target such a young age bracket and thus encountered Millennials the earliest. Over the last decade, they have been jettisoning their Xer-focused, '90s-era message of danger, adventure, and personal gain with a more Millennial message of tradition, discipline, and civic purpose. The U.S. Army Web site includes an award-winning video game that teaches players what daily life in the Army is really like. The Marine Corps officer recruiting Web site proclaims: "Before there was a nation, there were Marines." The National Guard launched a new "Citizen. Soldier." recruitment campaign. Some local public employers are also ahead of the curve. The Las Vegas police force Web site showcases its "vision, values, mission, and goals," including "I CARE" (Integrity, Courage, Accountability, Respect for people, and Excellence).

Like corporations, agencies can attract Millennials by emphasizing a structured work culture with clear expectations, a hierarchy of roles, and specific goals for each individual and department. The U.S. State Department's recruiting site includes a chart of the agency structure and an alphabetical listing of each office with explanations of their roles and internal organizations.

Once new employees are on board, agencies should continue to highlight mission and tradition—which most have in abundance. At orientation, provide a copy of your mission statement for employees to keep on their desks. Have senior executives discuss the agency's history, the importance of its work, and how new hires fit into its future. NASA, for example, schedules special tours for new employees in which the agency's mission is explained and demonstrated.

In certain other ways, government jobs are a less-than-perfect fit for conventional Millennials. Agencies' formal office rules and inflexible working hours impede the homey workplace atmosphere and work-life "blending" Millennials prize. According to Universum's *Ideal Employer Survey*, students see "lack of control over working hours" as one of the major weaknesses of government careers. When asked what employers can do to retain them, nearly one-third of young public employees chose "offer flexible working hours," and one-quarter chose "promote better work-life balance"—both significantly higher than for their peers in the private sector. To compete for top talent, agencies must do more to enable work-life blending. This means instituting flexible hours, allowing employees to keep in touch with parents and peers throughout the day, and creating comfortable common spaces where employees can make themselves at home after hours.

Millennials' conventionality will also have important implications for public policy.

For many decades, legislators have promulgated workplace rules and regulations by appealing to older institutional leaders, whom they view as more rule abiding than the younger rank and file. This will change. Over the next decade, the youth workforce will be increasingly seen as more rule abiding, while the older leadership will gain a reputation for defying convention. Policy makers will find that today's cadre of young professionals can play a special role in policing and reporting violations in the workplace. This will work better, in fact, than asking older managers to enforce the rules from the top down. Community leaders can also target calls for citizen monitoring and enforcement to the young (as with the successful Census 2000 program that targeted K–12 students to improve response rates).

Millennials will make some rules harder to police. This generation's work-life blending will blur the line being "punched in" and "punched out." Hourly work-limits may become harder to regulate, requiring legislators to rethink the traditional employer-employee relationship.

Millennials' attachment to their parents, and the resulting resurgence of the extended family, could generate dramatic and positive fiscal dividends. Perhaps the greatest fiscal challenge America faces over the next half-century is funding expensive entitlements like Medicare and Social Security while the massive Boomer Generation moves fully into retirement. If a much higher share of

Boomer elders live with or near their grown children, legislators may be able to cut the cost of these programs without affecting retiree living standards. Long-term care facilities could be scaled back in favor of less costly at-home care. Closer lifelong parent-child relationships could also help families carry out an array of important social functions now often served by government programs, from finding jobs and daycare for children to providing an emergency economic safety net. The fiscal dividends generated by a stronger extended family could then be used to invest in other public purposes, or given back to young families in the form of tax cuts.

In politics, as in the workplace, the Millennials will seek a new atmosphere of well-behaved professionalism. Surveys show that today's youth feel more strongly than older generations that policy debates should have a lot less attitude and a lot more informed discussion. The slogan of Millennial-run youth advocacy group Youth Entitlement Summit sums up this new attitude: "Governance, not politics."

11
Pressured

"Members of this generation—many of whom have had their young lives planned out for them to the last detail by their overachieving Boomer parents—also want something else: a clear career path laid out before them. They already know where they're going. And they expect you to make sure they get there."

— *HUMAN RESOURCE EXECUTIVE* MAGAZINE (2008)

"They want to have a very clear expectation of what they have to do to succeed. Like a 'roadmap.' They seem to be thinking, 'if I take this job, what's my next job.' They want to be able to predict the future."

— **STEVE CANALE**, RECRUITING AND STAFFING SERVICES MANAGER, GE (2008)

Pressured

According to our *LifeCourse-Chartwells College Student Survey*, both college undergraduates and their parents agree by an overwhelming (roughly six-to-one) margin that kids today spend more time planning for the future than their parents did at the same age. The majority of today's high school students say they have detailed five- and ten-year plans for their future. Most have given serious thought to college financing, degrees, salaries, and employment trends. For Millennials coming of age, the heat is on and the pressure is rising—as it has been throughout most of their lives.

During the 1990s, the sale of student day planners soared from one million to fifty million as kids coped with mounting schoolwork, more frequent testing, and greater urgency about getting into college. Since 2000, digital technology has inundated them with an incessant stream of phone calls, emails, and instant messages. Throughout their childhood, time diary logs have pointed to steadily fewer hours per week spent sleeping or engaging in open-ended play. The pressure continues as these heavily scheduled young people enter the workplace. They worry if they have made the right choices and gotten the right preparation—and if they have prepared soon enough or well enough.

The growing Millennial focus on long-term goals represents a major reversal from the trend set by older generations. Young Boomers famously rebelled against pressure from societal expectations. They refused to attach themselves to permanent life plans, insisting that they "find themselves" first. Young Gen Xers were seldom bothered by long-term goals because, by then, youth simply assumed that institutions could not be trusted to keep long-term promises. The Gen-X youth doctrine was to take risks, seize moments, and rebound from mistakes.

But today's Millennials are subscribing to a new credo: Success in life is the predictable reward for effort plus planning. They are often amazed by the haphazard life stories of older adults. They wonder if having too many options at age 22 leads to too many roommates at age 32. And maybe if Mom and Dad had been profile-matched online, they'd still be together. Come to think of it, why didn't Dad start worrying about his retirement income *before* age 55?

As students, Millennials are looking for well-marked paths. As job seekers, they seek continuity over time. Rather than having to change from one employer to the next, they would prefer a single, trusted employer who will change for them. A growing share of high school seniors report that they plan to hold only one or two jobs within their first ten years of employment. According to the annual Universum survey, graduating college seniors are identifying a steadily growing list of preferred long-term benefits, from retirement plans to health insurance for dependents.

In the workplace, this generation flourishes under daily pressure to get things done. Far more than their parents at the same age, they have grown used to it. What demoralizes them is not pressure *per se*, but rather situations in which their best effort under pressure does not ensure success. What haunts them is uncertainty and risk: not knowing what a supervisor expects or how they will be evaluated, having no idea how well they are meeting workplace standards, or not knowing what their next career step will be. Employers are reporting a rising share of young workers who prefer weekly or even daily feedback to ensure their work is on track.

Implications for Educators

In school, today's future-oriented Millennials feel more pressure than ever before to pick a career path early and plan accordingly. A growing share of students are surrounded by tutors, coaches, and hands-on parents helping them choose a specialized direction and avoid "wasting time" anywhere else—and those students who aren't subjected to all the extra adult pressure are feeling rising competitive pressure from those who are. Some employers are now asking to see high school transcripts, test scores, and even attendance records as early evidence of good conduct. Teens are crowding to take AP courses, AP tests, and "practice" PSAT tests at ever-earlier ages. Across the board, postsecondary and professional schools report being deluged with email and phone queries about "exactly what I have to do" to make it. The recessionary lull in new hiring is turning up the heat even more on college and professional admissions.

The response of most educational institutions thus far can only be described as woefully inadequate. Just over half of all high school students report that no one at the school has given them *any help at all* in career or college planning— and nearly all report that their own parents seem much more knowledgeable and focused on their future options. Similarly, at many colleges, the "placement" office is not taken seriously. According to a recent study of middle school through college students by the National Association of Manufacturers, "students expressed palpable frustration with what they viewed as significant pressure to become successful in their careers on the one hand, and the near total lack of guidance or career-planning tools on the other." A 2007 study of the California State University system concluded that too many undergrads "leave college still wondering what to do when they 'grow up.'"

Apparently, many K–12 systems believe their only objective is to "graduate" classes—which helps explains why bright and ambitious students continue to drop out soon after they reach the next level. Many four-year public and small liberal-arts colleges believe that career planning is somehow beneath their lofty mission—which helps explain why enrollment at community and for-profit colleges has been growing so much faster. All schools complain about insufficient funding for career planning. But whether the funding is large or small, schools rarely think carefully enough about how it's spent. Many educators simply have not acknowledged that a new generation of students is demanding something different from their institutions. In the years to come, as late-wave Millennials begin to show up with their bottom line-focused Gen-X parents, these demands will become overpowering.

To meet these demands, educators should think big and integrate hands-on career guidance and comprehensive life-skills training into the core mission of their institution. To carry out this mission, they should develop a formal career services curriculum that adds graduated structure to the task of settling on a career and finding the best first job. Students should regard each year of their education, from middle school through college graduation, as a step along a directed learning path leading to career launch, with special courses and workshops teaching basic workplace skills: how to locate a job, how to get hired for a job, and what to do on the job. Ideally, the path would dovetail with economic and financial literacy modules on the one hand and with project-based and profession-simulating teaching styles on the other.

This curriculum need not be difficult or expensive to implement. Middle and high schools can leverage Web-based learning tools like *knowhow2go.com* and a growing number of state "career pathway" programs that break down the hopelessly vast work world into a discrete number of directions and stages. Small colleges can get help by contracting out to career-counseling firms, many of which can set up training modules for specialized job-search skills from résumé-writing to interview protocol. All colleges should establish firm connections with local employer networks (since nearly all colleges, even top-tier liberal-arts colleges, have a regional focus). Schools that do all this right will get a reputation boost and earn the heartfelt gratitude of both students and parents.

For any student planning to pan out in reality, entire regions must start making brutally candid assessments of the alignment between their middle school, high school, and postsecondary levels—to make sure all those pathways and stepping stones actually go somewhere. Today's forward-planning students fear nothing worse than working as hard as they are asked to at one level of school only to discover they are unprepared for the next. (According to one survey, 80 percent of college freshmen taking remedial courses are surprised they need extra help.) Because Millennials are more likely than the Gen Xers who preceded them to trust the system and want to advance within it, the consequences of alignment failure are more serious today than they were ten or twenty years ago. "Yesterday's luxury of an education beyond high school has become today's necessity," declared the National Commission on the High School Senior Year. Nearly all Millennials and their parents would agree.

Although alignment requires systemic changes beyond the reach of any single teacher or counselor, some educators and institutions can take leadership roles. Superintendents can propose participating in statewide "K–14" and "K–16" initiatives that aim to align the curricula of high schools and

The "Career Pathways" Movement

In recent years, educators across the country have launched new efforts to create continuous, benchmarked pipelines for students to transition between educational levels (in K–12 and college) and also from school into the workplace. This new movement—often called the "career pathways" movement—encompasses everything from P–16 initiatives and career aptitude tests to career cluster programs and career academies.

All of these programs use two basic strategies: contextualizing learning and improving alignment. Rather than "tracking" academics and vocational learning, the new approach is to integrate academics with guided career exploration and hands-on job skills. Rather than simply ask, "How can we get students to pass this level of school?" the new question is, "How can we make sure they succeed at the next level?" The overall goal is to improve students' internal motivation to achieve by connecting class work to a personal career plan.

It is no surprise that the career pathways movement has gained momentum during the Millennial student era, since it offers just what this generation wants—a long-term plan for achievement that is guided, benchmarked, monitored, and continuous.

How do career pathway programs work? Many states have programs with multiple course "clusters," often paired with internships or job shadowing, that are geared towards different fields of work. There is no common terminology for these programs—some states talk about career "pathways," others about "clusters," "career majors," or "individual learning plans." Whatever the name, most of these clusters are quite broad, with requirements that students try out

a variety of different specialty options. Maryland, for example, has ten career clusters ranging from "Arts, Media, and Communication" to "Health and Biosciences" to "Manufacturing, Engineering, and Technology." As students reach the older K–12 grades, they can narrow their focus and develop an individualized career plan—that helps them decide on, and prepare for, the right postsecondary education option.

P-16 initiatives have also been growing in popularity as a way to coordinate statewide pipelines from preschool through college and beyond. Typically, a regional council will convene local education leaders from K–12 systems, universities, and community colleges as well as representatives from local businesses, government, and the community. Like the career cluster programs, these councils go by varying names ("K–16" integrates kindergarten through a bachelor's degree, "P–14" integrates preschool through an associate's degree, etc.), and they have widely varying structures, funding, and influence. Yet their common purpose is to align standards and assessments, smooth transitions between levels, and raise student achievement. Their most common initiatives include setting up data systems that track students from kindergarten

through college and promoting programs that allow students to "dual-enroll" in college while still in high school.

In the years ahead, one important objective will be to bring programs, funding, and best practices to scale nationwide. This is in line with the needs of Millennials, who prefer to measure themselves by national standards (one reason why a rapidly rising share take Advanced Placement exams). The National Association of State Directors of Career Technical Education Consortium has developed a common model of sixteen career clusters, which many states are now beginning to use. Meanwhile, educators and policy makers are trying to develop a nationwide system for forecasting labor market trends and "backward-designing" school curricula so that student skills will match high-demand careers. Such initiatives are already emerging on the state and local level. For example, Michigan's statewide exam to assess the effectiveness of high school curricula now includes components from the ACT WorkKeys, a job-skills assessment broadly used by professionals. Schools nationwide may follow suit and begin measuring the success of their curricula based on a unified set of standards for career readiness.

colleges. Community colleges can take the regional lead in connecting high school curricula to college curricula and college curricula to the expectations of nearby employers. Both high schools and community colleges can offer all students an electronic audit of regional careers for which he or she is qualified both by achievement-to-date and by completion of intended course of study. The National Association of Manufacturers is sponsoring a "National Career Readiness Certificate" that community colleges can issue to graduates who meet several specific standards of employability.

Because Millennials are most likely to make poor choices or drop out when advancing from one school level to the next, schools are also expanding and strengthening their "transition" programs. Most high schools and colleges now have some form of small learning community (perhaps a special seminar, academy, or living-learning program) for incoming freshmen. To keep upper-classmen motivated, many high schools have started dual enrollment programs (like early college and middle college) to plug them into college life. Public colleges in some states are developing summer "bridge" programs to give new high school graduates early remediation and help them organize what they will study in the fall. Even professional schools are trying to fill the gaps—like the UCLA law school, which has just launched a "transition to practice" program for graduates.

Time is another source of pressure for Millennials. Every year longer in school is one year more of steep tuition payments and one year less of income from a salary. The most effective means of easing time pressure is (paradoxically) to inform students earlier about their career options and to encourage them to make earlier choices about their concentration or major field. That way, students can avoid the wasted steps that lead to a financially burdensome fifth or sixth year of college. If students need more time to decide, counselors can advise them to stop out of college entirely for a year, thereby reducing, in many cases, their future debt overhang.

Many Millennials (and, increasingly, their Gen-X parents) see technical colleges and trade schools as a practical alternative to a four-year college—or see two years of community college as a more cost-effective route to a four-year college degree. A few liberal-arts colleges are reintroducing three-year BAs. Meanwhile, students who earn a BA are favoring shorter graduate programs, such as a one-year master's and three-year PhD programs, often abroad. A new two-year professional science master's degree, called PSM, is rising in popularity as a shorter, more career-oriented alternative to natural science PhDs. In the years ahead, other professional fields are likely to follow suit, perhaps with two-year law degrees and six-year MDs.

Career counselors are sometimes personally unsettled by their encounters with this new pressured generation of students. For decades—ever since the Boomer youth era—"student development theory" has emphasized the counselor's role in helping students discover who they really want to be. Yet now counselors are meeting students who want to be told where and how they fit in. They report rising student interest in personalized psychological evaluations (Myers-Briggs Type Indicator, Strong Interest Inventory, ACT WorkKeys, CareerScope) that objectively locate the overlap between interests and skills and identify a life path. Some Boomers lament that we are returning to the "trait and factor" methods of the 1950s, often ridiculed as the "square-peg, square-hole" approach to career counseling. Yes, the times they are a-changin'. For youthful Boomers, the journey was the destination. But today's Millennials are likely to disagree: The destination, they insist, is the destination.

Career Aptitude Tests

Test	Source
Johnson O'Connor Aptitude Tests	Johnson O'Connor Foundation
Pathfinder Career Testing Program	Rockport Institute
Strong Interest Inventory	CPP Inc.
Myers-Briggs Career Aptitude Test	CPP Inc.
The Career Key	Careers Inc.
Keirsey Temperament Sorter	Keirsey.com
Kingdomality Personal Preference Profile	Career Management International
Discover Your Perfect Career Quiz	MonsterTrak
WorkKeys	ACT
CareerScope	Vocational Research Institute

Many Boomers also complain that the rising pressure to focus so early on career plans is unhealthy, and indeed the trend does have its dangers. Students who specialize young may not have the chance to explore a wide range of options and get to know themselves as whole people. College professors complain about the rising number of students who focus only on grades and avoid taking any intellectual risks. As the executive director of Duke University's career services recently observed, students often arrive freshman year "prepackaged and not willing to explore different options." But to get today's students to take chances exploring themselves and their latent talents, educators need to first allay their fears. They'll experiment here and there—but only when they've been assured they can make it on time to life's train station with a stamped and validated ticket.

Implications for Employers

As pressure mounts for students to plan careers earlier, recruiters need to attract the interest of Millennials earlier. In effect, employers need to partner with educational institutions to "grow their own" crop of future employees while they're still students. Many employers reach out to students as early as middle school with mentoring, job-shadowing, and after-school programs. Texas Instruments, Exxon Mobil, Kaiser Permanente, and Boeing support career-driven summer camps to promote kids' interests in fields ranging from aerospace engineering to computer security to pharmacology. Goldman Sachs introduces college students to investment banking at "GS Camp," while Morgan Stanley's summer mentoring program puts high school students to work on its trading floor. Against the abstract background of coursework and theory, students will generally gravitate to a real pipeline to a real career.

Some employers like to support local programs that can grow into a convenient "feeder base" of talent to recruit later on—for example, community hospitals funding and drawing employees from health-care academies at a nearby high school, or utility companies doing the same with nearby engineering academies. This is a smart move. Since Millennials (and their parents) increasingly prefer career opportunities in their own communities, employers often do better by focusing more on their own communities as well. Over time, this local focus tends to create a dominant theme for career academies, institutes, and graduate programs in any one region. The Seattle theme is computers and aerospace, the Los Angeles theme is design and game AI, the New York City theme is finance and law. Employers not only need to grow their own Millennial workers, they need to grow them in their own backyard.

Internship programs offer another key opportunity to connect with pressured students who want to jump-start their careers early and sign on with someone they already know—and who dread the uncertainty of the open labor market. By every measure, internships have been rising steeply in importance for today's young hires. NACE reports that, over the last twenty years, the share of college graduates participating in at least one internship has risen from less than 10 percent to over 80 percent. Meanwhile, the share who get their first full-time post-graduation job through an internship has risen from 5 to 30 percent. Not long ago, summer internships meant mostly busywork or mere exposure to an office environment. Today, both employers and interns are recogniz-

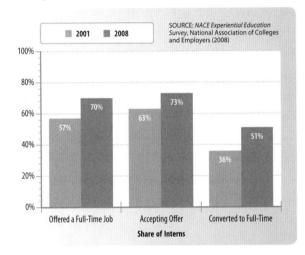

SOURCE: *NACE Experiential Education Survey*, National Association of Colleges and Employers (2008)

◀ **Figure 27**

Internships: National Survey of Over 1,000 Employers

ing their value as pipelines into full-time jobs. According to a recent Michigan State University study, four out of five employers reported that the return on their internship investment was "good to excellent"—making internships the highest-rated recruiting strategy.

The internship screening process often rivals the regular hiring process. Boston Consulting Group gives successful candidates five interviews each, and General Motors administers a timed online test with questions on logic and ethics. What's more, the competition for internships is happening at ever-younger ages as employers try to accommodate the students' ever-longer job-planning horizon. Students who have just entered college make up a rising share of JPMorgan Chase's summer program, and Proctor and Gamble is starting to take interns right after high school graduation.

All of this early résumé-stuffing reflects a deeper trend: the Millennials' rising anxiety over the significance of their "first real job." Employers trying to attract Millennials should remember that today's students—and their parents—often consider their first job as a strategic career launcher, the payoff for all the stress, time, money, and shared ambitions that have gone into the students' lives. Excruciating first-job pressure is leading a growing number of graduates to opt to live at home and remain unemployed, and perhaps even to take temporary unskilled jobs, rather than make the wrong first career move.

Gen Xers were content to hop from one job to another looking for a better break—but Millennials prefer to find the ideal single institutional setting that will support their long-term ambitions. According to a 2008 PricewaterhouseCoopers study of its 3,000 new Millennial hires, just over three-quarters believe they will have only two to five employers during their entire careers. A 2008 survey by New Paradigm came to much the same conclusion: When given the choice, 74 percent of today's young adults said they would rather "work for one or two companies," while only 26 percent preferred to "work for a variety of companies."

To attract the best and the brightest, employers should therefore position themselves as long-term partners in achieving Millennials' career aspirations.

Figure 28 ▶

Asked of U.S. Youth
Age 16 to 29,
in 2007:
*Which would
you rather do?*

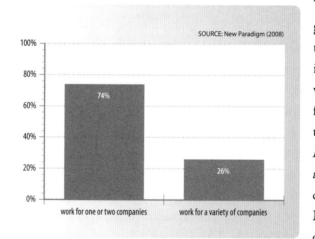

SOURCE: New Paradigm (2008)

Today's students cite growth opportunities as one of the most important factors when choosing their first job, according to MonsterTRAK's *High School Graduate Survey.* Some companies get it. McDonald's, for example, is scrapping its old high-turnover "McJobs" brand (a positive and iconic image back in the Gen-X youth era) and fashioning for itself a new brand as a permanent employer, with TV spots showcasing corporate management careers. Other companies don't get it and continue to lure youth with no-benefit, high-risk jobs. When their new hires soon quit in favor of other opportunities, these companies (ironically) congratulate themselves for having been right all along about the short time horizons of "Generation Y."

To be sure, most Millennials would prefer variety in their careers. But they would be hugely grateful if your company could support their variety of life-long career goals *within* your organization. Large companies can do this by letting young workers rotate positions within the company. A recent Deloitte & Touche survey found that today's students highly value different experiences in their prospective careers. Deloitte responded by introducing an internal career counseling center where its workers can confidentially explore a variety of future options within the company. The center significantly increased employee retention. Govplace in Irvine, California allows new hires to switch roles within the company after a year, also boosting the retention rate. Small companies can easily support career growth and mobility by allowing young workers to participate in a broader range of less specialized tasks. Many Millennials find small businesses attractive for this very reason.

As soon as young hires have settled in, employers should position themselves as a partner in their continuing education and career development, both inside and outside the workplace. IBM is currently launching "learning 401(k)s," where the company makes a 50 percent match to the "lifelong learning accounts" of employees who have been with the company for at least 5 years. Employees can use the money to further their education in order to meet their own professional goals. Many other companies, such as BJC HealthCare, CVS Caremark, and Boeing, offer similar plans. They send a message to today's young workers that their employer supports their careers for the long haul.

On a day-to-day level, employers should monitor the skills of young workers with tight cycles of feedback. As educators have already learned, Millennials do well under pressure so long as they know they are doing their job right or, if they are not, why they are not and exactly what they can do to improve their skills. Annual high-stakes performance reviews with limited feedback in between are simply not enough for Millennials—most of whom want formal evaluations at least once per quarter and at least some informal feedback from their bosses *every day*. A growing number of workplaces are already develop-

How Can Managers Give Effective Feedback to Millennials?

■ **Balance the negative with positive.** Explain not just what the employee is doing wrong, but what aspects of the job she or he is doing right. Millennials need to feel like a valued team member, so emphasize how their work contributes to the group—and how, by making changes, they can contribute even more.

■ **Be specific and behavioral.** Boomers often approach problems holistically or theoretically. But to Millennials, who are far more focused on behavioral "dos" and "don'ts," this comes across as vague, confusing, and negative. Managers should offer detailed, specific instructions about how young employees can adjust their behavior to optimize performance.

■ **Create a co-solution.** Millennials will respond well to having their input sought and valued, even in a conversation about poor performance. Rather than simply dictating, ask if they have any ideas about what they could do differently. Many will have constructive suggestions—and they will be more motivated if they feel they are part of the solution.

■ **Establish a follow-up regimen.** Create a concrete plan for how the employee will get his or her work where it needs to be, with measurable benchmarks along the way. Check in at regular intervals to make sure he or she stays on track with this plan. When you see any specific improvements, let the employee know you noticed and give positive feedback on the spot.

ing Millennial-friendly feedback plans. At PricewaterhouseCoopers, managers have 30 days to respond to employee requests for feedback after a project ends. The accounting firm Clifton Gunderson cut its turnover in half by instituting a high-touch guidance policy. Managers there now schedule at least one formal in-person meeting per week with employees to offer guidance, and touch base informally with them daily.

Millennial recruits will also be impressed by long-term benefits that would never have hit the radar screen of Boomers or Gen Xers at the same age, including retirement plans and even life insurance. A 2005 survey by Diversified Investment Advisors found that 37 percent of Millennials expect to start saving for retirement before they reach age 25, and 46 percent of those already working are already saving. Forty-nine percent say retirement benefits are a very important factor in their job choices, and 70 percent of those who are eligible contribute to their 401(k) plan. According to NACE's 2006 *Graduating Student and Alumni Survey*, one of Millennials' top criteria when choosing an employer is "good benefits package/stability (provides secure future)."

Students rated 401(k) retirement plans third out of twenty job benefits, life insurance fifth, and pension plans eighth.

Again, this rising trend is generational. Young Boomers regarded long-term benefits as a relic of the old regime and seldom paid much attention to them. Young Gen Xers never met a long-term benefit they didn't want to cash out—which, with the introduction of "total rewards" packages, they often did. By the late-'90s dot-com bubble, the hottest benefits for college grads were all of the short-term variety—flextime, incentive travel, extra vacation, and bonuses. Young Millennials, pressured by their parents and their own step-by-step life plans, are looking more favorably on the perks that Boomers rejected and Gen Xers ignored. When companies hold staff meetings to discuss retirement benefits, employees in their late twenties often express as much—or even more—interest than employees in their late thirties. Even the need to prepare for old age puts a bit of pressure today's rising generation.

Implications for the Public Sector

Like private companies, many public agencies are trying to reach out early to pressured Millennials, from NASA's Girl Scout Recognition Program to the Air Force's Space Camp. At the FBI's youth Web site, kids can follow cases, take a "special agent challenge," and check out a "day in the life" of an agent. State and local governments can use local programs to create a "feeder base" of talent. The YMCA Youth and Government program, active in forty states, organizes Model Government programs, including training modules and mock state conferences in which middle and high school students learn about state government and practice different jobs. Some cities field programs (like San Francisco's YouthWorks) that funnel high school students into paid internships with city agencies so they can explore government careers.

Although private companies are successfully reaching out to Millennials earlier through internships, the public sector is notably failing to exploit the same opportunity. In 2007, private employers converted 51 percent of their internships into permanent jobs, while the federal government converted only 7 percent, according to NACE and the Partnership for Public Service. Private firms filled 40 percent of their permanent entry-level vacancies with former interns, while the federal government filled only 9 percent.

Why is the public sector so far behind? At most levels of government, the civil service has a more structured and regulated employment entry process, and tends to view internships as "back-door entries" that cheat the gatekeepers. This is why the vast majority of federal agencies hire interns under programs that are not designed to lead to permanent employment (the so-called "STEP" program). Only a few use the career-focused "SCEP" program. Meanwhile, students have to search for federal internships by locating ad-hoc agency invitations, since there is no central registry. Both federal and state employers must work harder to leverage internships to attract full-time hires. According to North Carolina's 2008 study, a top reason young employees accepted state jobs was a successful internship or temporary assignment.

Once young employees are on board, most public employers do a good job of offering career guidance and exploration within the organization. The Department of Health and Human Services' new "emerging leaders program" rotates selected employees through diverse assignments during a two-year training and mentoring regimen. The Presidential Management Fellows Program allows high-achieving young professionals to "float" among various agencies for two years. Public agencies should do much more to advertise these programs in recruitment materials. For example, Vermont's state recruitment site describes the "rich and rewarding professional path" of working for the state, declaring, "nowhere in Vermont will you find so many opportunities with one employer."

No one can rival public employers in the long-term benefits Millennials value, and this strength, if properly presented, can make up for lower salaries. While Millennials express some concern about low starting salaries in public jobs, surveys show that they value long-term earning potential and benefits just as highly. Benefits like the federal Student Loan Repayment Program, which permits agencies to repay up to $60,000 of their employees' student loans, will be a particularly powerful incentive for this debt-pressured generation.

Millennials' sense of pressure will also have important implications for public policy.

In the years ahead, policy makers will face increased demands to protect Millennials from inappropriate career pressure at a young age. To avoid endless competition by employers to engage students (and by students to meet employers) at ever-earlier ages, federal and state legislators may want to build "firewalls" that set grade limits on corporate contact with the classroom— or age limits on internships. Legislators may also be asked to monitor any conflicts of interest that arise between major corporate employers and the career colleges and training programs that they sponsor. When businesses and educational institutions work together, the result is usually positive for local youth—but the relationship needs to be constructive and transparent.

Policy makers will feel pressure to continue strengthening the alignment between middle school and high school, between high school and college, and between college and the workplace. There will be further efforts to structure and facilitate the transition from one level to the next through policies like early and middle college, career academies, and "P–16" or "P–14" initiatives. Today, every state has different academic standards for high school graduation, and only a few align these standards with postsecondary curricula or with employer needs. Voters may ultimately demand national alignment standards. Top officials from the Education and Labor Departments publically pledged in 2009 to align federal education and labor programs.

With rising college tuition looming large for most families, policy makers will be called on to put downward pressure on price by enlarging the career pipeline and by helping to expand the supply of career-oriented postsecondary institutions. Traditional four-year colleges may offer a high-quality education, but are limited in number and are often not oriented towards workplace training. Private for-profit colleges and trade schools, today's fastest-growing postsecondary sector, do offer career training—but often lack accreditation and quality control. Government officials currently lack even an accurate count of how many of these institutions exist. Policy makers will need to bridge this gap by fostering the growth of accredited private colleges, trade schools, and community colleges.

Policy makers may be called on to help students cope with the high cost of college retroactively, especially if youth and young-adult unemployment remains high. Policy initiatives may include debt forgiveness based on a sliding income scale or requirements for institutions to collect and publish data on graduates' career outcomes. Such data will offer future incoming students a better estimate of the value of their educational investment—and of the odds that they will be able to bear the associated debt burden.

12
Achieving

"Teenagers today are much more career-focused and thinking more about the future. They're looking at even their first job to learn skills they can use later or put on a résumé."

— **AUSTIN LAVIN**, CEO, *MYFIRSTPAYCHECK.COM* (2008)

"The message from Millennials is clear: To lure them into the workplace, prospective employers must provide state-of-the-art technologies."

— **GARY CURTIS**, GLOBAL MANAGING DIRECTOR, ACCENTURE TECHNOLOGY CONSULTING (2010)

Achieving

Every year, high-achieving Millennials astound older Americans by showing off their academic prowess. Back in the twentieth century, pre-Millennial eighth graders could win the National Spelling Bee with words like *knack* (1932), *therapy* (1940), *vouchsafe* (1973), or *lyceum* (1992). Consider the winning words of the new millennium, starting in 2001: *succedaneum, prospicience, pococurante, appoggiatura, autochthonous, ursprache, serrefine,* and *Laodicean.* The spelling bee itself has taken on a whole new Millennial flavor: highly structured, fussed over by doting teachers and intrusive parents, and captured in the full-on glare of the media.

Twenty years ago, teens wrote term papers on lined paper and won science fairs with paper-mâché geology. Today, teens turn in multi-media presentations that resemble "Mission Impossible" briefings and win science fairs with discoveries that often lead to new business startups, with one in five National High School Science Fair finalists now applying for a patent.

Over the last twenty years, as the glorification of "dumb" among youth (recall *Wayne's World*) has been replaced by the glorification of "smart," a rapidly rising share of youths have been taking standardized aptitude and admissions tests—and the average scores on those tests have been rising. In settings with clear achievement benchmarks, today's young people are using disciplined preparation to perform at a level far beyond what was expected of prior generations of youth.

The Millennial achievement orientation should come as no surprise. Throughout this generation's childhood, accountability and higher educational standards have risen to the top of America's political agenda, with a widening torrent of grades, rankings, aptitude tests, weekly online-interim reports, and the like. Forty years ago, young Boomers launched a growing resistance to being ranked and sorted by "the system." Today, Millennials are bringing back the desire to achieve and find a place *within* the system. Academic summer camps, once filled with students in need of remediation, are now filled with students seeking that extra edge to help them excel. Instead of taking drugs to tune out, like young people did in decades past, today's youth are taking "smart drugs" like Ritalin and Adderall to help them plug in. Their résumés brim with checklisted accomplishments, as if to say: I have tried to prepare for whatever skill you need.

Millennials will not reach their full potential—indeed, may not even reach minimal competence—unless schools and companies engage this achievement orientation. Educators must lay down clear and objective learning goals so that Millennials know exactly what they are expected to master. They must contextualize and apply their content so that Millennials know why it's important. And they must truly challenge a generation that wants to prove itself. Employers are beginning to notice that Millennials don't stop trying to achieve after they've been hired. They are also finding out that the only way they can fully harness the energy of Millennials is to invite them to excel—an invitation that usually requires definable "missions," measurable benchmarks, ongoing professional development, and cutting-edge technology.

Implications for Educators

Many educators are puzzled by the Millennial focus on achievement. Yes, they notice that today's students strive to excel. Unlike Boomers or Gen Xers at the same age, Millennials don't want to question or evade the high standards, they want to meet or beat the high standards. Yet they also notice that many students who graduate from high school with good grades remain underprepared both for college and the workplace. Roughly one-third of college freshmen need to take at least one remedial course, and a large majority of employers express disappointment with at least some aspect of their new hires' speaking, writing, numeracy, or personal interaction skills. Even straight-A students with super test scores often strike college faculty or business supervisors as shell-shocked by real-world working environments. One common complaint is that young people lack "soft skills" (from phone and email etiquette to follow-through on independent tasks). Another is that they seem astonishingly deficient in basic "do-it-yourself" life skills—like simply knowing how to use a shovel, change a tire, or navigate with a map.

So where is the disconnect? Typically, the problem is not that Millennials don't focus on or excel at the learning tasks that educators set before them. The problem is that these learning tasks often don't impart the skills that Millennials will need in their future careers. The tasks leave certain critical skills unaddressed. Or they are taught in a directionless, hands-off manner. Or their applications are never made clear. Or they simply don't push students to a level that is sufficient to do them any good—or even sustain their interest.

Teaching Millennials requires particular care and method. Today's students work more diligently to learn skills in achievement-oriented settings than older generations did at the same age. But they also have fewer opportunities to acquire skills in any other setting. They are less likely to have summer or after-school jobs, less likely to acquire practical know-how from their parents, and less likely to try out their own projects in their own "free time." If the skill is not actually taught in some structured fashion, the odds are that Millennials won't learn it.

If educators want to help Millennials master necessary career skills, they will have to do a better job explicitly teaching those skills. Specifically, this means *formulating, directing, contextualizing, applying,* and *toughening* the curriculum. Do all five of these well, and you will fully harness the Millennials' desire to achieve.

First, educators should *formulate* what students learn in the classroom—translate content into a formula that is easy to grasp and that provides a structured framework around which students can fill in detail and complexity. This approach seems familiar enough when teaching chemistry, biology, or history (think of the periodic table, labeled cell diagrams, or event panoramas). But the approach also works well with the sorts of soft skills and life skills that employers prize and that Millennials have trouble acquiring. When teaching professional workplace behavior, for example, educators will see little progress if they simply complain every time they see a student do something inappropriate. Instead, they need to introduce a comprehensive, point-by-point rubric for proper diction, dress, or mannerisms—including always-do and never-do checklists—which enable students to evaluate, practice, and improve their conduct and feel a positive sense of mastery. Similarly, when teaching workplace safety or quality control, don't let students guess when they're making a mistake. Devise a learnable, step-by-step protocol by which students can make a habit out of doing it the right way every time.

Some educators (especially Boomers) resist formulating the content of any curriculum because they dislike, on principle, distilling knowledge down to mere steps or lists. But knowledge has to begin somewhere. And Millennials prefer it to begin, not with the Socratic method, but with a clear roadmap where progress can be sequentially tested until ultimate mastery can be achieved and celebrated. Millennials get excited by teachers who assure them that diligent practice of each lesson will likely earn them an excellent grade on the final. They rush to enroll in "Life-Skills 101" courses, which, though still uncommon, are beginning to proliferate in colleges and training institutes. Surveys show that minority and first-generation college students are especially likely to favor formulated content and testing because it levels the playing field. In effect, it reduces the importance of "tacit" or informal knowledge that is much easier to pick up from privileged family backgrounds.

Second, educators should *direct* the curriculum toward a mastery goal that students can grasp from the outset. Instead of designing courses to "cover" a certain amount of material, start with the precise skills students should have at the end of the course—or upon graduation—and then backward-design the curriculum to get them to that goal, jettisoning anything extraneous. When content is formulated, it should also be directed so that today's pressured students know for certain they are working towards a tangible, achievable goal. The National Association of Secondary School Principals has emphatically endorsed the concept of "backward-designed" curricula. This is especially effective in work-skills courses that merge practical activities with academic content, because the goals here can be described so tangibly to students: At the end of this module you will be able to... audit a corporate 10-K, engineer a roadbed, build a robot, diagnose an emotionally disturbed child, and so on.

Third, educators should *contextualize* what students learn in the classroom by having them engage in hands-on activities that simulate real-world use of what they are learning. This helps goal-oriented Millennials see more broadly and practically where all their hard work is actually heading. At the middle and high school level, districts are introducing career academies ("themed" around fields like finance or marine studies) that enable students to use academic skills in practical settings. Many old-style "vocational schools" are rebuilding themselves as math and science magnets, which occasionally (such as Bergen County Academies in New Jersey) attract long waiting lists. As a supplement to their regular curriculum, schools can turn to video-game simulations which pull students into immersive and complex decision-making environments. They can also use turn-key courses like those from Project Lead the Way, which introduce students to engineering and biomedical sciences through hypothetical problem solving.

At the college level, contextualizing content often means getting rid of the traditional classroom altogether. Many top research universities are cutting down on lectures in their big intro-level courses (or simply resourcing the lectures on podcasts) and using class time for workshops, experiments, and team projects. As Millennials fill professional schools, schools of all types are beginning to copy the same "case method" that was once used only in business schools, learning law by assembling a hypothetical defense, for example, or learning medicine by diagnostic exercises.

Fourth, educators should encourage students to *apply* what they're learning in real-world situations. Millennials want to go from context to actual practice as soon as possible, so that they can see themselves as professionals at work. According to a 2006 survey by Eduventures, college students considered "professional preparation" to be the most important criterion for assessing a degree program. In high school, educators should be creative about finding ways for teens to use their skills, such as donating trade or IT skills to the community or selling them to local families. A class of seniors in Fairfax County, Virginia, combined their craft skills and built a house that was later sold for just over $1.3 million.

In postsecondary schools, educators should encourage apprenticeships, job-shadowing programs, and internships and explore flexible new ways of linking students and employers—for example, "online" internships. In the most popular grad school programs, the faculty invite students to team up and join them in their research projects. The key is to be imaginative and look for opportunities. When setting out to improve infrastructure and equipment, for example, schools should always ask themselves: Rather than turning to an outside contractor, could we create a perfect applied-learning opportunity—plus save money and customize the outcome better to our needs—by having our own students accomplish this? (With anything related to IT, the answer is almost always yes.)

Finally, educators often need to *toughen* the curriculum. The problem is not just that low standards fail to prepare students adequately for their next level of school, for their first job, or for their eventual career. By depriving these achievement-oriented students of challenge, low standards will also leave them entirely unmotivated. By hefty margins, most high school students want to be *more* challenged in school than they now are. Public Agenda reports, for example, that 80 percent of them (and a somewhat higher share for blacks and Latinos than for whites) say schools should hold them to higher standards even if it means summer school. Two-thirds of recent high school dropouts agree that "I could have worked harder if more had been expected of me." Perhaps it is no accident that the subject today's high school students say they find the hardest (math) is also the subject they like the most.

Educators are often tempted to lower the bar when students are having trouble meeting it. This is probably a risky strategy for any generation of students. But it is especially dangerous for Millennials, because it leads so quickly to a downward spiral of boredom, disengagement, and further lowering of standards. If Millennials are having trouble, educators first need to ask themselves whether the teaching method needs improvement. (For example, is the content formulated, contextualized, and applied?) Once Millennials are engaged and focused, educators often find they can increase motivation by raising the standard. Early and middle college programs, which enroll at-risk high school students in college-level courses, have been successful for precisely this reason.

As more educators understand the importance of higher standards in motivating all students, the old model of separately "tracking" vocational and college-bound students will continue to lose favor. And as that happens, the market for high-quality, career-oriented postsecondary institutions will take off. Already, research indicates that trade schools, community colleges, and career colleges often do a better job than traditional colleges in attracting diverse students and actually placing graduates in jobs in their fields.

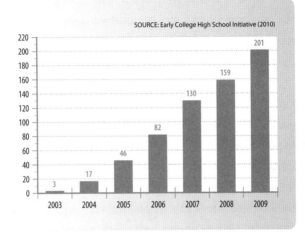

SOURCE: Early College High School Initiative (2010)

◀ **Figure 29**

Number of Early College High Schools,* 2003 to 2009

*"Early college" high schools take at-risk high school students and enroll them in a joint college-high school program, often on a college campus, where they earn both a high school diploma and one or two years of transferable college credit

And many of these fields are growing: According to the U.S. Bureau of Labor Statistics, eighteen of the twenty fastest growing occupations within the next decade will require career and technical education. Educators should expect the image of career-oriented postsecondary education to shift in the years ahead from a fall-back option for failing students to a legitimate path to successful achievement.

Implications for Employers

When strategizing over an employer image that will attract potential young recruits (what Fortune 1000 corporations call an "employer brand"), companies should always keep in mind this generation's achievement orientation. Quite simply, the best and brightest Millennials want to work for the best and brightest companies. They want to join high-achieving organizations that are doing more than others to change their industries and the world. Most large companies that enjoy such a reputation—like Google (in IT), Disney (in entertainment), or PwC (in business consulting)—eventually find themselves near the top of any Millennial list of favorite employers. Yet employers need not be large to be considered high achieving. When looking over a small company, talented Millennials will look closely at the quality of its product, the caliber of its workforce, and the prestige of its clients and customers. If they are impressed, they may be eager to sign up.

One obvious step companies can take to improve their best-and-brightest reputation is to take an active role in raising the achievement orientation of the educational system—for example, helping align school and college curricula with the needs of cutting-edge employers. Many companies are now helping out. Coca-Cola's Council for Corporate and School Partnerships promotes cooperation between regional businesses and schools. Xerox sends employee volunteers into high schools to teach hands-on science, with the goal of attracting students to engineering careers. A consortium of engineering companies is responsible for the popular "Project Lead the Way" teaching units. Several companies are developing entire graduate-school curricula— including IBM, which has partnered with North Carolina State University to develop a "services sciences" master's degree program. And what can look "smarter" than celebrating the nation's smartest kids? Raytheon sponsors a middle school "MathCounts" competition and Intel sponsors a middle school "Science Talent Search" competition, all as part of their programs to support innovation in the teaching of math and science.

Nothing better epitomizes the Millennial achievement ethic than how they use cutting-edge digital information technology. This generation believes that information technology will someday empower them to reshape the world— and non-college-degreed Millennials believe that high-tech skills are their best hope to keep up with their college-degreed peers. Whatever business they're in, employers must show that the digital revolution didn't pass them by. Some recruiters now hand out flash drives rather than brochures and schedule meetings via text message. Others are setting up virtual Q&A sessions, blogs written by first-year employees, podcasts on day-to-day workplace culture, and even user-generated digital videos. You don't need to dazzle potential hires with the latest hyped gadget. You do need to show them that your workplace integrates digital IT seamlessly and sensibly into your daily work routine.

Some industries need to think more about their achievement image than others. Like everyone else, Millennials are influenced by the global stereotype that associates high-achieving careers with a cosmopolitan, yuppified work-style in a creative, high-tech "corporate-campus" setting. When young job seekers consider a company that designs video games or sells research to CEOs, that stereotype pushes in the right direction. But when they look at a company that manufactures trucks, drills for oil, franchises motels, builds infrastructure, or manages temp workers, it pushes in the wrong direction. Not surprisingly, companies and professions that don't fit the stereotype need to work harder (with innovative Web sites, outreach to schools, and even on-site orientations) to persuade talented young people that, yes, we too use the best technology there is—and we too have a tradition of excellence and high standards.

The Millennial focus on achievement won't stop after they are hired. Once on board, Millennial employees will continue to focus on improving their skills—and they will do so in an explicit, employer-focused way that differs considerably from anything young Boomers or Gen Xers did.

To the extent young Boomers thought about workplace achievement, it was about gradually mastering their trade or profession, however they cared to define it, or about choosing their own mission or calling. If asked about "achievement" back in the 1960s and '70s, most Boomers would have talked about lofty professional standards and their own life ideals. In the 1980s and '90s, Gen Xers came of age with a more pragmatic notion of workplace achievement, which put much less emphasis on professional or personal ideals and much more on adapting and profiting in a fast-changing marketplace. Many Gen Xers came to see themselves as acquiring a "toolbox" of skills that they could sell to the highest bidder as they moved from company to company.

> ### High-Tech Employers in High Demand
>
> In a national survey of youth age 14 to 27:
>
> - 52 percent say state-of-the-art technology is an important consideration in selecting an employer.
> - More than 20 percent (of those who have had a job) say that employer-provided technologies do not meet their expectations.
>
> SOURCE: *New-Generation Workers*, Accenture (2008)

When Millennials reflect on how these older generations approach work, they find much to respect. Many admire the deep expertise and professionalism they observe in the Boomers at the top of their organizations. And they often find themselves emulating the creative resourcefulness and efficiency of

Training a Generation of Gamers

The era of video-game training has arrived. Long derided as a sign of cultural decline among youth, video games are now being hailed for their role in elevating the ability of players to estimate, analyze, plan, and problem-solve under pressure. Boomer kids didn't have video games. Xer kids had simple games (first-wavers had Atari, late-wavers Nintendo). Most Millennials, on other hand, have grown up since early childhood playing games featuring high-resolution graphics, warp speed, multi-thread complexity, and sophisticated AI engines. Thanks in part to video games, the "abstract reasoning" and "pattern recognition" scores for youth taking IQ tests are rapidly rising. Even retirees now play video games in the hope that it will ward off dementia.

Educators have been very slow to adapt any part of their K-12 or college curricula into video-game platforms, due partly to their limited resources and partly to their conservative preference for theory-first (rather than student-centered) teaching methods. Employers have shown no such hesitation. Managers favor training methods that are immersive and contextual. They are also finding that Millennials learn better by focusing on execution rather than just on concept. As an on-the-job training tool, video games are a natural.

For depth and extent of video-game training, no other employer can match the U.S. armed forces. The military has been using simulation games to train young soldiers since the 1980s, and now spends over $4 billion annually improving and expanding them. These range from popular Web-based games like *America's Army* and *Full Spectrum Warrior* to highly specialized (and often classified) games to train operators of individual weapons systems. In the years to come, with the growing deployment of unmanned Predator drones and infantry "bots," the very division between training and combat is likely to disappear. In 2009, remarkably, the U.S. Air Force was training more video-joystick drone pilots than in-the-air fighter and bomber pilots.

Private-sector employers are also investing heavily in video-game training. A recent survey by the Entertainment Software Association (ESA) found that 70 percent of large companies now use some form of interactive software and gaming to train employees. If the company wants to promote generic professional development, it can often turn to off-the-shelf games at very little cost—including excellent "management simulation" games such as *Capitalism, Air Bucks, The Movies,* and the various *Tycoon* games. If the company needs are more specific, it can build a game (typically the job is outsourced) for that specific purpose. Many companies build games that help orient new employees about their traditions and corporate culture. Others build games that teach particular skills, from customer service, delivery, or equipment repair to using a new accounting system or bidding on the trading floor.

Some of these custom-built games reach stunning levels of sophistication and complexity. Cisco Systems, Inc. has created a video game in which their technicians must practice constructing equipment under all sorts of simulated conditions, including a sandstorm on the planet Mars. Many hospitals are using video games to train surgeons in the most advanced laparoscopic surgery skills (better to make a mistake on a virtual patient than an actual one). VirtualHeroes, a leading simulation designer for the military, recently built the first totally interactive action-figure training game commissioned by the private sector. Called "Ultimate Team Player," it was built to train the hospitality service workers at Hilton Garden Inn.

Most custom-built games have simpler graphics and are a lot less complex. But as experts in serious gaming will attest, what makes an effective training game is not slick graphics—but rather a basic game design that is fun, informative, and keeps the player challenged every step of the way.

By the time Millennials reach midlife, Americans may be carrying out many of their daily activities through virtual, game-like interfaces. Consider how they'll eventually shop, go to class, watch sports, get their health care, monitor their factories, fight their wars, or participate in politics. Employers prepare: You might as well use video games today to teach on-the-job skills—since, in the future, these skills may come to look more and more like the games themselves.

their Gen-X supervisors. Yet if there are pieces of the elder approach they like to borrow, there are also pieces they reject.

Unlike Boomers, Millennials believe that achievement should be measured, monitored, and assessed according to objective benchmarks. Before they are hired, most have spent a lifetime focused on quizzes, test scores, letter grades, specialized credentials, and résumés overflowing with bulleted accomplishments. That won't change after they are hired. Millennials expect to receive not just frequent feedback from one supervisor, but collective feedback from every relevant superior, and even from coworkers, that gives them an updated and calibrated measure of how well they are performing. While Boomers may find this kind of scorekeeping bureaucratic and irksome, Millennials will find it reassuring (OK, I'm mostly doing fine), helpful (I get it, here's where I need to improve), and fair (since my evaluation is less likely to depend on the subjective, last-second opinion of just one person).

As young employees settle in, employers should motivate them by leveraging this notch-in-my-belt achievement ethic. Present new tasks to Millennials as challenges worthy of their qualifications, even as important "missions" for them to accomplish. When feasible, transfer routine training and performance reviews to video-game platforms, where the task and difficulty level automatically adjusts to the user and every "score" is saved. Couch even minor administrative chores as special assignments that are important to the overall success of the firm and that need to be done effectively and well. Couple your mentoring program with a "reverse-mentoring" program that allows Millennials to teach their own areas of expertise (especially their facility with IT) to older colleagues.

Instead of making young employees wait for that six-month review, set out smaller benchmarks that they can successfully achieve. The message should be that, at your company, workers are always reaching to achieve clear goals, never just treading water with nothing specific to accomplish.

Unlike Gen Xers, Millennials expect—or at least very much hope—that career advancement and skill development won't require frequent moves between employers. Millennials are more likely to fear the uncertainty of the labor market. They are also more likely to trust a large company, look forward to the (benefit) perks of seniority, and value the social capital they create by becoming a team member. Moving from community to community, Gen Xers believe they take all their skills with them, while Millennials worry that they may be leaving something important behind. The same 2007 Michigan State University survey showing that 81 percent of young job seekers rate "opportunities for promotion" as an important criterion for choosing a job also showed that 77 percent say the same about "learning new skills." Apparently, most Millennials think they can do both.

As they try to attract Millennials with the prospect of promotion, employers need to tie it closely to the acquisition of new skills and the prospect of entirely new job roles based on those new skills. Showcase the stories of young workers who have continually moved up within the company, give details on where entry-level jobs might lead, and explain any opportunities young workers will have to connect with higher ups in their desired fields. Employers should also emphasize that the company's achievement focus is not just a choice for individual employees, but a shared institutional expectation for all employees. Millennials will be impressed, for example, to notice widespread employee participation in communities of professional practice. Even beyond their own opportunities to excel personally, Millennials want to be part of an organization that collectively excels at whatever it does.

Among the recent initiatives at Wachovia to keep young workers engaged is a daily five-minute video report showing "where we are, where we are going, and why." For Millennials, it's not enough that they come in everyday, do their job, and get paid for it. They want to feel a sense of collective purpose at the beginning of the day—and a sense of collective accomplishment at the end.

Implications for the Public Sector

Like their private-sector competitors, public employers can attract young recruits by presenting themselves as state-of-the-art enterprises known for cutting-edge efficiency and innovation. The vast scale and unique public importance of many agency missions—like managing social services over an entire city, tracking criminals across the nation, or monitoring weather across the globe—often makes this an easy sell. (After all, what private enterprise could ever accomplish such tasks?) One way an agency can highlight its achievement orientation is to support activities that promote achievement in youth well before they reach workforce age. Some public agencies already do this, such as NASA with its famous Space Camp and Space Academy.

To attract Millennials, it also helps to project "cool" through a streamlined, Web 2.0 image. Unfortunately, most government agencies don't project any such thing: Their halting and low-tech application procedures often give Millennial applicants the upfront impression that they constitute a professional backwater. With some difficulty, agencies like the State Department have been working to change this image by reaching out with YouTube videos and glitzy recruiting Web sites. What's even more challenging is to follow through on this image by incorporating quality IT tools into daily operations. In fact, it's a near-impossible task for agencies that only make infrequent, large-scale tech investments, which quickly become outdated. Recruits into the armed forces and intelligence agencies, for example, often join with the expectation of working with super high-tech systems, only to realize that their day-to-day tools may be years behind what's available off-the-shelf at Best Buy.

Surveys show that Millennials highly value both career advancement and skill development—and, unlike Xers, expect to get both without having to switch employers. Public employers do fairly well on skill development, but fall short when it comes to career advancement. According to OPM, 64 percent of federal employees feel they are given opportunities to improve skills—four points higher than in the private sector. But only 39 percent are satisfied with their opportunities to get a better job within their organization, ten points lower than the private sector. Federal agencies face special obstacles because top positions are reserved for political appointees, placing an unbreakable glass ceiling over career civil servants. State governments fare slightly better, but still fall short of private-sector competitors. According to a 2009 Deloitte survey, 48 percent of young state employees are satisfied with their current career paths, compared with 61 percent of their private-sector peers.

As Millennials flood the workplace, they will insist that their advancement match their achievement. Public agencies will need to work harder to showcase advancement opportunities. If such opportunities simply don't exist in-house, they should create easy pipelines to sister agencies (for example, an inter-agency rotation or exchange for high-level civil servants) or into the private sector. Employers will also have to address the flip side of this issue— bureaucratic rules that prevent firing incompetent employees. Millennials eager to show their stuff will resent being tethered to coworkers who have nothing to show.

More easily than most private employers, public employers can often present their work as a worthy challenge or "mission" to Millennial recruits. Most agencies have yet to focus on this kind of branding. An interesting exception is the GAO, which recently changed its name from the "Government Accounting Office" to the "Government Accountability Office," in part to present a more attractive employer brand to young workers. The former name conjured up rows of eye-shaded clerks checking numbers. The new name suggests a team that makes sure our government carries out the will of the American people.

Millennials' achievement-orientation will also have important implications for public policy.

More than young Boomers or Xers, Millennials trust in the value of expertise and credentialed knowledge. They not only want to acquire such knowledge themselves, they want to see it in their leaders. This generation will expect policy debates to have a lot less attitude and a lot more informed discussion. They tend to trust experts in government to regulate decisions that individuals may not have the time or resources to make themselves. For example, surveys show they are more likely to favor contribution requirements for retirement savings—and are less bothered by government intrusions into their privacy. They will expect policy makers to harness cutting-edge technologies to make systems work better, for example through so-called "smart infrastructure" (high tech electricity grids, roads, and bridges).

Throughout their lives, Boomers have favored policies based on *moral* imperatives. Millennials, by contrast, favor policies based on *behavioral* imperatives, with specific goals whose achievement can be quantified (and collectively celebrated) over time. Legislators proposing new policies can galvanize Millennial support by including concrete targets and achievable benchmarks that monitor progress towards those goals. For example, Millennials will likely support the Xer-led "outcomes" movement in K–12 schools, demanding standards for student achievement and transparent data measuring how well schools are reaching those standards. The focus on outcomes is already spreading to post-secondary education, and may jump into the workplace as Millennials and Xers take over from more "holistic" senior Boomer managers.

AMERICA'S **MILLENNIAL FUTURE**

A Generation
of Destiny

"Every generation has its chance at
 greatness. Let this one take its shot."

— *NEWSWEEK* (2000)

"Relentless optimism and faith in collective
 action in the face of hardship is typical of civic
 generations such as the Millennials. And judging
 by history, their attitudes will serve them well."

— *LOS ANGELES TIMES* (2009)

A Generation of Destiny

Every generation has its own strengths and weaknesses, its own potential for triumph and tragedy. Some generations steer society toward outer-world rationality, others toward inner-world passion. Some focus on graceful refinement, others on the hardscrabble bottom line. The German historian Leopold von Ranke, who weighed many Old World generations on the scales of history, observed that "before God all the generations of humanity appear equally justified." In "any generation," he concluded, "real moral greatness is the same as in any other."

The Next Great Generation

The collective Millennial lifespan—and its influence on history—will stretch far into the twenty-first century. What will this generation provide for those who come after? It is this future contribution, not what they have done in their youth, which will be their test of greatness.

The first wave of this generation is already setting its course in life. In 2000 their first birth cohort—those born in 1982—graduated from high school and began entering the workforce. In 2002 they began graduating from community and career colleges, and in 2004 from bachelor's degree programs, pouring into the workplace in greater numbers. In 2006 they began graduating from business and professional schools, in 2007 from law schools, and in 2009 from medical schools and PhD programs, launching careers as credentialed professionals. In 2007 the first cohort of Millennial women reached the median age of first marriage and of giving birth to a first child. The first cohort of Millennial men reached that age in 2009.

Over the next two decades, the Millennials will fill the ranks of young-adult celebrities in the Olympics, pro sports, and entertainment—and the ranks of the military in any wars the nation may wage. From now through 2020, they will make a major mark on the youth pop culture. The new youth activism that began impacting national politics in the election of 2008 will strengthen and solidify in the elections of 2012 and 2016. Through the 2010s, Millennials will be giving birth in large numbers and swarming into business and the professions, no longer as apprentices. Some will enter state houses and the U.S. Congress. Around 2020, they will elect their first U.S. Senator—and around 2030, their first U.S. President.

In the 2020s the Millennials will begin taking over as senior managers in the workplace, and in the 2030s they will take over as CEOs, bringing their generational style to the highest echelons of corporate leadership. They will occupy the White House into the 2050s, during which period they will also provide majorities in the Congress and Senate, win Nobel prizes, and rule corporate boardrooms. Thereafter, into the 2070s, they will occupy the Supreme Court and be America's new elders. And along the way, they will make lasting contributions to literature, science, technology, and many other fields. Their children will dominate American life in the latter half of the twenty-first century—and their grandchildren will lead us into the twenty-second. Their influence on the American story, and the memory of their deeds and collective persona, will reach far beyond the year 2100.

As is true for any generation, history will intrude on the Millennials' collective life story, posing distinct challenges and opportunities. How they respond will alter the way others see them and the way they see themselves. What would one have said about the future of the G.I. Generation of youth back in the early 1930s, before World War II redefined who they were and how they lived their lives? What would one have said about the future of young Boomers back in the early 1960s, before the Consciousness Revolution? And what of Generation X in the early 1980s, before the digital and dot-com age?

Towards the close of his re-nomination address in 1936, President Roosevelt said:

There is a mysterious cycle in human events. To some generations much is given. Of other generations much is expected. This generation of Americans has a rendezvous with destiny.

When summoning "this generation" to a "rendezvous with destiny," Roosevelt was particularly referring to the G.I. Generation—those young men and women who had overwhelmingly voted him into office and who, within a few years, would rally behind his elder leadership with dedication, energy, courage, and intelligence. Together, all of America's adult generations—leaders, generals, and soldiers—fought and won a war civilization could not afford to lose, achieving a triumph we today honor with monuments and memorials.

For many decades Americans have especially revered this G.I. Generation, today's very old war veterans and their widows. As young people, the G.I.s understood how much older generations had given them. They wanted to give back, and they did—especially in World War II, and also by nurturing a new postwar generation of idealistic Boomers. Those Boomers have given birth to the first Millennials, and the story continues.

The Millennials' greatness as a generation has yet to reveal itself. When the strengths of this generation do appear, it is unlikely they will resemble those of their Boomer parents. Instead, their virtues are more likely to call to mind the confidence, optimism, and civic spirit of the high-achieving G.I.s.

It is possible that the Millennials will dominate the story of the twenty-first century to much the same degree as the G.I. Generation dominated the story of the twentieth. If Millennials face their own "rendezvous with destiny" as they come of age, much will be expected of them by older generations. Will future writers have reason to call them, on their record of achievement, another "great generation"?

We think it is likely—though of course only time will tell. Igor Stravinsky once wrote that every generation of youth declares war on its parents and makes friends with its grandparents. Already we see some signs of this in Millennials. When asked which of today's living generations has the highest reputation, and which they would most like to emulate, Millennial high school seniors say it is their grandparents' generation—the can-do, war-winning, "greatest generation."

Millennials and a Fourth Turning

What will happen over the course of the Millennials' lives is, of course, unknowable. But the record of history offers insight into the challenges this rising generation will likely face.

When William Strauss and I wrote *The Fourth Turning* in 1997, we forecast that, sometime in the first decade of this century, America would enter a new societal mood of historical urgency, sacrifice, and renewal—an era of crisis, a "fourth turning" comparable in significance to the American Revolution, the Civil War, and the era spanning the Great Depression and World War II. We predicted that this shift would occur when Boomers entered elderhood (as national leaders and cultural icons), when Gen Xers entered midlife (as managers of businesses and families), and when Millennials came of age (as young workers and networked activists). Today, these three generations are entering these new stages of life, and very much appear to be pushing America into a new era.

Much of what we forecast in 1997 is now coming to pass. The financial crisis that began in 2008 has sparked a new mood of national urgency. Society is growing less tolerant of personal risk-taking and more tolerant of civic risk-taking, including war. Worries about financial collapse, nuclear proliferation, terrorism, and global instability abound, making a national—and even global—crisis seem immanent.

The anxiety about a "fourth turning" is palpably on the rise among these three generations, each of whom will be a dominant player in the first half of the twenty-first century. In his inauguration speech in January, 2009, President Obama quoted the words of Thomas Paine, which George Washington invoked in 1776, during an earlier crisis era, the Revolutionary War: "Let it be told to the future world...that in the depth of winter, when nothing but hope and virtue could survive...that the city and the country, alarmed at one common danger, came forth to meet it." President Obama described an era in which the larger tides of history converge and society comes together to meet great and unusual challenges. This may well be the kind of era we are entering today.

If we do move into a new "fourth turning," the next two decades could involve substantial tests of America's society and place in the world. This could include

economic disruptions, a protracted War on Terror, a crisis of weapons proliferation, an energy shortage, a fiscal crisis and debt crash, new civil wars abroad,
a culture-war end game here at home—or any combination of all these things.

Whatever challenges our nation and world may encounter in the years
to come, the largest challenge and greatest call to sacrifice will be borne by
the generation now coming of age. Already, the Millennials are struggling to
enter the workplace and launch careers in the worst recession since the Great
Depression—the Depression that catalyzed America's last "fourth turning"
era.

The graver the national peril, the more the nation will focus on this generation. What they need will become a national priority, what they suffer a
source of national anguish, and what they achieve a source of national pride.
Whatever challenges history hands the Millennials—whether economic,
political, military, social, or environmental—today's youth will see in them
a lifetime agenda. And they will mobilize to meet these challenges with the
upbeat attitude, can-do confidence, and civic spirit that will enhance the prospects for a successful outcome.

Against this backdrop of history, the Millennials' generational personality
will continue to develop, and will profoundly impact America's life and institutions. History teaches that a Fourth Turning will only strengthen the traits
that make this rising generation so unlike Boomers and Gen Xers—and will
give them greater opportunities to transform the nation.

As the Millennials reach the zenith of their power in the decades ahead,
how will their presence and leadership make America feel different from the
society we know today? This rising generation of leaders will most likely create
the following social shifts:

* *A powerful new sense of national community.* The Millennials will become
  a political powerhouse generation, filling the void left by individualistic
  Boomers and Xers and revitalizing the connection between ordinary
  citizens and the national community. They will reject the negativism and
  moralism of the national politics they witnessed as children and use political organizing as a tool to turn collegial progress into civic progress.

* *Greater emphasis on avoiding economic, lifestyle, and career risks.* Most Millennials will avoid the high-risk career paths and the high-risk life-styles (from substance abuse to extreme sports) and that many Boomers and even more Xers have pursued. A crisis era will encourage risk-averse Millennials to place an even higher premium than they do now on ordered lifestyles, job security, and economic guarantees—goals they will certainly promote as government and corporate leaders.

* *Greater group cohesion in families, neighborhoods, and the workplace.* The Millennials will continue to use networked technology to maintain constant contact with extended families, local communities, and large circles of friends. They will place a new premium on how groups and teams produce not just social, but also economic value—which may lead them to create a refurbished, high-tech, and youth-oriented version of today's graying union movement.

* *More female leadership, yet also more cooperation between genders.* Leading the new focus on community, family, and security will be the alpha women of this generation. The "power-girls" at the forefront of so many Millennial youth trends will become the business and government leaders who assert their generation's new set of priorities. At the same time, gaps between gender roles will widen as mutual dependence between men and women no longer attracts controversy.

* *A unified, big-brand technology landscape.* Millennials will choose a limited number of preferred technologies from among the multitude of innovations of the last two decades—and make these big "winners" the basis for a new large-scale social infrastructure. This generation will transform information technology from a fragmented and individualized niche market to a nationwide force for action and community-building.

In combination with a "fourth turning," these social shifts will make the America Millennials pass on to their children a very different place from the America that Boomers and Gen Xers have passed on to them. The larger the crisis, the more likely it is that the basic rules of America's economy will fundamentally change, as society eliminates old institutions and creates new ones. We already see the beginning of this today.

What do these changes mean for the workplace? In the decades ahead, companies and organizations will forge new reputations in a shifting institutional landscape. Organizations that harness the power of Millennials and serve them well will find themselves on the right side of history.

The decades ahead will therefore be a time of historic opportunity for employers, as they help today's young people achieve greatness in their own time and generation.

About the Authors

Neil Howe is a historian, economist, demographer, and a renowned authority on generations in America. As president of the consulting firm LifeCourse Associates, he serves as a marketing, personnel, and government affairs consultant to corporate and nonprofit clients. He has spoken and written extensively on the collective personalities of today's generations—who they are, what motivates them, and how they will shape America's future. He is also a recognized authority on global aging, long-term fiscal policy, and migration. His current titles include: senior advisor to the Concord Coalition and senior associate to the Center for Strategic and International Studies (CSIS) in Washington, D.C.

Howe has coauthored many books on generations with William Strauss, all bestsellers widely used by businesses, colleges, government agencies, and political leaders of both parties. Their first book, *Generations* (1991) is a history of America told as a sequence of generational biographies. *Generations*, said *Newsweek*, is "a provocative, erudite, and engaging analysis of the rhythms of American life." Vice President Al Gore called it "the most simulating book on American history that I have ever read," and sent a copy to every member of Congress. Newt Gingrich called it "an intellectual tour de force." Howe's second book on generations, *13th Gen* (1993) remains the bestselling nonfiction book ever written about Generation X. Of Howe and Strauss's third book, *The Fourth Turning* (1997) Dan Yankelovich said, "Immensely stimulating... We will never be able to think about history in the same way." The *Boston Globe* wrote, "If Howe and Strauss are right, they will take their place among the great American prophets."

Howe and Strauss originally coined the term "Millennial Generation." Their fifth book, *Millennials Rising* (2000), has been widely quoted in the media for its insistence that today's new crop of teens and kids are very different from Generation X, and, on the whole, doing better than most adults think. "Forget Generation X—and Y, for that matter," says the *Washington Post*, "The authors make short work of most media myths that shape our perceptions of kids these days." LifeCourse Associates has since released several application books on Millennials—including a *Recruiting Millennials Handbook* for the United States Army (2001), *Millennials Go To College* (2003; second edition, 2007), *Millennials and the Pop Culture* (2005), and *Millennials and K–12 Schools* (2008). Howe's work with Millennials in colleges and in the military was recently featured by CBS' *60 Minutes*.

Previously, with Peter G. Peterson, Howe coauthored *On Borrowed Time* (1989; reissued 2004), a pioneering call for budgetary reform. According to Harvard's Martin Feldstein, former chairman of the President's Council on Economic Advisors, "This book should be read by everyone who wants to understand how government spending can be controlled."

Howe's articles have appeared in *The Atlantic*, the *Washington Post*, the *New York Times*, *American Demographics*, *Harvard Business Review*, *USA Weekend*, and other national publications. He has drafted several Social Security reform plans and testified on entitlements many times before Congress. He has written extensively on budget policy and aging and on attitudes toward economic growth, social progress, and stewardship. He co-edits the "Facing Facts" fax-letter for the Concord Coalition and coauthors numerous studies for CSIS (including the Global Aging Initiative's *Aging Vulnerability Index* and *The Graying of the Middle Kingdom: The Economics and Demographics of Retirement Policy in China*). In 2008, he coauthored *The Graying of the Great Powers* with Richard Jackson.

Howe grew up in California, received his BA at U.C. Berkeley, studied abroad in France and Germany, and later earned graduate degrees in economics (MA, 1978) and history (MPhil, 1979) from Yale University. He currently lives in Great Falls, Virginia.

Millennials in the Workplace is authored with Reena Nadler. She has co-authored a number of reports and articles with Howe, most recently the white paper "Yes We Can: Millennials as a Political Generation," published by the New America Foundation. She is also a contributing author to *Millennials in K–12 Schools* (2008) and worked extensively on *Millennials Go to College* (2007). Nadler is the Program Director at LifeCourse Associates, where she helps coordinate research, publications, and consulting across a broad range of topics, from education and workforce preparation to global generations and rhythms of history. She speaks frequently on generations in education and the workplace at meetings and national conferences. Nadler has a BA in Religion from Swarthmore College and studied abroad in France. A first-wave Millennial herself, she brings a first-hand perspective to LifeCourse's work on today's rising generation.

Sources

Given the vast range of topics covered in this book—and the numberless scholarly, journalistic, and pop-culture sources that bear some connection to them—there is no way to reference everything of interest. As a convenience, a brief list is provided here of the sources (from publications and Web sites to programs and agencies) that were of particular use in preparing this book.

Readers who want to find out more about the Howe-Strauss generational perspective on American history are invited to read two of the authors' previous books: *Generations* (1991) and *The Fourth Turning* (1997). Readers who want to find out more about their earlier treatments of the Millennial Generation are invited to read *Millennials Rising* (2000), *Millennials Go To College* (2003, 2007), Millennials and the Pop Culture (2006), and *Millennials in K–12 Schools* (2008).

Readers with further questions are invited to contact the authors at LifeCourse Associates, by emailing authors@lifecourse.com.

Major Sources on Economics, Education, Socio-Demographics, and Behavior

General Summary
The Child and Family Webguide (Tufts University), Web site
Child Trends DataBank (Child Trends), Web site
America's Children: Key National Indicators of Well-Being (U.S. Federal Interagency Forum on Child and Family Statistics), published annually and Web site
The State of America's Children (Children's Defense Fund), published annually
The Child and Youth Well-Being Index (Child and Youth Well-Being Index Project, Duke University), Web site

Births, Demographics, Households, Family Structure
U.S. Census Bureau
U.S. National Center for Health Statistics (Centers for Disease Control and Prevention)

The Network on Transitions to Adulthood, publications and Web site

Entry-Level Job Survey (MonsterTrak), published annually

For Nearly Half of America, Grass is Greener Somewhere Else (Pew Research Center), 2009

William H. Frey, *The Great American Migration Slowdown: Regional and Metropolitan Dimensions* (Brookings Institution), 2009

T.J. Matthews and Brady E. Hamilton, *Delayed Childbearing: More Women Are Having Their First Child Later in Life* (National Center for Health Statistics, U.S. Department of Health and Human Services), 2009

Jeffrey Arnett, *Emerging Adulthood: The Winding Road from the Late Teens Through the Twenties* (Oxford University Press), 2004

Frank F. Furstenberg, Sheela Kennedy, Vonnie C. McLoyd, Rubén G. Rumbaut, Richard A. Settersten, "Growing Up is Harder to Do" (*Contexts*, The American Sociological Association and University of California Press), 2004

Ethan Watters, *Urban Tribes: Are Friends the New Family?* (Bloomsbury USA), 2004

Zhu Xiao Di, Yi Yang, and Xiaodong Liu, *Young American Adults Living in Parental Homes* (Joint Center for Housing Studies, Harvard University), 2002

Alexandra Robbins and Abby Wilner, *The Quarterlife Crisis: The Unique Challenges of Life in Your Twenties* (Tarcher/Putnam), 2001

Frances Goldscheider, *Recent Changes in U.S. Young Adult Living Arrangements in Comparative Perspective* (Journal of Family Issues), 1997

Race and Ethnicity

U.S. Census Bureau

U.S. Bureau of Labor Statistics (Department of Labor)

Youth Employment, Consumption, and Family Income

U.S. Census Bureau

Economic Policy Institute

Harris Interactive YouthPulse Report (Harris Interactive), annual survey of spending by youth age 8 to 24

Taking Stock With Teens (PiperJaffray), semi-annual survey of teen spending

"Changes in U.S. Family Finances from 2004 to 2007: Evidence from the Survey of Consumer Finances" (*Federal Reserve Bulletin*), 2009

Oldest are Most Sheltered: Different Age Groups, Different Recessions (Pew Research Center), 2009

The Recession and Its Impact on the Youth Market (JWT AnxietyIndex), 2009

Julie L. Hotchkiss, *Changes in the Aggregate Labor Force Participation Rate* (Federal Reserve Bank of Atlanta), 2009

Rebecca Keller, "How Shifting Occupational Composition has Affected the Real Average Wage" (*Monthly Labor Review*), 2009

Tamara Draut, *Economic State of Young America* (Dēmos), 2008

Tamara Draut, *Strapped: Why America's 20- and 30-Somethings Can't Get Ahead* (Anchor), 2008

Teresa L. Morisi, "Youth Enrollment and Employment During the School Year" (*Monthly Labor Review*), 2008

Geoffrey Paulin, "Expenditure Patterns of Young Single Adults: Two Recent Generations Compared" (*Monthly Labor Review*), 2008

Economic Mobility: Is the American Dream Alive and Well? (Economic Mobility Project, The Pew Charitable Trusts), 2007

Generational Spending Patterns: A Study of the Spending Behavior of Echo Boomers and Boomers (Yankelovich), 2007

"Recent Changes in U.S. Family Finances: Evidence from the 2001 and 2004
  Survey of Consumer Finances (*Federal Reserve Bulletin*), 2006
What Is Happening to Youth Employment Rates? (Congressional Budget Office), 2004

Educational Achievement

The Nation's Report Card (National Assessment of Educational Progress, U.S.
  Department of Education), regular publications and Web site
Trends in International Mathematics and Science Study (TIMSS) (National Center for
  Education Statistics, U.S. Department of Education), regular publications and Web site
College-Bound Seniors (The College Board), annual publication
The AP Report to the Nation (The College Board), annual publication
High School Survey of Student Engagement (Indiana University
  School of Education), published annually
Annual Report (National Survey of Student Engagement), published annually
*Rising to the Challenge: Are High School Graduates Prepared
  for College and Work?* (Achieve, Inc.), 2005

Schools and Colleges

The Condition of Education (National Center for Education Statistics, U.S.
  Department of Education), annual publication and web site
Digest of Education Statistics (National Center for Education Statistics, U.S.
  Department of Education), annual publication and web site
Education Pays (The College Board), annual publication and Web site
Trends in College Pricing (The College Board), annual publication
Trends in Student Aid (The College Board), annual publication
*Can I Get A Little Advice Here? How an Overstretched High School Guidance
  System Is Undermining Students' College Aspirations* (Public Agenda), 2010
*Squeeze Play 2010: Continued Public Anxiety on Cost, Harsher Judgments
  on How Colleges Are Run* (Public Agenda), 2010
Changes in Postsecondary Awards Below the Bachelor's Degree: 1997–2007
  (National Center for Education Statistics), 2009
*College Enrollment Hits All-Time High, Fueled by Community
  College Surge* (Pew Research Center), 2009
A Portrait in Numbers (Early College High School Initiative), 2009
*With Their Whole Lives Ahead of Them: Myths and Realities about Why So
  Many Students Fail to Finish College* (Public Agenda), 2009
Kevin Carey, Frederick M. Hess, Andrew P. Kelly, and Mark Schneider,
  *Diplomas and Dropouts: Which Colleges Actually Graduate Their Students
  (and Which Don't)* (American Enterprise Institute), 2009
Diploma to Nowhere (Strong American Schools), 2008
Cheryl A. Almeida and Adria Steinberg, *Raising Graduation Rates in an Era of High
  Standards: Five Commitments for State Action* (Achieve, Inc. and Jobs for the Future), 2008
Nancy Hoffman, Janet Santos, and Joel Vargas, *On Ramp to College: A State
  Policymaker's Guide to Dual Enrollment* (Jobs for the Future), 2008
*Choosing Hispanic-Serving Institutions: A Closer Look at Latino
  Students' College Choices* (Excelencia), 2007.
Reality Check: How Black and Hispanic Families Rate Their Schools (Public Agenda), 2006
The Silent Epidemic: Perspectives of High School Dropouts (Civic Enterprises), 2006
*Smoothing the Path: Changing State Policies to Support Early College
  High School: Case Studies from Georgia, Ohio, Texas, and Utah* (Early
  College High School Initiative, Jobs for the Future), 2006

Cheryl Almeida, Cassius Johnson, and Adria Steinberg, *Making Good on a Promise: What Policymakers Can Do to Support the Educational Persistence of Dropouts* (Jobs for the Future), 2006

Stephanie Riegg Cellini, *Community Colleges and Proprietary Schools: A Comparison of Sub-Baccalaureate Institutions* (California Center for Population Research, UCLA), 2005

Dan M. Hull (ed.), *Career Pathways: Education With a Purpose* (Center for Occupational Research and Development), 2005

Raising the Graduation Rates of Low-Income College Students (Pell Institute), 2004

Children's Use of Time

Generation M2: Media in the Lives of 8- to 18-Year-Olds (Kaiser Family Foundation), 2010

Garey Ramey, Valerie A. Ramey, *The Rug Rat Race* (The University of California, San Diego and the National Bureau of Economic Research), 2009

American Time Use Survey (Bureau of Labor Statistics), 2008

Mary Dorinda Allard, "How High School Students Use Time: A Visual Essay" (*Monthly Labor Review*), 2008

Anne H. Gauthier and Frank F. Furstenberg, Jr., *Working More, Playing Less: Changing Patterns of Time Use Among Young Adults* (MacArthur Foundation Research Network on Transitions to Adulthood and Public Policy), 2004

F. Thomas Juster, Hiromi Ono, and Frank P. Stafford, *Changing Times of American Youth: 1981–2003* (Institue for Social Research, University of Michigan), 2004

Sandra L. Hofferth and John F. Sandberg, *Changes in Children's Time with Parents, U.S. 1981–1997* (Institute for Social Research and Population Studies Center, University of Michigan), 2001

Sandra L. Hofferth and John F. Sandberg, *Changes in American Children's Time, 1981–1997* (Institute for Social Research and Population Studies Center, University of Michigan), 1998

Youth Health and Risk Behaviors

U.S. National Center for Health Statistics

U.S. National Institute of Child Health and Human Development (National Institutes of Health, Department of Health and Human Services)

Youth Risk Behavior Surveillance System (U.S. Centers for Disease Control and Prevention), Web site and *National Youth Risk Behavior Survey: 1991–2005*, 2006

Youth Studies Group (Stanford Center for Research in Disease Prevention)

Teen Births and Abortions

U.S. National Center for Health Statistics

Alan Guttmacher Institute, publications and Web site

Family Dysfunction

U.S. Children's Bureau (Administration on Children, Youth and Families, of the Administration for Children and Families, Department of Health and Human Services)

Children's Welfare Information Gateway (Administration on Children, Youth and Families, of the Administration for Children and Families, U.S. Department of Health and Human Services)

Youth Crime and Drug Abuse

U.S. National Criminal Justice Reference Service (Department of Justice), publications and Web site

U.S. Substance Abuse and Mental Health Services Administration (Department of Health and Human Services), regular publications and Web site

National School Safety Center, publications and Web site

Partnership for a Drug-Free America, publications and Web site

Monitoring the Future (Institute for Social Research, University of Michigan), annual questions to students in grade 12 (since the class of 1975) and in grades 10 and 8 (since the class of 1991); publications and Web site

David Finkelhor and Lisa Jones, "Why have Child Maltreatment and Child Victimization Declined?" (*Journal of Social Issues*), 2006

Major Sources on Values, Attitudes, and Workplace Preferences

Accenture

Millennial Women Workplace Success Index (Accenture), 2010

New-Generation Workers (Accenture), 2008

CERI

Ready for Prime Time? How Internships and Co-ops Affect Decisions on Full-time Job Offers (Collegiate Employment Research Institute, University of Michigan and MonsterTrak), 2008

How Central is Work to Young Adults? (Collegiate Employment Research Institute, University of Michigan and MonsterTrak), 2007

Important Characteristics of Early Career Jobs: What do Young Adults Want? (Collegiate Employment Research Institute, University of Michigan and MonsterTrak), 2007

Today's Young Adults: Surfing for the Right Job (Collegiate Employment Research Institute, University of Michigan and MonsterTrak), 2007

Phil Gardner, *Moving Up or Moving Out of the Company? Factors that Influence the Promoting or Firing of New College Hires* (Collegiate Employment Research Institute, University of Michigan), 2007

Phil Gardner, *Parental Involvement in the College Recruiting Process: To What Extent?* (Collegiate Employment Research Institute, University of Michigan), 2007

Deloitte

Managing Talent in a Turbulent Economy (Deloitte LLP), 2009

Bill Chafetz, Josh Ensell, and Robin Adair Erickson, "Where Did Our Employees Go?: Examining the Rise in Voluntary Turnover During Economic Recoveries" (*Deloitte Review*), 2009

W. Stanton Smith, *Decoding Generational Differences* (Next Generation Initiatives, Deloitte LLP), 2008

Gallup Polls

The Gallup Youth Survey: Major Issues and Trends (regularly published surveys on youth attitudes, e.g. *Teens & Alcohol, Teens & Career Choices, Teens & Family Issues, Teens & Sex, Teens Religion & Values*, etc.), reports issued in various years

Girl Scout Research Institute

Good Intentions: The Beliefs and Values of Teens and Tweens Today (Girl Scout Research Institute), 2009

The New Leadership Landscape: What Girls Say about Election 2008 (Girl Scout Research Institute), 2009

Change it Up: What Girls Say about Redefining Leadership (Girl Scout Research Institute), 2008

Harvard University Institute of Politics

Biannual Youth Survey on Politics and Public Service (Harvard University
Institute of Politics), annual publication and Web site

HERI

The American Freshman (Higher Education Research Institute, University of
California at Los Angeles) published annually, yearly surveys since 1966
John H. Pryor, Sylvia Hurtado, Victor B. Saenz, José Luis Santos, William
S. Korn, *The American Freshman: Forty Year Trends* (Higher Education
Research Institute, University of California at Los Angeles), 2007

Horatio Alger

The State of Our Nation's Youth (Horatio Alger Association), annual publication and Web site

JWT

AnxietyIndex Quarterly (AnxietyIndex, JWT), published quarterly since spring 2009
The Recession and Its Impact on the Youth Market (AnxietyIndex, JWT), 2009
Millennials at Work: Myths vs. Reality (JWT), 2008

Monitoring the Future

Monitoring the Future (Institute for Social Research, University of Michigan),
annual questions to students in grades 12 (since the class of 1975) and in
grades 10 and 8 (since the class of 1991); reports issued in various years

NACE

Moving On: Student Approaches and Attitudes Toward the Job Market (National
Association of Colleges and Employers), annual publication
NACE Job Outlook (National Association of Colleges and Employers), annual publication
NACE Career Services Benchmark Survey for Four-Year Colleges and Universities
(National Association of Colleges and Employers), annual publication
Salary Survey (National Association of Colleges and Employers), annual publication since 1962
"NACE Research: High Tech in a High-Touch World" (*NACE Journal*), 2009

NASSP

The Mood of American Youth (National Association of Secondary School Principals),
1974, 1983, and 1996; students age 13–17 interviewed early in each year

New Paradigm (now nGenera)

Paul Artiuch and Deepak Ramachandran, *Harnessing the Global
N-Gen Talent Pool* (New Paradigm), 2007
Bill Gillies and Janet Hardy, *Attracting and Engaging the
N-Gen Employee* (New Paradigm), 2007
Neil Howe and William Strauss, *Helicopter Parents in the Workplace* (New Paradigm), 2007

Pew Research Center

Millennials Less Religiously Active Than Older Americans (Pew
Research Center for the People and the Press), 2010
The Millennials: Confident. Connected. Open to Change. (Pew
Research Center for the People and the Press), 2010

Teen and Young Adult Internet Use (Pew Research Center for the People and the Press), 2010

Forty Years After Woodstock, A Gentler Generation Gap (Pew
   Research Center for the People and the Press), 2009

Gen Next Squeezed by Recession, But Most See Better Times Ahead (Pew
   Research Center for the People and the Press), 2009

Latino Youths Optimistic, but Beset by Problems (Pew Research
   Center for the People and the Press), 2009

Teens, Video Games, and Civics (Pew Research Center for the People and the Press), 2008

Writing, Technology, and Teens (Pew Research Center for the People and the Press), 2008

Young Voters in the 2008 Election (Pew Research Center for the People and the Press), 2008

*How Young People View Their Lives, Futures, and Politics: A Portrait of "Generation
   Next"* (Pew Research Center for the People and the Press), 2007

Teens and Social Media (Pew Research Center for the People and the Press), 2007

Teens, Privacy, and Online Social Networks (Pew Research
   Center for the People and the Press), 2007

Public Agenda

*Can I Get a Little Advice Here? How an Overstretched High School Guidance System
   Is Undermining Students' College Aspirations* (Public Agenda), 2010

*With Their Whole Lives Ahead of Them: Myths and Realities About Why
   So Many Students Fail to Finish College* (Public Agenda), 2009

*Life After High School: Young People Talk about Their Hopes
   and Prospects* (Public Agenda), 2005

*All Work and No Play?: Listening to What Kids and Parents Really
   Want from Out-of-School Time* (Public Agenda), 2004

*Kids These Days '99: What Americans Really Think about the
   Next Generation* (Public Agenda), 1999

Universum

Ideal Employer Survey, annual publication

American Student Survey, annual publication

Other Sources

Roper Youth Report (Roper Starch Worldwide), published annually, results reported irregularly

2010 Kids and Careers Survey (Junior Achievement and ING), 2010

Age & Generations: Understanding Experiences at the Workplace (Sloan
   Center on Aging & Work, Boston College), 2009

The Family GPS: The Generation Gap Narrows (Nickelodeon
   Research and Harris Interactive), 2009

Ellen Galinsky, Kerstin Aumann, and James T. Bond, *Times Are Changing: Gender
   and Generation at Work and at Home* (Families and Work Institute), 2009

Nicole A. Lipkin and April J. Perrymore, *Y in the Workplace:
   Managing the "Me First" Generation* (Career Press), 2009

Don Tapscott, *Grown Up Digital: How the Net Generation Is
   Changing Your World* (McGraw Hill), 2009

Bruce Tulgan, *Not Everyone Gets a Trophy: How to Manage Generation Y* (Jossey Bass), 2009

LexisNexis Technology Gap Survey (LexisNexis), 2008

Millennial Magnets (Fortune magazine and the Great Place to Work Institute), 2008

*A Report on the Opinions and Attitudes of the Millennial Generation toward the
   United States Public Service Academy* (U.S. Public Service Academy), 2008

World at Work (Randstad), 2008

Ron Alsop, *The Trophy Kids Grow Up: How the Millennial Generation is Shaking Up the Workplace* (Jossey-Bass), 2008

Workplace Connections & Their Impact on Retention, Recruiting, and Productivity (SelectMinds Research), 2007

2006 Cone Millennial Cause Study (Cone, Inc.), 2006

Lowell C. Rose and Alec M. Gallup, *The 38th Annual Phi Delta Kappa/ Gallup Poll of the Public's Attitudes Toward the Public Schools*, 2006

Jean M. Twenge, *Generation Me* (Free Press), 2006

Voices Study: Research Findings (America's Promise), 2005

Lynne C. Lancaster and David Stillman, *When Generations Collide* (Harper Business), 2002

Generation 2001 Survey (Northwestern Mutual Life), 1999

The Shell Poll (Shell Oil Company), 1999

The PRIMEDIA/Roper National Youth Opinion Survey (PRIMEDIA, Inc., and Roper Starch Worldwide, Inc.), 1998; students in grades 7–12 interviewed in Nov, 1998

Drexel University Futures Poll: Teenagers, Technology and Tomorrow (Drexel University), 1997

Annual Survey of High Achievers (Who's Who Among American High School Students), "high-achieving" high school students interviewed annually since 1967 (discontinued in 2000)

Youth Attitude Tracking Survey (Defense Manpower Data Center, U.S. Department of Defense), survey of potential high school-aged recruits, published annually since 1975 (discontinued in 1999)